The Mormon Contradiction:

In Their Own Words

By Marcia Van Outen

authorHOUSE®

AuthorHouse™ UK Ltd.
500 Avebury Boulevard
Central Milton Keynes, MK9 2BE
www.authorhouse.co.uk
Phone: 08001974150

Published by AuthorHouse 10/31/2012

ISBN: 978-1-4490-7067-0 (sc)
ISBN: 978-1-4678-9349-7 (e)

INTRODUCTION

My aim was not to write an anti-Mormon book. The vast majority of Mormons are good honest, decent citizens trying to follow God, with the "truth" which they believe only they possess.

My personal quest was to find out what the truth really is and to hopefully save myself and my family from the sure destruction of mind, body, and spirit, which staying in the Mormon Church ensured if I continued to stay within its grasp. To all ex-Mormons who read this book I hope that you find something that will help you as you try to deal with the lie you gave your life to, even if it was for a short or a very long time. It is not easy, consider yourself one of the lucky ones to be out of the deception and not living a lie till the day you die as many others have done and continue to do so.

As it happened the choice was made for me. The time came that I could no longer physically drag my emotionally abused body, mind, and crushed spirit out to their various meetings. I had suffered so much spiritual abuse. After too many years (of trying to endure to the end!) my body put up the white flag saying "ENOUGH". I stopped going to church not because I wanted to but because I physically couldn't anymore. One day after shedding many tears and praying, I picked up my scriptures; my hands shook as I tried to read for they were associated to the Church that was literally killing me.

They opened to *Ezekiel 34 verses 1, 2, & 10* in the Old Testament

1 And the word of the Lord came unto me, saying,

2 Son of man, prophesy against the shepherds of Israel, prophesy, and say unto them, Thus saith the Lord God unto the shepherds; Woe be to the shepherds of Israel that do feed themselves! Should not the shepherds feed the flocks?

10 Thus saith the Lord God; Behold, I am against the shepherds; and I will require My flock at their hand, and cause them to cease from feeding the flock; neither shall the shepherds feed themselves any more; for I will deliver My flock from their mouth, that they may not be meat for them.

Thus began another painful journey, but this time being able to think and reason for myself, which did not come easy in the beginning, for one loses the ability to reason when all one's beliefs are tied up in the doctrines of the Mormon Church. The Mormon Church does not brainwash you in one fell swoop, that would be easy to detect. In the Church we are told that we learn the doctrines line upon line, precept upon precept. And this is the insidious way the brainwashing occurs. I transgressed in no way, but the church leaders did. I suffered tremendously as a result. It is my hope and prayer that this book will spare others what I suffered and prevent anyone else from joining the great delusion that is Mormonism.

Dictionary definitions

De·lu·sion:

- A fixed false belief that is resistant to reason or confrontation with actual fact:
- An erroneous belief that is held in the face of evidence to the contrary.
- An idiosyncratic belief or impression maintained despite being contradicted by reality or rational argument.

Spiritual Abuse is a very real trauma. It's not something that is imagined. It affects the mental, emotional, physical and, of course, the spiritual state of the sufferer. I believe that my experiences are of no use if I keep them to myself, they have to be shared so hopefully others can benefit, that is why so many others publish their own stories, for each story is similar yet unique, as indeed so are we all.

The true history of the Mormon Church is contained within these pages. Books that portray the Church in an unfavourable light are termed anti-Mormon literature even if the facts from their own Mormon History are

To Ashish,
Lots of love
Marcia Van Outen x

published. The Church leaders will say that people who write against the Church are trying to pull the members from the Church and are inspired by the devil. This I now know is not the case, what they are trying to do is bring the truth to others so that they too can get their lives back before it's too late.

The Church also states the reason there is so much opposition to the Mormon Church is because it is the only "True Church" on the face of this Earth. The Church of Jesus Christ of Latter-day Saints is its official name, commonly referred to as The Mormon Church. I used to correct anyone referring to the Church as the Mormon Church, but since coming to know the truth I will hereafter refer to it as the Mormon Church. This book is a compilation of the facts for those who wish to inform themselves about this Church. After many months of painful research I wrote it in a way that I thought would be helpful. It is basically the book I wished I'd had when I was going through my roller coaster, emotional, painful, and exhausting journey.

The Mormon Church uses lies and deceit in order to perpetuate "the truth". And unfortunately they make it up as they go along.

All Bible scriptures are taken from the King James Version which is the version the Mormon Church uses as part of their Standard Works.

In the Book of Doctrine and Covenants which is revered by the Mormons as revealed scripture.

D&C 88:81

"Behold I sent you out to testify and warn the people, and it becometh every man who hath been warned to warn his neighbour."

They use this "scripture" in relation to their gospel; I will use it in relation to them. I am warning my neighbour about what their gospel truly is. My reason for doing so can be summed up in the story of The King's Highway.

THE KING'S HIGHWAY

Once upon a time, a king had a great highway built for the people who lived in his kingdom. After it was completed, but before it was opened to the public, the king decided to have a contest. He invited as many of his subjects as desired to participate. The challenge was to see who could travel the highway the best, and the winner was to receive a box of gold.

On the day of the contest, all the people came. Some of them had fine chariots; some had fine clothing and fancy food to make the trip a luxurious journey. Some wore their sturdiest shoes and ran along the highway on their feet to show their skill. All day they travelled the highway, and each one, when he arrived at the end, complained to the king about a large pile of rocks and debris that had been left almost blocking the road at one point, and that got in their way and hindered their travel.

At the end of the day, a lone traveller crossed the finish line warily and walked over to the king. He was tired and dirty, but he addressed the king with great respect and handed him a small chest of gold. He said, "I stopped along the way to clear a pile of rocks and debris that was blocking the road. This chest of gold was under it all. Please have it returned to its rightful owner."

The king replied, "You are the rightful owner."

"Oh no," said the traveller, "This is not mine. I've never known such money."

"Oh yes," said the king, "You've earned this gold, for you won my contest. He who travels the road best is he who makes the road better for those who will follow."

Author Unknown

CHAPTER ONE

An introduction to the Mormon Church usually comes through two missionaries knocking on doors or through meeting someone who is a member. They will more often present a person with pamphlets and a copy of the Book of Mormon. The Book of Mormon is presented as Another Testament of Jesus Christ. This book (they will say) is a record of the ancient inhabitants of the American continent who came from Israel around 600 BC. It is also a record of another group of people. This other group is known as the Jaredites, who came out at the confusion of the tongues in ancient Babylon whilst trying to build the Tower of Babel. The Mormons claim that all of these people are the ancestors of the Native American Indians.

The crowning glory in the book of Mormon is the visitation of the resurrected Jesus Christ after His death in Jerusalem.

Where did this book come from? The Mormons say that an angel visited Joseph Smith (who was then a fourteen-year old boy) and told him there was a record deposited in a hill in Palmyra, that it was written on brass plates and that he (Joseph Smith) would be able to translate it by the gift and power of God. The missionaries will urge the investigator to read the book and pray to find out if it is true. The book tells of a man named Lehi and his family who were led out of Jerusalem around 600 BC. They travelled on foot for a considerable time and then proceeded to build a ship to carry them across the ocean. They sailed to the American Continent. After the death of Lehi, contention broke out between two brothers (Nephi and Laman) so they each went their separate ways. One group was called Nephites after the righteous brother (Nephi) and the other group called Lamanites after the unrighteous brother (Laman). The Lord caused a skin of blackness to come upon the unrighteous brother and his followers because of their iniquities.

I told the missionaries that I believed this passage to be racist. Their explanation was that it was done so the seed of the unrighteous could be distinguished from the seed of the righteous and the two would not intermingle.

Introduction page in the Book of Mormon

The Book of Mormon is a volume of Holy Scripture comparable to the Bible. It is a record of God's dealings with the ancient inhabitants of the Americas and contains, as does the Bible, the fullness of the everlasting gospel. Many ancient prophets by the spirit of prophecy and revelation wrote the book. Their words, written on gold plates, were quoted and abridged by a prophet-historian named Mormon. The record gives an account of two great civilizations. One came from Jerusalem in 600 B.C., and afterward separated into two nations, known as the Nephites and the Lamanites. The other group came much earlier when the Lord confounded the tongues at the Tower of Babel. This group is known as the Jaredites. After thousands of years, all were destroyed except the Lamanites, and they are the principal ancestors of the American Indians.

The crowning event recorded in the Book of Mormon is the personal ministry of the Lord Jesus Christ among the Nephites soon after his resurrection. It puts forth the doctrines of the gospel, outlines the plan of salvation, and tells men what they must do to gain peace in this life and eternal salvation in the life to come. After Mormon completed his writings, he delivered the account to his son Moroni, who added a few words of his own and hid up the plates in the hill Cumorah. On September 21, 1823, that same Moroni, then a glorified resurrected being, appeared to the Prophet Joseph Smith and instructed him relative to the ancient record and its destined translation into the English language. In due course the plates were delivered to Joseph Smith, who translated them by the gift and power of God.

The record is now published in many languages as a new and additional witness that Jesus Christ is the Son of the living God and all who will come unto him and obey the laws and ordinances of his gospel may be saved.

Concerning this record the Prophet Joseph Smith said: "I told the brethren that the Book of Mormon was the most correct of any book on the earth, and the keystone of our religion, and a man would get nearer to God by abiding by its precepts, than any other book." In addition to Joseph Smith, the Lord provided for eleven others to see the gold plates for themselves and to be special witnesses of the truth and divinity of the Book of Mormon. Their written testimonies are included herewith as "The Testimony of Three Witnesses" and "The Testimony of Eight Witnesses".

We invite all men everywhere to read the Book of Mormon, to ponder in their hearts the message it contains, and then to ask God, the Eternal Father, in the name of Jesus Christ if the book is true. Those who pursue this course and ask in faith will gain a testimony of its truth and divinity by the power of the Holy Ghost. (See Moroni 10: 3-5.)

Those who gain this divine witness from the Holy Spirit will also come to know by the same power that Jesus Christ is the Savior of the world, that Joseph Smith is His revelator and prophet in these last days, and that The Church of Jesus Christ of Latter-Day Saints is the Lord's kingdom once again established on the earth, preparatory to the second coming of the Messiah.

The investigator will be told if he/she prays with real faith and a sincere heart, the Holy Ghost will testify of the truthfulness of the Book of Mormon. I was very curious about their claims and wanted to know if this was indeed Another Testament of Jesus Christ. I prayed to find out if what they were telling me was true, not knowing how an answer was going to be obtained.

The Book of Mormon

28 *Now, we will compare the word unto a seed. Now, if ye give place, that a seed may be planted in your heart, behold, if it be a true seed, or a good seed, if ye do not cast it out by your unbelief that ye will resist the Spirit of the Lord, behold, it will begin to swell within your breasts; and when you feel these swelling motions, ye will begin to say within yourselves—It must needs*

be that this is a good seed, or that the word is good, for it beginneth to enlarge my soul; yea, it beginneth to enlighten my understanding,yea, it beginneth to be delicious to me.

Alma, Chapter 32

This is referred to as the burning in the bosom. I received this "testimony" and believing it to be from God through the power of the Holy Ghost I felt there was no going back for me. I had received what I believed to be a true witness from God through the power of the Holy Ghost.
Thus the delusion began. I remained faithful to this "testimony" for nearly twenty years.

Mormonism can make your heart burn because it applies to emotion, but when you search it out intellectually the truth fails.

The Old Testament

"He that trusteth in his own heart is a fool: but whoso walketh wisely, he shall be delivered".

Proverbs, Chapter 28 verse 26

CHAPTER TWO

The Book of Mormon

Where did it really come from?

Solomon Spalding was born in 1761 in Connecticut, U.S.A. He attended Dartmouth College in preparation for the ministry and graduated in the year 1787. Through association with the Windham Congressional Association he was ordained in that denomination.

He married Miss Matilda Sabine In 1795

They moved to New York where he joined his brother Josiah who ran a mercantile business. In 1799 he retired from the ministry due to his failing health. His brother Josiah moved his mercantile business to Richfield. Solomon and his wife moved to Salem, Ohio in 1809. Due to ill health Solomon was unable to work much and to pass the time he began to write novels. The first novel was titled Manuscript Story. He didn't complete Manuscript Story but used what he had learned to write a new novel titled Manuscript Found. He then moved to Pittsburgh, Pennsylvania with the hope of selling his novel Manuscript Found to help pay off his debts. The Spalding's then moved to Amity.

Solomon's health deteriorated and he died in 1816.

Solomon Spalding had a great desire to know the history of the American continent, so much so that he wrote his own history of the Americas. He would share these stories to anyone who would listen to them. He came to be known as 'Old came to pass' after his favourite literary phrase. 'And it came to pass'. Friends of Solomon stated that his novel Manuscript Found had been stolen from the printers in Pittsburgh and that it resurfaced again in 1830 with some revisions and modifications as The Book of Mormon.

John Spalding wrote of his brother[1]

Solomon Spalding was born in Ashford Connecticut in 1761, and in early life contracted a taste for literary pursuits. After he left school, he entered Plainfield Academy, where he made great proficiency in study, and excelled most of his classmates. He next commenced the study of law in which he made little progress, having in the meantime turned his attention to religious subjects. He soon after entered Dartmouth College with the intention of qualifying himself for the ministry where he obtained the degree of A.M., and afterwards was regularly ordained.

After preaching three or four years, he gave it up, removed to Cherry Valley, N.Y., and commenced in the mercantile business, in company with his brother Josiah. In a few years he failed in business, and in the year 1809 removed to Conneaut, in Ohio. The year following, I removed to Ohio, and found him engaged in building a forge. I made him a visit in about three years after, and found that he had failed, and was considerably involved in debt. He then told me he was writing a book, which he intended to have printed, the avails of which he thought would enable him to pay all his debts. The book was entitled the "Manuscript Found", of which he read to me many passages.

It was an historical romance of the first settlers of America, endeavouring to show that the American Indians are the descendants of the Jews, or the lost tribes. It gave a detailed account of their journey from Jerusalem, by land and sea, till they arrived in America, under the command of Nephi and Lehi. They afterwards had quarrels and contentions and separated into two distinct nations, one of which he denominated Nephites, and the other Lamanites. Cruel and bloody wars ensued, in which great multitudes were slain. They buried their dead in large heaps, which caused the mounds so common in this country.

Their arts, sciences and civilization were brought into view in order to account for all the curious antiquities found in various parts of North and South America. I have recently read the Book of Mormon and to my great surprise I find nearly the same historical matter, names, &c., as they were in my brother's writings. I well remember that he wrote in the old style, and commenced about every sentence with "And it came to pass," or "Now it came to pass," the same as in the Book of Mormon, and according to the best of my recollection and belief, it is the same as my brother Solomon wrote, with the exception of the religious matter. By what means it has fallen into the hands of Joseph Smith, Jun., I am unable to determine.

(Signed)

John Spalding

Solomon Spalding's sister in-law Martha Spalding affirmed[2]

I was personally acquainted with Solomon Spalding, about twenty years ago. I was at his house a short time before he left Conneaut; he was then writing an historical novel founded upon the first settlers of America. He represented them as an enlightened and warlike people. He had for many years contended that the aborigines of America were the descendants of some of the lost tribes of Israel, and this idea he carried out in the book in question. The lapse of time which has intervened, prevents my recollecting but a few of the leading incidents of his writings; but the names of Nephi and Lehi are yet fresh in my memory, as being the principal heroes of this tale. They were officers of the company which first came off from Jerusalem. He gave a particular account of their journey by land and sea, till they arrived in America, after which disputes arose between the chiefs, which caused them to separate into different bands, one of which was called Lamanites, and the other Nephites. Between these were recounted tremendous battles, which frequently covered the ground with the slain; and their being buried in large heaps was the cause of numerous mounds in the country. Some of these people he represented as being very large.

I have read the Book of Mormon, which has brought fresh to my recollection the writings of Solomon Spalding; and I have no manner of doubt that the historical part of it is the same that I read and heard read more than twenty years ago. The old obsolete style and the phrases of "And it came to pass," & c., are the same.

(Signed) Martha Spalding

Henry Lake was Solomon Spalding's business partner[3]

I left the State of New York, late in the year 1810, and arrived at this place [Conneaut], about the first of January following. Soon after my arrival, I formed a co partnership with Solomon Spaulding, for the purpose of rebuilding a forge, which he had commenced a year or two before. He very frequently read to me from a manuscript, which he was writing which he entitled "Manuscript Found," and which he represented as being found in this town. I spent many hours in hearing him read said writings, and became well acquainted with its contents. He wished me to assist him in getting his production printed, alleging that a book of that kind would meet with a rapid sale.

I designed doing so, but the forge not meeting our anticipations, we failed in business, when I declined having anything to do with the publication of the book. This book represented the American Indians as the descendants of the lost tribes, gave account of their leaving Jerusalem, their contentions and wars, which were many and great. One time, when he was reading to me the tragic account of Laban, I pointed out to him what I considered an inconsistency, which he promised to correct: but by referring to the Book of Mormon, I find to my surprise, that it stands there just as he read it to me then. Some months ago I borrowed the Golden Bible, put it in my pocket, carried it home, and thought no more of it.

About a week after, my wife found the book in my coat pocket, as it hung up, and commenced reading it aloud as I lay on the bed. She had not read twenty minutes, till I was astonished to find the same passages in it that Spaulding had read to me more than twenty years before, from his "Manuscript Found." Since that, I have more fully examined the said Golden Bible, and have no hesitation in saying that the historical part of it is principally, if not wholly, taken from the "Manuscript Found". I well recollect telling Mr. Spaulding that the so frequent use of the words "and it came to pass," "now it came to pass," rendered it ridiculous. Spaulding left here in 1812, and I furnished him the means to carry to Pittsburgh, where he said he would get the book printed and pay me. But I never heard any more from him or his writings, till I saw them in the Book of Mormon.

(Signed) Henry Lake

In 1814 Solomon Spalding operated a temperance tavern in Amity, not far from Pittsburgh.

Joseph Miller a neighbour worked in Amity during this period and spent many evenings in the Spalding home often listening to Solomon read his novel.

Joseph Miller's knowledge of the Manuscript Found 1869[4]

When Mr. Spaulding lived in Amity, Pa., I was well acquainted with him. I was frequently at his house. He kept what is called a tavern. It was understood that he had been a preacher, but his health failed him and he ceased to preach. I never knew him to preach when he came to Amity. He had in his possession some papers, which he had written. He used to select portions of these papers to amuse us of evenings.

These papers were detached sheets of foolscap. He said he wrote the papers as a novel. He called it the "Manuscript Found or "The Lost Manuscript Found. "He said he wrote it to pass away time when he was unwell; and after it was written he thought he would publish it as a novel, as a means to support his family. Some time since, a copy of the Book of Mormon came into my hands. My son read it for me, as I have nervous shaking of the head that prevents me from reading. I noticed several passages, which I recollect having heard Mr. Spaulding read from his "Manuscript."

One passage on the 148th page (the copy I have is published by J.O. Wright & Co., New York) I remember distinctly. He speaks of a battle, and says the Amalekites had marked themselves with red on their foreheads to distinguish them from the Nephites. The thought of being marked on the forehead was so strange that it fixed itself in my memory. This together with other passages I remember to have heard Mr. Spaulding read from his "manuscript". Those who knew Mr. Spaulding would soon all be gone and I among the rest. I write that what I knew may become a matter of history; and that it may prevent people from being led into Mormonism, that most seductive delusion of the devil. From what I know of Mr. Spaulding's "Manuscript" and the book of Mormon, I firmly believe that Joseph Smith, by some means, got possession of Mr. Spaulding's "manuscript" and possibly made some changes in it and called it the "Book of Mormon."

(Signed) Joseph Miller Sr.

In two letters submitted by John Storrs to the Boston Recorder, the first one by John Storrs, the second one written by Matilda Davison[5]

Matilda Davison was Solomon's Spaulding's wife. She remarried after his death.

Letter one. *To the Editor of the Boston Recorder*

Dear Sir, -- As the Pastor of the Congregational Church and society in this town, I have had occasion to come in contact with Mormonism in its grossest forms. Consequently, I have been led to make inquiries relative to its origin, progress, and, so far as they have any, the peculiar sentiments of its votaries. My object in this has been, as a faithful pastor, so far as possible, to arrest the progress of what I deem to be one of the rankest delusions ever palmed on poor human nature.

However, not supposing that the readers of the Recorder would be interested in the details of Mormonism in general, I send you for publication in your valuable periodical, the following communication, as a paper of unusual importance, giving a certified, sufficiently well attested and true account of the origin of the "Book of Mormon," or "Golden Bible," as it is sometimes called; on which the whole system mainly depends. And here, perhaps it should be said, that the leaders of the delusion pretend that the book was dug out of the ground, where it had been deposited for many centuries; that it was written on certain metallic plates, in a peculiar character or hieroglyphic; that the finder, a man of *money-digging* memory who was accustomed to look into the ground by aid of a peculiar stone, was in a similar manner enabled to read and translate it! Hence what is sometimes called the Mormon bible. But not such was its origin, according to the following communication.

The occasion of the communication coming into my hands, is as follows. Having heard incidentally that there was a lady in Monson, Ma., whose husband now dead was the author of the book, I requested in a note, Rev. D. R. Austin, Principal of Monson Academy, to obtain of her, for my benefit, and to be used as I should think proper, a certified account of its origin with her husband; for the character of which lady I wished the venerable Dr. Ely and himself to avouch. The following highly satisfactory document came in reply.

You are requested to insert it in the Recorder, not so much because it will interest the majority of your readers, but that the facts well attested may be laid up in memory, and the number of your paper containing them being kept, may afford the means to an enlightened community, to refute so great an imposition on the world. I would not only respectfully bespeak its publication in the Recorder, but in other papers; I would it were published throughout the land. For many Mormons are struggling throughout the country endeavoring to propagate their notions; and with some success, with a peculiar class of people. The origin of this pretended revelation being thus *completely authenticated*, may save many minds from delusion, fanaticism and ruin.

Yours respectfully,
John Storrs, Boston Recorder. HOLLISTON, APRIL 8, 1839

Letter from Matilda Davison

Origin of the "Book of Mormon," or "Golden Bible"

As this book has excited much attention, and has been put by a certain new sect in place of sacred scriptures, I deem it a duty which I owe to the public to state what I know touching its origin. That its claims to a divine origin are wholly unfounded needs no proof to a mind unperverted by the grossest delusions. That any sane person should rank it any higher than any other merely human composition is a matter of the greatest astonishment; yet it is received as divine by some who dwell in enlightened New England, and even by those who have sustained the character of devoted Christians. Learning recently that Mormonism has found its way into a Church in Massachusetts, and has impregnated some of its members with some of its gross delusions, so that ex-communication has become necessary, I am determined to delay no longer doing what I can to strip the mask from this monster of sin, and to lay open this pit of abomination.

Rev. Solomon Spalding, to whom I was united in marriage in early life, was a graduate of Dartmouth College, and was distinguished for a lively imagination and a great fondness for history. At the time of our marriage he resided in Cherry Valley, New York. From this place we removed to New Salem, Ashtabula County, Ohio, sometimes called Conneaut, as it is situated on Conneaut Creek. Shortly after our removal to this place, his health sunk, and he was laid aside from active labours. In the town of New Salem there are numerous mounds and forts, supposed by many to be the dilapidated dwellings and fortifications of a race now extinct. These ancient relics arrest the attention of the new settlers, and become objects of research for the curious. Numerous implements were found and other articles, evincing great skill in the arts.

Mr. Spalding being an educated man and passionately fond of history, took a lively interest in these developments of antiquity, and in order to beguile the hours of retirement and furnish employment for his lively imagination, he conceived the idea of giving an historical sketch of this long lost race. Their extreme antiquity of course would lead him to write in the most ancient style; and as the Old Testament is the most ancient book in the world, he imitated its style as nearly as possible. His sole object in writing this historical romance was to amuse himself and his neighbours. This was about the year 1812. Hull's surrender at Detroit occurred near the same time, and I recollect the date well from this circumstance. As he progressed in his narrative, the neighbours would come in from time to time to hear portions of it read, and a great interest in the work was excited among them. It is claimed to be written by one of the lost nation, and to have been recovered from the earth, and assumed the title of "Manuscript Found".

The neighbours would often enquire how Mr. Spalding progressed in deciphering the "manuscript", and when he had a sufficient portion prepared, he would inform them and they would assemble to hear it read. He was enabled from his acquaintance with the classics and ancient history to introduce many singular names, which were particularly noticed by the people, and could be easily recognized by them. Mr Solomon Spalding had a brother, Mr John Spalding, residing in the place at the time, who was perfectly familiar with the work, and repeatedly heard the whole of it read.

From New Salem we removed to Pittsburgh, Pa. Here we found a friend in the person of Mr. Patterson, an editor of a newspaper. He exhibited his manuscript to Mr.P, who was very much pleased with it, and borrowed it for perusal. He retained it for a long time and informed Mr. S. that if he would make out a title page and preface he would publish it, and it would be a source of profit. This Mr. S. refused to do, for reasons, which I cannot now state. Sidney Rigdon, one of the leaders and founders of the sect, who had figured so largely in the history of the Mormons, was at this time connected with the printing office of Mr. Patterson, as he is well known in that region, and as Rigdon himself has frequently stated. Here he had ample opportunity to become acquainted with Mr. Spalding's manuscript, and to copy it if he chose.

It was a matter of notoriety and interest to all who were connected to the printing establishment. At length the manuscript was returned to its author, and soon after we removed to Amity, Washington County, Pa., where Mr. S. deceased in 1816. The manuscript then fell into my hands, and was carefully preserved. It has frequently been examined by my daughter, Mrs Mc Kinstry, of Monson Mass., with whom I now reside, and by other friends. After the Book of Mormon came out, a copy of it was taken to New Salem, the place of Mr. Spalding's former residence, and the very place where "Manuscript Found" was written. A Mormon preacher appointed a meeting there, and in the meeting read and repeated copious extracts from the "Book of Mormon".

The historical part was immediately recognized by the older inhabitants as the identical work of Mr. Spalding in which they had been so deeply interested years before. Mr John Spalding was present, who is an eminently pious man, and recognized perfectly the work of his brother. He was amazed and afflicted that it should have perverted to so wicked a purpose. His grief found vent in a flood of tears, and he arose on the spot, expressed in the meeting his deep sorrow and regret that the writings of his sainted brother should be used for a purpose so vile and shocking. The excitement in New Salem became so great that the inhabitants had a meeting and deputed Dr. Philaster Hurlbut, one of their number, to repair to this place and to obtain from me the original manuscript of Mr. Spalding, for the purpose of comparing it with the Mormon Bible to satisfy their own minds and to prevent their friends from embracing an error so delusive.

This was in the year 1834. Dr.Hurlbut brought with him an introduction and request for the manuscript, signed by Messrs. Henry Lake, Aaron Wright and others, with all of whom I was acquainted, as they were my neighbours when I resided in New Salem. I am sure that nothing would grieve my husband more, were he living, than the use, which has been made of this work. The air of antiquity, which has been thrown about the composition, doubtless suggested the idea of converting it to purposes of delusion. Thus an historical romance, with the addition of a few pious expressions and extracts from the sacred scriptures, have been constructed into a new Bible, and palmed off upon a company of poor deluded fanatics as divine. I have given the previous narration that this work of deep deception and wickedness may be searched to the foundation and its author exposed to the contempt and execration he so justly deserves.

(Signed)
Matilda Davison

In the newspaper the *Quincy Whig* the following letter appeared.

Quincy Whig, Argus, &c.

By S. M. Bartlett.   Quincy, Illinois, Sat., Nov. 16, 1839.   Vol. 2 - No. 29

Copy of a letter written by Mr. John Haven of Holliston, Middlesex county, Massachusetts, to his daughter, Elizabeth Haven, of Quincy, Adams co., Ill.

Your brother Jesse passed through Monson, where he saw Mrs. Davidson, and her daughter, Mrs. McKinestry, and also Dr. Ely, and spent several hours with them, during which time he asked them the following questions, viz:

Did you, Mrs. Davidson, write a letter to John Storrs, giving an account of the origin of the Book of Mormon? Answer: I did not. Ques. Did you sign your name to it? Ans: I did not, neither did I ever see the letter until I saw it in the Boston Recorder, the letter was never brought to me to sign. Ques. What agency had you in having this letter sent to Mr. Storrs? Ans: D. R. Austin came to my house and asked me some questions, took some minutes on paper, and from these minutes wrote that letter. Ques. Is what is written in the letter true? Ans: In the main it is.

Rebuttal letter from Sidney Rigdon to The Boston Recorder[6]

May 27, 1839.

Messrs. Bartlett & Sullivan: --- In your paper of the 18th inst., I see a letter signed by somebody calling herself Matilda Davison…. It is only necessary to say, in relation to the whole story about Spaulding's writing being in the hands of Mr. Patterson, who was in Pittsburgh, and who is said to have kept a printing office, and my saying that I was connected in the said office, &c., & c., is the most base of lies, without even the shadow of truth. There was no man by the name of Patterson, during my residence at Pittsburgh, who had a printing office; what might have been before I lived there I know not. Mr. Robert Patterson, I was told, had owned a printing office before I lived in that city, but had been unfortunate in business, and failed before my residence there. This Mr. Patterson, who was a Presbyterian preacher, I had a very slight acquaintance with during my residence in Pittsburgh. He was then acting under an agency in the book and stationary business, and was the owner of no property of any kind, printing office or anything else, during the time I resided in the city.

If I were to say that I ever heard of the Rev. Solomon Spaulding and his wife, until Dr. P. Hurlbut wrote his lie about me, I should be a liar like unto themselves. Why was not the testimony of Mr. Patterson obtained to give force to this shameful tale of lies? The only reason is that he was not a fit tool for them to work with; he would not lie for them; for if he were called on, he would testify to what I have here said. Let me here, gentlemen give a history of this Dr. P. Hurlbut and his associates who aided in getting up and propagating this batch of lies.

I have seen and heard, at one time and another, by the persecutors and haters of the truth, a great deal about the eminent physician, Dr. Hurlbut. I never thought the matter worthy of notice, nor probably ever should, had it not made its appearance in your paper, or someone of equal respectability. And I believe, gentlemen, had you have known the whole history of this budget of lies, it would never have found place in your paper. But to my history this said Doctor was never a physician at any time, nor anything else, but a base ruffian. He was the seventh son and his parents called him Doctor; it was his name, and not the title of his profession. He once belonged to the Methodist Church, and was excluded for immoralities. He afterwards imposed himself on the Church of Latter-Day Saints and was excluded for using obscene language to a young lady, a member of the said Church, who resented his insult with indignation, which became both her character and profession.

After this exclusion he swore-- for he was vilely profane-- that he would have revenge, and commenced his work. He soon found assistance; a pious old Deacon of the Campbellite Church, by the name of Onis Clapp, and his two sons, Thomas J. Clapp, and Matthew S. Clapp, both Campbellite preachers, abetted and assisted by another Campbellite preacher, by the name of Adamson Bentley. Hurlbut went to work catering lies for the company. Before Hurlbut got through, his conduct became so scandalous that the company utterly refused to let his name go out with the lies he collected, and he and his associates had made, and they substituted the name of E.D. Howe. The change, however, was not much better. There were scandalous immoralities about the Howe family of so black a character that they had nothing to lose, and became good tools for this holy company to work with.

A man of character never would have put his name to a work, which Hurlbut was concerned in. The tale in your paper is one hatched up by this gang before the time of their expulsion. It has always been a source of no ordinary satisfaction to me to know that my enemies have no better weapon to use against me, or the cause in which I am engaged, than lies; for, if they had any better, they would certainly use them. I must confess, however, that there is some consistency in our persecutors; for, as truth can never destroy truth, it would be vain for our persecutors to use truth against us, for this would only build us up; this they seem to know, and lay hold of the only available means they have, which are lies. And this indeed, is the only weapon, which can be, or ever has been used against the truth.

As our persecutors are endeavouring to stop the progress of truth, I must confess that they act with a degree of consistency in the choice of means, namely, lies; but, if truth would do it, they would surely have recourse to lies. In order to give character to their lies, they dress them up with a great deal of piety; for a pious lie, you know has a great deal more interest with an ignorant people than a profane one.

Hence their lies came signed by the pious wife of a pious deceased priest. However, this last act of piety seems to have been to write a bundle of lies, themselves being witnesses; but then great piety sanctifies them, and lies become holy things in the hands of such excessive piety, particularly when they are graced with a few Reverend's sanctions; the intelligent part of the community of all parts of the country, know that Reverends are not more notorious for truth than their neighbours.

The only reason why I am assailed by lies is that my opposers dare not venture on argument, knowing that if they do they fall. They try, therefore, to keep the public from investigating, by publishing and circulating falsehoods. This I consider a high encomium on both myself and the cause I defend.

Respectfully

S. Rigdon

(*Author's Note: Eber Dudley Howe was the founder and editor of the Painsville Telegraph. He was also the author of one of the first anti-Mormon* books, "Mormonism Unvailed" {sic}. Some would dispute this and say that Philaster Hurlbut was the actual author and E.D. Howe published the book under his own name.)

THE

"MANUSCRIPT FOUND"

---- OR ----

"MANUSCRIPT STORY "

OF THE LATE

REV. SOLOMON SPAULDING;

FROM A

VERBATIM COPY OF THE ORIGINAL

NOW IN THE CARE OF PRES. JAMES H. FAIRCHILD,
OF OBERLIN COLLEGE, OHIO.

INCLUDING CORRESPONDENCE

TOUCHING THE MANUSCRIPT, ITS PRESERVATION
AND TRANS-
MISSION UNTIL IT CAME INTO THE HANDS OF
THE PUBLISHERS.

LAMONI, IOWA:
PRINTED AND PUBLISHED BY THE REORGANIZED
CHURCH OF
JESUS CHRIST OF LATTER DAY SAINTS.
1885

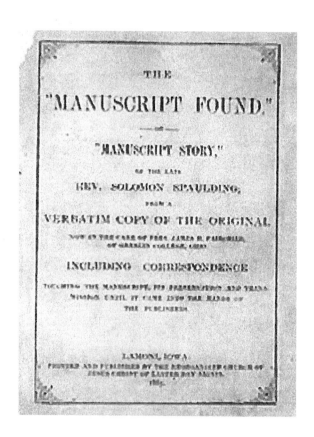

Original title page of the Manuscript Found

In a letter to Arthur B. Deming, Solomon Spaulding's daughter Mrs. M.S. Mc Kinstrey gives the following words on The Manuscript Found or Manuscript Story which Arthur B. Deming had sent to her.

Mrs. Mc Kinstrey[7]
WASHINGTON -- Nov. [20] th /86
Mr. A. B. Deming,

Dear Sir,

I have read much of the Manuscript Story Conneaut Creek which you sent me. I know that it is not the Manuscript Found which contained the words "Nephi, Mormon, Maroni, and Lamanites. Do the Mormons expect to deceive the public by leaving off the title page -- Conneaut Creek and calling it Manuscript Found and Manuscript Story?

Mrs. M. S. McKinstry

The last statement of Solomon Spaulding's daughter with her signature
A. B. DEMING

The 1885 Reorganized LDS edition of the Oblerlin Spalding manuscript was the first publication of the entire text. The typescript for the 1885 edition was furnished to the RLDS Church by James H. Fairchild

Manuscript Found or Manuscript Story

The following Correspondence explains the manner in which the Manuscript was preserved and placed in the hands of the present publishers. (Reorganized Church of Jesus Christ of Latter Day Saints)

James H. Fairchild's writings from the Bibliotheca Sacra were republished in many leading journals east and west.

Bibliotheca Sacra is the theological journal published by Dallas Theological Seminary. First published in 1844, it is the oldest theological journal in the

United States. It was originally published by Union Theological Seminary in 1843, moved to Andover Theological Seminary in 1844, then to Oberlin College in 1884, and to Xenia Seminary in 1922. Dallas Theological Seminary (then the Evangelical Theological Seminary) took over publication in 1934.

James H. Fairchild[8]

"The theory of the origin of the Book of Mormon in the traditional manuscript of Solomon Spaulding will probably have to be relinquished. That manuscript is doubtless now in the possession of Mr. L.L. Rice, of Honolulu, Hawaiian Islands, formerly an anti-slavery editor in Ohio, and for many years State printer at Columbus. During a recent visit to Honolulu, I suggested to Mr. Rice that he might have valuable anti-slavery documents in his possession which he would be willing to contribute to the rich collection already in the Oberlin College Library. In pursuance of this suggestion Mr. Rice began looking over his old pamphlets and papers, and at length came upon an old, worn, and faded manuscript of about 175 pages, small quarto, purporting to be a history of the migrations and conflicts of the ancient Indian tribes which occupied the territory now belonging to the states of New York, Ohio and Kentucky. On the last page of this manuscript is a certificate and signature giving the names of several persons known to the signer, who have assured him that, to their personal knowledge, the manuscript was the writing of Solomon Spaulding. Mr. Rice has no recollection how or when this manuscript came into his possession. It was enveloped in a coarse piece of wrapping paper and endorsed in Mr. Rice's handwriting "A Manuscript Story."

There seems no reason to doubt that this is the long-lost story. Mr. Rice, myself, and others compared it with the Book of Mormon, and could detect no resemblance between the two, in general or in detail. There seems to be no name or incident common to the two. The solemn style of the Book of Mormon, in imitation of the English Scriptures, does not appear in the manuscript. The only resemblance is in the fact that both profess to set forth the history of lost tribes. Some other explanation of the origin of the Book of Mormon must be found, if any explanation is required.

Signed, James H. Fairchild

Letter from Mr. Lewis L. Rice to Pres. Fairchild of Oberlin College
HONOLULU, H. I., June 12, 1885

PRESIDENT J. H. FAIRCHILD[9]

Herewith I send to you the Solomon Spalding Manuscript, to be deposited in the Library of Oberlin College, for reference by any one who may be desirous of seeing or examining it. As a great deal of inquiry has been made about it since it became known that it was in my possession, I deem it proper that it be deposited for safe keeping, where any one interested in it, whether Mormon or Anti-Mormon, may examine it. It has been in my possession forty-six years -- from 1839 to 1885 -- and for forty-four years of that time no one examined it, and I was not aware of the character of its contents.

I send it to you enclosed in the same wrapper, and tied with the same string that must have enclosed it for near half a century -- certainly during the forty-six years since it came into my possession. I have made and retain in my possession a correct literal copy of it, errors of orthography, of grammar, erasures and all. I may allow the Mormons of Utah to print from this copy, which they are anxious to do; and a delegation is now in the Islands, awaiting my decision on this point. They claim that they are entitled to whatever benefit they may derive from its publication; and it seems to me there is some justice in that claim. Whether it will relieve them in any measure, from the imputation that Solomon Spalding was the author of the Book of Mormon, I do not attempt to decide. It devolves upon their opponents to show that there are or were other writings of Spalding -- since it is evident that this writing is not the original of the Mormon Bible.

P. S. -- The words "Solomon Spaulding's Writings" in ink on the wrapper were written by me, after I became aware of the contents. The words "Manuscript Story -- Conneaut Creek," in faint penciling, were as now when it came into my possession.

L.L. R. Truly, yours, &c.,

L. L. RICE

Letter to Joseph Smith lll from Mr. L. L. Rice[10]
Joseph Smith lll was the Prophet of the Reorganized Church of Jesus
Christ of Latter Day Saints, and the son of Emma and Joseph Smith Jnr.
the founder of Mormonism.

MR. JOSEPH SMITH; Dear *Sir:* --

I am greatly obliged to you for the information concerning Mormonism, in
your letters of April 30th and May 2d. As I am in no sense a Mormonite,
of course it is a matter of curiosity, mainly, that I am interested in the
history of Mormonism.

Two things are true concerning this manuscript in my possession: First,
it is a genuine writing of Solomon Spaulding; and second. It is *not* the
original of the Book of Mormon.

My opinion is, from all I have seen and learned, that this is the *only*
writing of Spaulding, and there is no foundation for the statement of
Deming and others, that Spaulding made another story, more elaborate,
of which several copies were written, one of which Rigdon stole from a
printing office in Pittsburgh, &c. Of course I can not be as certain of this,
as of the other two points. One theory is, that Rigdon, or some one else,
saw this manuscript, or heard it read, and from the hints it conveyed, got
up the other and more elaborate writing on which the Book of Mormon
was founded. Take that for what it is worth. It don't seem to me very
likely.

Another letter from L.L.Rice to Joseph Smith lll
Mr. Joseph Smith:[11]

The Spaulding Manuscript in my possession came into my hands on
this wise. In 1839-40 my partner and myself bought of E.D. Howe the
Painsville Telegraph, published at Painsville, Ohio. The transfer of the
printing dept, types, press, &c., was accompanied with a large collection of
books, manuscripts, &c, this manuscript of Spaulding among the rest.

On 26th Feb.1886 Lewis L. Rice writes one of his last letters to Mr.James A. Briggs. At this point Rice still did not accept any connection between the writings of Spalding and the Book of Mormon. However, at about this same time Rice receives information from Briggs which helped him change his mind and give the Spalding authorship claim more serious consideration.

James Alfred Briggs, Esq. Was a prominent attorney in Cleveland, Ohio, and New York State. He, at various times, worked as a civil official, financial journalist, temperance advocate; political supporter of Abraham Lincoln, NY correspondent to several newspapers, and was also briefly the editor of the *Cleveland True Democrat* in 1848-49.

HON. JAMES A. BRIGG'S STATEMENT[12]

The manuscript of Rev. Solomon Spaulding, Conneaut, Ohio, found by Mr. L. L. Rice, of Honolulu, Sandwich Islands, and now in the archives in the Library of Oberlin, Ohio, and published by the reorganized Church of Jesus Christ of Latter Day Saints, Lamoni, Iowa, throws no more light upon the authorship or origin of the "Mormon Bible" or "Book of Mormon" or the "Golden Bible" than it does upon the real authorship of the Letters of Junius.

The manuscript came in the possession of Mr. Rice legitimately being among the effects of the Painsville *Telegraph*, bought by him of its former owner, Mr. E. D. Howe, who published, in 1834, a book "Mormonism Unveiled." Now, Mr. Joseph Smith of Lamoni, Iowa, you assume altogether too much when you say the newly found missing link completes the chain of evidence which proves that the "Manuscript Found" never was, and never could be made the occasion, cause or germ of the "Book of Mormon." I have just read the Manuscript Story you sent me a few days ago, by request of my old and much valued friend, Mr. L. L. Rice, of Honolulu, and in my opinion it settles nothing, save that the author of the story was a very weak brother, and if written by Rev. Solomon Spaulding, he was a man of indigent talents, and the money paid for his college expenses was wasted.

Allow me to doubt if he wrote it. You must get some better and more positive link in the chain of evidence than this story, recently printed, to convince the world that the original "Manuscript Found," written by Solomon Spaulding, was not the basis for the historical portion of your Mormon Bible. Let me state some stubborn facts, not only from my own memory, but substantiated by witnesses; from Oct., 1832, until the first of April, 1834, I lived in the village of Willoughby, some two and one-half miles from the village of Kirtland, where your first Mormon temple was built, and yet stands. I heard much of Mormonism, heard its most eloquent champion, Rev. Sidney Rigdon, preach.

In the winter of 1833-34, or in the early spring of 1834, a number of gentlemen in Willoughby who felt an interest in the Mormon question appointed themselves a committee to look into the matter. They were Judge Nehemiah Allen, who had been an associate Judge of the county of Cuyahoga, a representative in the Legislature; Dr. George W. Card, an intelligent physician, Samuel Wilson, an active and energetic business man; Jonathan Lapham, a lawyer of many years at the bar, and myself, a very young lawyer.

We met at the house of Mr. W. Corning, in Mentor, now the Garfield place, a well-to-do and independent farmer. Dr. P. Hurlbut also met with us. He lived in Kirtland and during the winter and spring had given much time in looking up evidence and documents to prove that Mormonism was a delusion. He had much of the evidence that he had collected with him. Now I am very sure he had the identical story that you have printed with him. I remember about the ancient fort at Conneaut Creek, the mound, and the statement of finding the manuscript about the Indians.

I have no doubt that Hurlbut, as he says, gave the story to Mr. E. D. Howe. But I believe he had also with him, and we had before us in that investigation, the original "Manuscript Found" written by Rev. Solomon Spaulding. I have said and believed for more than fifty years that I have seen and had in my hands the original "Manuscript Found" from which the Mormon Bible was made.

I have no doubt we had the "Manuscript Found" before us, that we compared it with the Mormon Bible, that the style in which the "Manuscript Found" was written was the same as that of the Mormon Bible. The names -- peculiar -- were the same, not to be forgotten. The names Lehi, Nephi, Maroni, etc., and the expression "and it came to pass" often repeated. This manuscript did not go to Mr. Howe. What did Hurlbut do with it?

Some few years ago I wrote to him and asked him who had it -- what he did with it. He did not answer my letter. He received it, as it was not returned to me. Dr. Hurlbut died in Ohio two years ago last June. He is silent now, the grave closed over him. Of Dr. Hurlbut and this "Manuscript Found" the Rev. D. R. Austin, of Munson, Mass, writes in a letter to Rev. Dr. Clark, June 28, 1841. "He, Dr. Hurlbut, stated some time after he had received it, the Manuscript, he had made four hundred dollars out of it." Whether Dr. H. sold the Manuscript in question or not, it is certain he did not give it to Howe with the other documents and the Manuscript Story is not the "Manuscript Found" of Spaulding. Was there more than one Manuscript of Spaulding? John N. Miller writes in 1833, as follows:

"In 1811 I was in the employ of Henry Lake and Solomon Spaulding at Conneaut. I boarded and lodged in the family of Spaulding for several months. I was soon introduced to the Manuscript of Spaulding and perused it as I had leisure. He had written two or three books or pamphlets on different subjects, but that which particularly drew my attention was one which he called "Manuscript Found." I have recently examined the "Book of Mormon" and found in it the writings of Solomon Spaulding from beginning to end." Several of the witnesses who knew Spaulding intimately and well and heard him read, and had read themselves, the "Manuscript Found," certify that they recognized the names of the Manuscript in the "Book of Mormon." They are positive; they admit of no doubt. The statements of Mr. Robert Patterson, of Pittsburgh, Pa., the son of Mr. R. Patterson, the printer with whom Spaulding left his "Manuscript Found," in his history of the "Book of Mormon" shows how the Rev. Sidney Rigdon was mixed up with it".

Letter from L.L.Rice to the Daily Bulletin[13]

The Daily Bulletin

Vol. IX. No. 1273.   Honolulu, Wednesday, March 11, 1886.   50 ¢ per mo.

MORMONISM

EDITOR BULLETIN:-- As you have taken interest enough in the Mormon question to publish an account of the Spaulding Manuscript recently in my possession, it occurs to me that a more specific statement of some points connected with Mormonism and the Mormon Bible, may be of interest to you and your readers; especially as it is alleged, with some evidences of probability, that the Utah Mormons contemplate establishing a large colony of their followers on these Islands, and even of transferring their headquarters here.

The Spaulding Manuscript recently discovered in my possession, and published by the Mormons, in no wise determines the question as to the authorship of the Book of Mormon, or of Spaulding's connection with the latter. It shows conclusively that *this writing* of Spaulding was not the original of the Book of Mormon -- nothing more in that regard. It gives the Mormons the advantage of calling upon their opponents to produce or prove that any other Spaulding Manuscript ever existed -- and that is the gist of the whole matter.

Until lately I have been of the opinion that there was no tangible evidence that any other production of Solomon Spaulding, bearing upon the question, could be shown as having ever existed. But correspondence and discussions growing out of the publication of this document, have shaken my faith in that belief, and indeed produced quite a change of opinion on that subject. I will refer to several items productive of that change of opinion.

Mr. A. B. Deming, of Painesville, Ohio, who has investigated the subject thoroughly, writes to me that he has evidence that Spaulding, after writing the story which has recently come to light, without finishing it, changed his plan, and got up a more elaborate story, which he denominated

29

"Manuscript Found," of which he made two or more copies, and sent one to Pittsburgh for publication -- from whence Sidney Rigdon obtained it -- and on which the historical part of the Book of Mormon was based.

(It is to be noted that the title "Manuscript Found," is not given in the manuscript recently in my possession, at all. It was added by the publisher of the copy furnished you by Prof. Alexander.)

Colonel William H. Leffingwell, a well-known teacher in Northern Ohio., says recently, in the St. Louis Republican.

"Long ago in the past, I have forgotten the year. Mr. Spalding wrote a drama called "The Book of Mormon," in a hotel at Conneaut, Ashtabula County, Ohio, where I had been teaching school. I was known through the country as a good grammarian and possessing an accurate knowledge of the English language. My father had been principal of the Meadville school, at Meadville, Penn., for eight years, a position which I subsequently filled on my father retiring to a farm. Mr. Spalding was a lawyer by profession and had taught school. He had never been a reverend, as some accounts give that prefix to his name. He was about 35 years of age when I first fell in with him, was very poor, and sick with consumption, and toward the last nearly lost his voice, so that he could not plead at the bar. He said he wanted to make some money, and wrote the drama, which he handed me for correction. It was full of Bible expressions, and as I had read the Bible from lid to lid I knew the proper phraseology to use. I corrected the grammar, and had to reconstruct and transpose entries to make good English out of it. I was engaged three months, and my notes and pencil marks may be found on every page."

There were no such "notes and pencil marks" on the pages of my manuscript.

James A. Briggs, Esq., was a well known and reputable lawyer in Northern Ohio for many years, and for a dozen years past a public officer in New York City, resided at Willoughby, Ohio, four miles from Kirtland, when the Mormons first located at the latter place. In a letter to the New York *Tribune,* dated Jan. 29, 1886

Mr. Briggs says: --

"In the winter of 1833-34, a self constituted committee, consisting of Judge Allen, Dr. Card, Samuel Wilson, Judge Lapham, W. Corning and myself, met at Mr. Corning's house, in Mentor, now known as the Garfield farm, to investigate Mormonism and the origin of the Mormon Bible. Dr. D.P. Hurlburt, whose name is mentioned in the article in your paper this morning, was employed to look up testimony. He was present with the committee and had Spaulding's original manuscript with him. We compared it, chapter by chapter with the Mormon Bible. It was written in the same style, many of the names were the same, and we came to the conclusion, from all the testimony before us, that the Rev. Sidney Rigdon, the eloquent Mormon preacher, made the Mormon Bible from this manuscript. Of this the committee had no doubt whatever.

About this time Dr. Hurlburt had some trouble with the Mormons at Kirtland, where they had built a temple, and he had the prophet, Joseph Smith, arrested on a warrant of a justice of the peace for assault and battery. He had an examination before two justices in the Old Methodist Church in Painesville. It lasted three days. Judge Benjamin Bissell was the attorney for Smith and I was the attorney for Dr. Hurlburt. The examination produced much interest. Cowdery, Hyde and Pratt, Mormon leaders, were there with "Joe" Smith. I said to Mr. Bissell, let us get from 'The Prophet' his history of the finding of the 'golden plates.' Mr. B. consented and for two days we had the Prophet, 'Joe' Smith, on the witness stand. He swore, that is, under oath, that he found the golden plates buried in the earth in a field in Palmyra, N.Y., and when he found them he was kicked by an unseen foot out of the hole in which they were placed. All present knew that it was a Mormon lie. Rigdon was a natural orator, and had much native genius. He got the manuscript in Pittsburgh at the printing office of Mr. Robert Patterson, the father of the present Mr. Robert Patterson, who has published an interesting history of Mormonism, showing without doubt that the Rev. Sidney Rigdon was the compiler of the Book of Mormon.

In 1879, Dr. Hurlburt was living at Gibsonburg, Ohio.

In a letter to Mr. Patterson, of Pittsburgh, he says: 'I gave the manuscript with all my other documents connected with Mormonism to Mr. Howe.' Mr. Rice was the successor of Mr. Howe in *The Telegraph*, and this accounts for his possession of the 'manuscript found' at this late day in an island in the Pacific Ocean."

This testimony of Mr. Briggs is entirely reliable. I was acqu[a]inted {sic} with all the members of the "self-constituted committee" of which he speaks.

The mooted question now is what became of the Manuscript before the Committee, which they "compared chapter by chapter with the Mormon Bible," and found them to correspond so perfectly? Mr. Deming, already referred to, says that Dr. Hurlburt sold it to the Mormons for $400 with which he purchased the farm he occupied at Gibson's burgh, at the time he wrote to Mr. Patterson, as related by Mr. Briggs. My belief is, from the above and other testimony in my possession, that either Hurlburt or Howe sold it to the Mormons, who of course destroyed it, or put it out of the way.

Yours for the truth and the right
L. L. RICE
Honolulu, March 4, 1886

L.L. Rice[14]

L.L.Rice was born in Otsego Co., N. Y., in 1801. As a young man he went to New York City where he learned the printing business early in this century. While living there he was led to take the total abstinence pledge, and enrolled himself upon that platform, and has done much for the cause of temperance during a long life, the most of which found him identified with the newspapers of Ohio. He went to that State before 1830, and for fifty years was one of her leading citizens. About 1830 he began the publication of an anti-Masonic paper. A few years later he removed to Cleveland where for many years he was the editor and publisher of a paper which was the predecessor of the *Cleveland Leader* and was dedicated to the agitation of anti-slavery principles.

In 1848 he went to Columbus, the capital of the State, and began the publication of a paper in that city. For more than twenty-five years he was identified with the public life of Columbus, at first as an editor, then as State printer, and in other positions.

The following letter was published in the Daily Press Vol. II. No. 40 Honolulu, Thursday, April 15, 1886

THE MORMON BIBLE[15]
Col. W. H. Leffingwell's revision of the Spalding Manuscript

He Details His Visit to the Temple of the Saints at Kirtland, Ohio.

The venerable Col. Wm. H. Leffingwell, accompanied by an old Mormon friend from Utah, was met by a Republican reporter yesterday afternoon on Olive Street. The colonel's friend remarked to the reporter: "Did you know that Leffingwell corrected the manuscript of the Mormon Bible alleged to have been written by Rev. Solomon Spalding?"

This was something like a new revelation, and on Col. Leffingwell stating that it was a fact, and as all parties knowing the circumstances are now dead, except Mr. Leffingwell, he was asked to add to the truth of history by telling what he knew about the origin of the Mormon bible. The colonel readily consented but his Mormon friend, observing his readiness to do so, walked on and beckoned to the colonel to come along, evidently objecting to having the story told for publication.

Col. Leffingwell commenced by saying: "Long ago in the past, I have forgotten the year, Mr. Spalding wrote a drama called 'the Book of Mormon,' in a hotel at Conneaut, Ashtabula county, O., where I had been teaching school. I was known through the country as a good grammarian and possessing an accurate knowledge of the English language. My father had been principal of the Meadville school, at Meadville, Pa., for eight years, a position which I subsequently filled on my father retiring to a farm. Mr. Spalding was a lawyer by profession and had taught school. He had never been a reverend, as some accounts give that prefix to his name. He was about [35] years of age when I first fell in with him, was very poor, and sick with consumption, and towards the last nearly lost his voice, so that he could not plead at the bar. He said he wanted to make some money, and wrote the drama, which he handed me for correction. It was full of Bible expressions, and as I had read the Bible from lid to lid I knew the proper phraseology to use. I corrected the grammar, and had to reconstruct and transpose entries to make god English out of it. I was engaged three months, and my notes and pencil marks may be found on every page.

NEVER PAID FOR IT

"He wanted it to conform to Bible language. He never paid me a cent for my labor. It was entitled the Book of Mormon, and he told me he was going to Pittsburgh to sell the manuscript. I afterwards learned that he got hold of Sidney Rigdon, and I knew within six months that Spalding sold it, and that Rigdon got it. Rigdon was a preacher in the Cumberland Presbyterian church. He was a scholar and a smart fellow. I had seen him baptizing converts in Mahoning County, Ohio. Some years afterward I was on a lecture tour in Ohio, lecturing on grammar and the construction of English language.

I went to Kirtland in a buggy accompanied by a young lawyer, to see Joe Smith and the Mormon leaders. We drove up in front of a large tent and Sidney Rigdon came out. I told him that I corrected the Mormon Bible when it was Spalding's manuscript. I assured him I gave it the proper construction and what grammar it had. He smiled and said that was all right, but requested me to say nothing about it. I told Rigdon that we came over there to see him and Joe Smith. He said, 'It is just our dinner time; you can't see Joe Smith because he is marking goods at the store.' they having received forty wagon-loads from the lake shore the day before. Afterwards we were introduced to the prophet. Joe Smith had a round face, and his hair was cut short down on his forehead. The color of his hair was between a deep brown and dark red. He sent a young man with us into the temple, which was but newly finished. The front had a projecting roof, supported by pillars. We entered the portico, when the young man, our guide, said: "Take off your hats!" I replied; "Our hats are already off, sir. We've a long ways to drive, and want you to hurry up, sir!"

THE TEMPLE DIVIDED

"We were then conducted into the interior of the temple. A broad aisle ran through the middle of the temple with a cross aisle in the centre, above which a curtain hung, dividing the temple into two parts, Sidney Rigdon occupying, we were told, the eastern portion and Joe Smith the western portion, which included the grand altar. The arrangement seemed to be thus made in consequence of the incomplete conditions of the temple. By mounting on one another's shoulders, we were enabled to pull ourselves up through a hole in the attic where we were shown several mummies including that of Joseph and other patriarchs mentioned in the Bible. After visiting the temple we were invited into the tent where we were provided with a good dinner, and taking leave of the saints we drove out of Kirtland well satisfied with our visit."

Concerning John C. Dowen's statement[16]

This affidavit was taken by Arthur B. Deming from John C. Dowen in January 1885. The original is a five page typed document (all in capital letters) on file in the A. B. Deming section of the Mormonism Collection of papers and letters in the Chicago Historical Society Library.

CENTENNIAL MEMORIAL EDITION

NAKED TRUTHS ABOUT MORMONISM.

Also a Journal for IMPORTANT NEWLY APPREHENDED TRUTHS, and Miscellany.
IN MEMORY OF ARTHUR B. DEMING. ALL RIGHTS RESERVED.
Published irregularly by A.B. DEMING SOCIETY, Berkely, California

VOL. II.	BERKELEY, CAL., DECEMBER, 1988.	NO. 1.

This obscure paper from 1988-89 was reportedly intended as a limited-print edition, but the project was abandoned. Proof sheets for the pilot issue remain in a private collection. The abortive publication was evidently never copyrighted.

[pg. 1 col. 3]

STATEMENT OF J C DOWEN

I came to Kirtland, Ohio, from Oneida Co., N.Y., in June 1832. I bought the Allen Farm one mile south of the Mormon Temple, in Kirtland, July 6, 1832. In 1833, and again in 1836, I was elected Justice of the Peace on the Democratic ticket. I have been a full-blooded Democrat and Temperance man all my life. I was steward of the Methodist Church; some said I was boss, and all hands. I refused three-fourths of the demands for warrants. I tried over two hundred cases. I frequently held court at my house, but generally at Johnson's Brick Tavern at the flats. Bissel, one of Ohio's ablest lawyers, who lived at Painesville, was always counsel for the Mormons in important cases. He had 52 cases before me.

Bissel said Squire Russell, who proceeded me, by noticing drunken fights had made over one thousand dollars cost to the town. He told me if two men fought over a bottle of whiskey, and one man killed the other, not to notice it, and he would see me through. There was a distillery opposite the Temple, and I never saw so much drunkenness elsewhere. I threatened to complain to the State authorities. While quarrelling, a Mormon woman drew a butcher knife through Mrs. Ellis's, a Methodist woman's hand. Joe Smith took sides, and Jacob Bump, with Martin Harris, came to the trial. I told Jo, Martin told me a certain day that he found the plates of the Book of Mormon; Martin said I lied. I told him he must not say that again in my house. He said God never made a man who could harm him. I took him by the shoulder and pulled him to the floor on his hands and feet, and walked him to the door. I took him by the collar and seat of the breeches and threw him out and kicked him. Jo said he was sorry I did not hear him through. Martin was very kind to me ever after. I got the name of the Fighting Justice.

I issued a writ for Jo and his brother, Sam Smith, for non-attendance at training. I decided that as Rev. Coe, the Presbyterian minister, was exempt, I excused, Joe because he was a preacher, which pleased him very much. Sam I fined $1.75. He appealed. I placed him under $50 bond. It cost him considerable. Bissel said Judge Allen or the Devil put that in my head. Joe, his brother Bill, and others had a fight, I did not notice it. They were raising the devil all the time. Colonel John Morse, brother of Harvey, applied to me for a writ against Jo Smith for an assault. Joe begged me not to issue a writ against him. He told me every three or four days a writ was served on him to go to Chardon. Col. Ames, who was a drunken constable and slow pay, had owed me some time. I met him one Sunday at Johnson's Hotel. He said if it was not Sunday he would pay me. I told him it was not and he could not get out of paying. I gave Johnson a quarter.

[pg. 1 col. 4: Dowen continued]

I heard Dr. P. Hurlbut, who had been a Mormon preacher, preach a good sermon, and then deliver his first lecture in the Methodist Church in Kirtland, Ohio, on the origin of the Book of Mormon. He said he had been in New York and Pennsylvania and had obtained a copy of Spaulding's Manuscript Found. He read selection[s] from it, then the same from the Book of Mormon. He said the historical part of it was the same as Spaulding's Manuscript Found. He read numerous affidavits from parties in N.Y. and Penn. showing the disreputable character of the Mormon Smith Family.

Hurlbut staid {sic} at my house every three or four days for as many months. I read all of his manuscript, including Spaulding's Manuscript Found, and compared it with the Book of Mormon, the historical part of which is the same as Spaulding's Manuscript Found, which is about the size of the papyrus Jo had with his Egyptian mummies. Hurlbut said he would kill Jo Smith. He meant he would kill Mormonism. The Mormons urged me to issue a writ against him. I did, as recorded in my Docket, Dec. 27, 1833, on complaint of Joseph Smith, warrant returnable to William Holbrook, Esq., at Painesville, Ohio. He was brought to trial and over 50 [15?] witnesses were called. The trial lasted several days, and he was bound over to appear at the Court of Common Pleas at Chardon. Hurlbut let E. D. Howe, of Painesville, have his manuscript to publish. I should not be surprised if Howe sold Spaulding's Manuscript Found to the Mormons. There was all kinds of iniquity practiced at that time.

I knew Brigham Young as well as my adopted daughter. He had been to Methodist meetings with me in Kirtland, and we sang from the same book, knelt down and we both prayed. The Young's were lazy and distressedly poor. Brigham worked for me at farming one month. He said I was the only independent man in Kirtland. I was on good terms with the Mormons. I always had from one to five at my table and in my employ. My adopted son joined them. My wife's sister, Hester said she believed in spiritual wives and went West with them. It was claimed that more than forty of the leading Mormons had sealed to them spiritual wives, which were the same as any. Dr. Lattin Seeley, a brother of Dr. Seeley at Mentor, who lived at the flats, urged me to arrest leading Mormons for adultery and polygamy. But I refused. I never had any confidence in Rigdon; I believed the Mormon Leaders were dishonest and deceivers. There were some who were bright intelligent and good citizens; the majority were low, mean and dirty set, very poor and ignorant. I knew, but have forgotten, the names of Joe Smith's two spiritual wives in Kirtland. He claimed to receive revelations to lie with certain women, and had accomplished his purpose by the aid of a favorite woman. I had excellent opportunities of judging the character of Mormons and studied them closely.

The Smiths were a coarse, ignorant, rough set, I doubt if God ever made a meaner man than the Prophet Joe Smith. Joe Smith's sister once said to me, "How much better we live since we became Mormons." Oliver Cowdery told me he baptized Joe and then Joe baptized him. Joseph Coe, who owned a mill, told me he let Rigdon ride his horse from Mo. to Kirtland and he walked. He wanted to go again against his wife's wishes, she was past reproduction, but she wore a pillow and told her husband she was in an interesting condition. He believed all things were possible to Mormons and did not go to Missouri.

[pg. 1 col. 5: Dowen continued, etc.]

The Mormons warned Justice of the Peace, Hanson, out of town. He had much property and did not leave. Rigdon never came to my house. He knew I never believed in his doctrine. Mr. Wetherbee, a Mormon whose farm joined mine, told me the Mormons drank a barrel of liquor at the endowment or dedication of the Temple at communion. I always ask[ed] questions so as to obtain information I desired from the Mormons. The Mormons were not permitted to marry couples. They often had me perform the legal marriage ceremony and afterward Joe Smith would, as he claimed, marry them according to the gospel.

I married a number of Mormons near the flats and narrated the history of our First Parents, and alluded to taking Adam's rib to form Woman. There were many young women present, including Polly Johnson, who thought they would ascertain if Man had the full number of ribs. They took John Johnson, a Willoughby school teacher, no relation to Polly, threw him on the floor. He fought and kicked. They held him, unbuttoned his shirt bosom and counted his ribs. They said men had the right number. Many other things equally ridiculous were frequently done by Mormons at weddings.

I was present when the corner stone of the Mormon Temple was laid. They put the trinkets in the south east corner, near the road. Grandison Newell hated me. He was too fast in egging P. P. Pratt. The majority of the Mormons were Democrats. Joe Smith['s] attempts to walk on the water and raise a dead child occurred a short time previous to my arrival in Kirtland. If I should tell you all that was said to me about the conduct of the Mormons, in and about Kirtland, it would make a book much larger than you want. Some cases were so offensive I would not disgrace my docket with them, and did not try them after issuing warrants for arrest. I believe I know more of the history of Mormonism in Kirtland than any man living.

I have heard Mr. Deming read this statement distinctly and make it as the last important act of my li[fe], hoping it will prevent people from embracing the Mormon Delusion.

J. C. DOWEN.

Witnessed by:

HATTIE C. STRONG grand daughter
JOHN H. STRONG, grand son. *Willoughby, Lake Co., Ohio.* Sworn to and subscribed to before me this 2d. Day of Jan., 1885 A. P. BARBER, Justice of the Peace.
At J. C. Dowen's request I was present and heard A. B. Deming read distinctly this statement to Mr. Dowen before being signed, which he said was correct. A. P. ARBER

John C. Dowen died February 2nd, 1885, in the eighty-ninth year of his age.

Notes

1. Howe E.D., *Mormonism Unvailed* [Sic] pp. 278-280
2. Ibid. 281-282
3. Ibid., p.284
4. Creigh, Alfred History of Washington Pa, pp.90-91) Harrisburg B.Singerly, Pub, 1870, 71)
5. Boston Recorder Published by Nathaniel Willis April 8, 1839
6. Boston Recorder Published by Nathaniel Willis No 16-Vol XXlV Friday, April 19, 1839
7. Arthur B. Deming's *Naked Truths About Mormonism* ll (Berkeley, California: A.B. Deming Society) [Pg.1 col 5:]
8. The Manuscript Found. P 5-6 Published by the Reorganised church of Jesus Christ of Latter Day Saints.
9. The Manuscript Story. P. 10
10. Letter to Joseph Smith lll from L Rice. The Manuscript Story published by the Reorganised church of Jesus Christ of Latter Day Saints.
11. The Manuscript Story Page 6
12. John Codman *"Mormonism"* The International Review Xl: 3 (NYC: A.S. Brarnes &Co, Sept. 1881) Page 4 col. 4-5
13. The Daily Bulletin Vol lX No 1273 Honolulu March 11, 1886
14. Daily Press Vol. 11. No 40 Honolulu, Thursday, April 15, 1886
15. Daily Missouri Republican Vol LXXVll May 29, 1885
16. Arthur B. Deming's *Naked Truths About Mormonism II December 1988 No 1* (Berkeley, California: A. B. Deming Society) Page 1 col. 3, 4 &5

Chapter Three

Sidney Rigdon

Sidney Rigdon was born February 19, 1793 near the present village of Library, Allegheny Co., Pennsylvania. He attended in boyhood an ordinary country school. He joined the Baptist Church near his home May 31, 1817. He studied divinity with a Baptist preacher named Clark in Beaver County, Pa., and in the winter of 1818-19, was licensed to preach. He then went to Warren Ohio, where he was ordained. He returned to Pittsburgh where he became pastor of the First Baptist Church there Jan. 28, 1822, and for doctrinal errors was excluded from the Baptist denomination Oct. 11, 1823.

He continued to preach in the court-house to his adherents, but in 1824, according to one account, he removed to the Western Reserve, Ohio. According to another he engaged in the tanning business in Pittsburgh until 1826, and then removed to the Reserve, residing for brief periods at Bainbridge, Mentor, and Kirtland. At this time he was connected with the Campbellite or Disciples' Church, and preached its doctrines, mingled with extravagant conceits of his own, until in 1830 he joined the Mormons.

Isaac King[1] a highly-respected citizen of Library, Pa., and an old neighbor of Rigdon, states in a letter to the present writer, (Robert Patterson Jnr.) dated June 14, 1879, that Sidney lived on the farm of his father until the death of the latter in May, 1810, and for a number of years afterwards, farming with very indifferent success; "it was said he was too lazy and proud to make a good farmer:" received his education in a log school-house in the vicinity; "began to talk in public on religion soon after his admission to the Church, probably at his own instance, as there is no record of his licensure:" went to Sharon, Pa., for a time, and was there ordained as a preacher, but soon returned to his farm, which he sold

(June 26, 1823) to James Means, and about the time of the sale removed to Pittsburgh.

Charles A. Shook[2]

At R and J. Patterson's print shop Rigdon became friends with a printer by the name of J.H. Lambdin. This is the print shop that Solomon Spalding brought his manuscript to. Solomon Spalding lived in Pittsburgh between 1812 and 1814 and then moved to Amity In 1814 leaving a copy of the manuscript in the print shop.

After Spalding moved to Amity, his manuscript disappeared from Patterson's Print Shop. Spalding told Dr. Cephas Dodd (Solomon's physician) and Rev. Joseph Miller that he suspected Rigdon of the theft. Spalding died in 1816. The physician who attended Spaulding during his last illness was Dr. Cephas Dodd. Spaulding was very confidential, and confided to him his suspicions of the theft. After the death of Spaulding, Dr. Dodd purchased a copy of the Book of Mormon, and, after reading it, inscribed the following on one of the fly-leaves, June 6, 1831:

This work, I am convinced by facts related to me by my deceased patient, Solomon Spaulding, has been made from writings of Spaulding, probably by Sidney Rigdon, who was suspicioned by Spaulding with purloining his manuscript from the publishing-house to which he had taken it; and I am prepared to testify that Spaulding told me that his work was entitled, "The Manuscript Found in the Wilds of Mormon; or Unearthed Records of the Nephites." From his description of its contents, I fully believe that this Book of Mormon is mainly and wickedly copied from it.

CEPHAS DODD
JUNE 6, 1831

Robert Patterson Jr.[3]

In 1817 Rigdon was accepted into the membership of the First Baptist Church near his hometown of Library.

He was ordained during 1818 or 1819. He married Phoebe Brooks In 1820. Rigdon became the minister of the First Baptist Church of Pittsburgh in 1822, and it was during this time that he showed Spalding's manuscript to Dr. Winter. On October 11, 1823 Rigdon was excommunicated from the First Baptist Church for teaching irregular doctrine.

Rev.John Winter, M.D., was one of the early ministers of the Baptist Church, labouring in Western Pennsylvania, and Eastern Ohio. During a portion of the time when Sidney Rigdon was pastor of the First Baptist Church in Pittsburgh, Dr. Winter was teaching a school in the same city, and was well acquainted with Rigdon. Upon one occasion during this period, 1822-23, Dr. Winter was in Rigdon's study, when the latter took from his desk a large manuscript and said in substance.

"A Presbyterian minister, Spaulding, whose health had failed, brought this to the printer to see if it would pay to publish it. It is a romance of the Bible." Dr. Winter did not read any part of it, and paid no more attention to it until after the Book of Mormon appeared, when he heard that Mr. Spaulding's widow recognized in it the writings of her husband.

The authority for the above statement is Rev. A. G. Kirk, to whom Dr. Winter communicated it in a conversation at New Brighten, Pa., in 1870-71. Dr. Winter died at Sharon, Pa., in 1878. Mr. Kirk conveyed this information to the present writer (Robert Patterson Jnr).by letter, March 23.

Joseph Smith became a candidate for President of the United States in 1844. Sidney Rigdon was nominated as his running mate and took up residence in Pittsburgh to carry on the campaign. He was in Pittsburgh when news arrived of Joseph Smith's murder. He hastened to Nauvoo to offer himself as a "guardian of the Church," promising to act as such until Joseph Smith was resurrected from the dead. At a meeting in Nauvoo on August 8, 1844, Church members rejected him as guardian. The Twelve Apostles were sustained as the head of the Church.

Rigdon undertook to establish a rival leadership. He was excommunicated in September 1844 and left with a few disciples for Pennsylvania, where they organized a Church of Christ. He lost most of his followers in less than two years. In 1863, he made another effort, founding the Church of Jesus Christ of the Children of Zion. From 1847 to his death in 1876, Rigdon resided in Friendship, New York, usually in a state of emotional imbalance and unhappiness.

Robert Patterson, Jr.

Sidney Rigdon died in Friendship, New York, On July 14, 1876

The Salt Lake Daily Tribune

Vol. XXXIIII.   Salt Lake City, Utah, Sunday, April 15, 1888.   No. 155.

THE "GOLDEN BIBLE."

**Sidney Rigdon's grandson says their family
understood it to be a fraud.**

J.H. BEADLE

EDITOR TRIBUNE: -- In the intervals of my literary labors here I have many talks with men who were in Utah at a very early day, and occasionally with original Mormons or their sons, which would be interesting had I the time to detail them. But my chance talks with one of these are so agreeable that I report him briefly for you. Mr. Walter Sidney Rigdon is a citizen of Carrolton, Cattaraugus County, N. Y., and a grandson of Sidney Rigdon, the partner of Joe Smith. He talked with old Sidney hundreds of times about the "scheme of the Golden Bible," and his father still has many of the old Sidney's documents.

"Grandfather was a religious crank," says Mr. Rigdon, "till he lost money by it. He started in as a Baptist preacher, and had a very fine congregation for those days, in Pittsburg. There was no reason at all for his leaving, except that he got 'cracked.' At that time he had no ideas of making money. Indeed, while he was with the Mormons, his chances to make money were good enough for most men; but he came out of it about as poor as he went in."

B. -- "But how did he change first?"

"Well, he tried to understand the prophecies, and the man who does that is sure to go crazy. He studied the prophets and baptism, and of course he got 'rattled.' Daniel and Ezekiel and Revelations will 'rattle' any man who gives his whole mind to 'em -- at any rate they did him, and he joined Alexander Campbell. Campbell then believed that the end of the world was nigh --his *Millennial Harginger* shows that they 'rattled' all who listened to them in Ohio and other places; then grandfather got disgusted and decided on a new deal.

He found Joe Smith and they had a great many talks together before they brought out the plates. None of us ever doubted that they got the whole thing up; but father always maintained that grandfather helped get up the original Spaulding book. At any rate he got a copy very early and schemed on some way to make it useful. Although the family knew these facts, they refused to talk on the subject while grandfather lived. In fact, he and they took on a huge disgust at the whole subject.

Grandfather died at Friendship, Alleghany County, N. Y. in 1876, over eighty years old. His son Sidney, my father, was born at Mentor in 1827 and remembers the stirring times of Mormonism. He lives where I do. Grandfather had preached to his old neighbors in Alleghany and taken converts to Nauvoo, so after the break up in 1844, he returned to live at Friendship. For a while he spoke of Mormonism as an attempt to improve Christianity; but the later phases of the thing in Utah were totally different from what he had taught. His daughter Nancy Rigdon is now Mrs Ellis of Pittsburgh, and her husband is a journalist in that city. Her testimony against Joe Smith is very strong. The Prophet was no doubt a thoroughly bad man, etc."

I only report that part of Mr. Rigdon's talk which shows the history of the "Golden Bible," as accepted in the family. Of course, if Sidney Rigdon had wanted the world to believe the Smith story of the plates, he would have told them so. But, though the family do not care to ventilate it, he evidently taught them to treat the whole thing as a fraud.

J.H. BEADLE

NEW YORK, April 7, 1888

A daughter of Dr. Winter, Mrs. Mary Irvine[5]
Sharon, Pennsylvania. April 5, 1881

I have frequently heard my father {Dr. Winter} speak of Rigdon having Spalding's manuscript, and that he had gotten it from the printers to read it as a curiosity; as such he showed it to my father; and that at that time Rigdon had no intention of making the use of it that he afterwards did; for father always said Rigdon helped Smith in his scheme by revising and making the Mormon Bible out of Rev. Spaulding's manuscript.

Rev. A. J. Bonsall[6] pastor of the Baptist Church at Rochester, Pa, and a stepson of Dr. Winter, authorizes the statement that he repeatedly heard Dr. Winter say that Rigdon had shown him the Spaulding manuscript romance, purporting to be the history of the American Indians, which manuscript he had received from the printers.

It was the impression of these three witnesses that Dr. Winter had himself committed his recollections of his above-mentioned interview with Rigdon to writing, as he intended to do, and was even understood to say he had done, but a careful search among his papers has thus far proved unavailing to find it. Dr. Winter was noted for his retentive memory and for his scrupulous accuracy in treasuring up conversations with brethren in the ministry and incidents in their history, many of which he contributed to the press in the form of sketches of Western Church history. The reliability of the persons who have, in the interest of truth, related his statement to them will be confidently vouched for by all who know them; and Dr Winter's evidence, thus attested, is of itself sufficient to establish the certainty that Rigdon, in 1822-23, had possession of Spaulding's manuscript.

Mrs. Amos Dunlap[7]
Warren, Ohio. Dec. 7, 1879

When I was quite a child I visited Mr. Rigdon's family (1826-1827). He married my aunt. They at the time lived in Bainbridge, Ohio. During my visit Mr. Rigdon went to his bedroom and took from a trunk, which he kept, locked a certain manuscript. He came out into the other room and seated himself by the fireplace and commenced reading it. His wife at that moment came into the room and exclaimed, "What! You're studying that thing again?" Or something to that effect. She then added, "I mean to burn that paper." He said, "No indeed, you will not. This will be a great thing some day." Whenever he was reading this he was so completely occupied that he seemed entirely unconscious of anything passing around him.

Stephen H. Hart's statement[8]

I came to Mentor, O., in 1826 and have since resided here. I was well acquainted with Sydney Rigdon and other Mormon leaders. Isaac Morley and his brother-in-law, Titus Billings, and others through Rigdon's influence, established a Communistic Society on Morley's farm and claimed to have all things in common. I attended Rigdon's preaching and heard him urge the Church to put their property in the common fund and have all things common. I have heard Mrs. Mann and other members of Rigdon's Church say that weeks before he joined the Mormons, he took the Bible and slapped it down on the desk and said that in a short time it would be of no more account than an old almanac; that there was to be a new Bible, a *new* Revelation, which would entirely do away with this.

It caused the Church to distrust him and but few followed him into Mormonism. It was said that Jo and Rigdon ordered the poor Mormons, who had no money, to work five days on the Temple and one for their families. There was much suffering among them. It was commonly reported and believed that Jo Smith told his followers that they were the Saints and were to possess all things, and that they could take anything they chose from the Gentiles. Mr. McWhithey, who was a Mormon and pretty well off, frequently visited me. I have heard him for hours at a time tell his experience with the Mormons. They urged him repeatedly to put his property in the Lord's treasury to help build the Temple, but he declined.

Jo Smith said they would all know it was the work of the Lord when the Temple was dedicated. He said he attended a service which lasted from 10 A. M. until 4 P. M., and there was another service in the evening. The Lord's Supper was celebrated and they passed the wine in pails several times to the audience, and each person drank as much as he chose from a cup. He said it was mixed liquor, and he believed the Mormon leaders intended to get the audience under the influence of the mixed liquor, so they would believe it was the Lord's doings. He said they had a white dove which they intended to have light on Jo, the prophet, but it became entangled in the twine and the scheme failed. When the liquor was repassed, Mr. McWhithey told them he had endowment enough, and said he wanted to get out of the Temple, which was densely crowded. He retained his property.

The Mormons claimed they established the Kirtland Safety Society Bank by direct revelation from heaven. Martin Harris, who furnished the money to pay for publishing the "Book of Mormon," worked off and on for fifteen or twenty years for me. His judgment about farming was good. When we had finished hoeing the corn he would raise his hands toward the field and pronounce a blessing and say he was sure of a good crop with his blessing. One night he went upstairs to bed without a light, but soon came down and said the devil had stirred his bed. My wife went upstairs with the light and found that the bed was all right; Martin said the devil had made it all right.

There was a pile of bedding we supposed he had felt of instead of the bed. One night he fell down-stairs; he said the devil came to his bed and he had a tussel {sic} with him and the devil threw him downstairs. Every wrong he attributed to the devil. Martin claimed he would renew his age and be translated like Enoch. He said people would provide for his wants, because he was a prophet of the Lord. When old and unable to work he frequently came to my house, and would follow my wife about the house and talk Mormonism to her several days at a time. When she could endure it no longer, she would ask him if the Lord told him to marry Caroline Young, his second wife, who left him and went to Utah. He always became angry at that and would leave.

Martin, when closely questioned about the plates from which the "Book of Mormon" purports to have been taken, would say he saw the plates by the eye of faith. He often compared himself to Enoch, Elijah, Paul and other Bible persons. I never doubted that he was insane on Mormonism. My wife said she taught school in Mentor, and boarded with Preserved Harris, when Martin first came to Ohio. One night he talked Mormonism and all went to bed. She finally slipped into her room and shut the door. Martin kept on walking and talking Mormonism until late in the night.

[Signed] STEPHEN H. HART

Witnessed by:
A. B. DEMING.
Mentor, Ohio, Nov., 1884

Amos S. Hayden[9]

The following statement from the hand of that pillar of truth and justice, Bro. D. Atwater, just lately (May 28, 1873) laid down to rest, will be read with special interest:

Rev. Darwin Atwater's letter to his brethren in the Church

MANTUA STATION, *April 26, 1873*

DEAR BRO. A. S. HAYDEN:

The infant Church at Mantua was left small and inexperienced. I was the only one who had been accustomed to take an active public part. There were Bro. Seth Sanford, and Bro. Seth Harmon, both very young in the Christian profession, with a number of excellent sisters. In our weak state, in the midst of so much opposition, we were poorly prepared to take care of the Church.

March 21, 1830, I was ordained elder, (in my youth), and Bro. Seth Harmon was ordained deacon -- Adamson Bentley officiating.

At this time, Oliver Snow, an old member of the Baptist Church, united with us. His talents, age and experience, ought to have been very useful to us, but they were more frequently exercised in finding fault with what we attempted to do, than in assisting us. This only increased our embarrassment. Soon after this, the great Mormon defection came on us. Sidney Rigdon preached for us, and notwithstanding his extravagantly wild freaks, he was held in high repute by many.

For a few months before his professed conversion to Mormonism, it was noticed that his wild, extravagant propensities had been more marked. That he knew before of the coming of the book of Mormon is to me certain, from what he said the first of his visits at my father's, some years before. He gave a *wonderful description* of the *mounds* and other antiquities found in some parts of America, and said that they must have been made by the Aborigines. He said *there was a book to be published containing* an account of those things.

He spoke of these in his *eloquent, enthusiastic* style, as being a thing *most extraordinary.* Though a youth then, I took him to task for expending so much enthusiasm on such a subject, instead of things of the gospel. In all my intercourse with him afterward he never spoke of antiquities, or of the wonderful book that should give account of them, till the book of Mormon really was published. He must have thought I was not the man to reveal that to.

In the admiration of Sidney Rigdon, Oliver Snow and his family shared very largely; so, when he came with his pretended humility, to lay all at the feet of Mormonism, it caused a great shock to the little Church at Mantua. The force of this shock was like an *earthquake,* when Symonds Ryder, Ezra Booth and many others, submitted to the "New Dispensation."

51

Eliza Snow, afterward so noted as the *"Poetess"* among the Mormons, led the way. Her parents and sister, and three or four other members of the Church, were finally carried away. Two of these were afterward restored. From this shock the Church slowly recovered. Bro. Ryder returned and exposed Mormonism in its true light. The Mormon character soon exposed itself.

Marcus Bosworth continued to preach for us. Symonds Ryder soon resumed his public labors with us, and regained the confidence of the community. In the year 1834, there were several additions to the Church. Its growth has never been rapid. We never had very large accessions, or very low depressions.

In 1839 we built a meeting-house at the center of Mantua, and commenced to occupy it late in the fall. It was soon after this that you labored for us. About this time, (January 19, 1840), John Allerton and wife, from the Church at Euclid, and Selah Shirtliff and wife united, from the Church in Shalersville -- all the same day. Of the events during your labors for the Church at Mantua, in 1840 and 1841, I need not write.

After much prayerful consideration, the Church ordained Selah Shirtliff and John Allerton as elders, and Seth Sanford, deacon. This was done August 21, 1841. In the above, I should have mentioned that Walter Scott preached for us several times. Father Thomas Campbell a number of times. Alexander Campbell once and Bro. Alton once. Jacob Osborne several times before our organization, and once afterward. Adamson Bentley once or more. John Henry one meeting of days. William Hayden many times.

D. Atwater

Dr. Storm Rosa[10]

Doctor Storm Rosa was a prominent physician in the state of Ohio.

Dr. Rosa's letter is dated *Painesville, Ohio, June 3d,* 1841

Following extract.

* * * "I think the history of Mormonism as published by E. D. Howe -- a copy of which can he obtained in our place -- contains all the material truths connected with the rise and progress of that miserable deception. There are occasionally new doctrines introduced and incorporated with their faith, such as *being baptized for the dead.* This is a common custom here. When a member is satisfied that his father, mother, or brother, or any other friend is in hell, he steps forward and offers himself to the Church in baptism for that individual, and when properly baptized the tormented individual will instantly emerge from his misery into perfect happiness. There are many such follies which the simple hearted are ready and willing to believe. There is no permanent separation in the socirty {sic}. There were a few seceders a few years since, some of whom left them entirely, and became infidels, and others held to the original purity of the doctrines as they termed it.

As to Martin Harris -- of late I have heard but little of him. My acquaintance with him induces me to believe him a monomaniac; he is a man of great loquacity and very unmeaning, ready at all times to dispute the ground of his doctrines with any one. He was one of the seceders, and for a time threatened the Mormons with exposure, as I have been informed; but where he is now I cannot say.

Jo Smith is regarded as an inspired man by all the Mormons.
Sidney Rigdon is at the western settlement; he embraced the Mormon religion in the latter part of October, 1830.

In the early part of the year -- either May or June -- I was in company with Sidney Rigdon, and rode with him on horseback a few miles. Our conversation was principally upon the subject of religion, as he was at that time a very popular preacher of the denomination calling themselves '*disciples*' or Campbellites.

He remarked to me, that it was time for a new religion to spring up; that mankind were all rife and ready for it. I thought he alluded to the Campbellite doctrine -- he said it would not be long before something would make its appearance -- he also said that he thought of leaving for Pennsylvania, and should be absent for some months. I asked him how long -- he said it would depend upon circumstances. I began to think a little strange of his remarks, as he was a minister of the Gospel.

I left Ohio that fall, and went to the state of New York, to visit my friends, who lived in Waterloo -- not far from the mine of golden Bibles. In November I was informed that my old neighbor, E. Partridge, and the Rev. Sidney Rigdon were in Waterloo, and that they both had become the dupes of Joe Smith's necromancies: it then occurred to me that Rigdon's new religion had made its appearance, and when I became informed of the Spalding manuscript I was confirmed in the opinion that Rigdon was at least accessory if not the principal in getting up this farce. Any information that I can give shall be done cheerfully.

Respectfully, your obedient servant,

S. Rosa

Communications to Robert Patterson Jr.[11]

Mrs. Rebecca Johnston Eichbaum who worked in the Pittsburgh post-office during the time Rigdon and Spalding were there.

My father, John Johnson, was postmaster at Pittsburgh for about eighteen years, from 1804 to 1822. My husband William Eichbaum, succeeded him, and was postmaster for about eleven years, from 1822 to 1833. I was born August 25, 1792, and when I became old enough, I assisted my father in attending to the post-office, and became familiar with his duties. From 1811 to 1816, I was the regular clerk in the office, assorting, making up, dispatching, opening and distributing the mails.

Pittsburgh was then a small town, and I was well acquainted with all the stated visitors at the office who called regularly for their mails. So meagre at that time were the mails that I could generally tell without looking whether or not there was anything for such persons, though I would usually look in order to satisfy them. I was married in 1815, and the next year my connection with the office ceased, except during the absences of my husband. I knew and distinctly remember Robert and

Joseph Patterson, J Harrison Lambdin, Silas Engles, and Sidney Rigdon. I remember Rev. Mr. Spaulding, but simply as one who occasionally called to inquire for letters. I remember there was an evident intimacy between Lambdin and Rigdon.

They very often came to the office together. I particularly remember that they would thus come during the hour on the Sabbath afternoon when the office was required to be open, and I remember feeling sure that Rev. Mr. Patterson knew nothing of this, or he would have put a stop to it. I do not know what position, if any, Rigdon filled in Patterson's store or printing office, but am well assured he was frequently, if not constantly, there for a large part of the time when I was clerk in the post-office. I recall Mr. Engles saying that "Rigdon was always hanging around the printing office." He was connected with the tannery before he became a preacher, though he may have continued the business whilst preaching.

Mr. Zeb Rudolph[12] father of Mrs. Gen. Garfield, knew Sidney Rigdon very well, and has stated that "during the winter previous to the appearance of the Book of Mormon, Rigdon was in the habit of spending weeks away from his home, going no one knew where and that he often appeared very preoccupied and would indulge in dreamy, imaginative talks, which puzzled those who listened. When the Book of Mormon appeared and Rigdon joined in the advocacy of the new religion, the suspicion was at once aroused that he was one of the framers of the new doctrines, and probably was not ignorant of the authorship of the Book of Mormon." *Robert Patterson. Who wrote the Book of Mormon? 188. Page 434*

Mrs. Sophia Munson[13] a neighbour also noticed Rigdon's absences. She was living directly across from the Rigdon family at the time in question and, although a young girl, knew Rigdon and his wife well and observed Rigdon's more eccentric practices.

My parents settled on Mentor road, four miles west of Painesville, Ohio, in 1810, when I was six weeks old. I well remember when Elder Rigdon came and lived opposite our house in 1827. He was very poor, and when he had much company would send his children to the neighbours to borrow knives, forks, dishes and also for provisions.

Father kept his horse and goat gratis. Rigdon was a very lazy man; he would not make his garden and depended on the Church for garden supplies. He would sit around and do nothing. He was away much of the time, and sometimes claimed he had been to Pittsburgh, Pa. I was quilting at his house until 1 o clock at night the day four Mormons came to convert Rigdon. I heard some of their conversation in the adjoining room. Orson Hyde boarded at our house and attended a select school, also to Rigdon, who taught some evenings. My parents joined the Campbellite Church, in Mentor, during Eld. Adamson Bentley's protracted meetings, I think in 1828. Mrs. Rigdon was an excellent woman, and never complained of their poverty.

(Signed)

Mrs. Sophia Munson
Witnessed by:
A. B. DEMING.

Charles A. Shook
(1876-1939)
True Origin of Book of Mormon

Charles A. Shook[14]

I now have the pleasure of presenting to the reader two letters touching upon this point that have never been published before. The first of these was written by Mr. Thomas Gregg, of Hamilton, Illinois, the author of "The Prophet of Palmyra;" the second is the reply to the same, written by Mr. Lorenzo Saunders, of Reading, Hillsdale County, Michigan, who was an intimate acquaintance of the Smiths. Mr. Gregg died before he had the opportunity of publishing Mr. Saunders' letter, and later the correspondence was turned over to Mr. R. B. Neal, of Grayson, Kentucky, secretary of the American Anti-Mormon Association, who has kindly loaned these documents to me to publish in this book. The letters have been carefully copied from their originals and appear just as they were formerly written, except that in that of Saunders a number of errors in spelling, capitalization and punctuation have been corrected. Saunders was an aged man, and this, coupled with his poor educational advantages as a boy, accounts for the errors which appear. I regard his letter as one of the most important documents which we have bearing on the present question.

The letter of Mr. Gregg is as follows:

HAMILON, Hancock Co., Ill., January 19, 1885.

MR. LORENZO SAUNDERS,

Dear Sir: -- Permit me, a stranger, to "interview" you by letter. Mr. J. H. Gilbert, of Palmyra, N. Y., introduces us. He names you among the very few left, who know something about the origin of Mormonism, and the life and career of Joe Smith, the pretended Prophet. I am engaged on a work -- mainly a History of the Mormon Era in Illinois -- but with which I wish to incorporate the Rise and Progress of the miserable fraud in and about Palmyra. A main point I wish to investigate is as to how the *Spaulding Manuscript[s]* got into Smith's hands previous to 1829 when the B. of M. was first printed.

Some think Cowdery was the medium -- some that it was Rigdon. Of course, it is hard to remember after a period of 50 or 60 years, little occurrences unimportant at the time; but I am induced to apply to you, as a neighbor of the Smiths, hoping you may be able to recall events that may help me out. What can you recall of *Cowdery's* career? His first appearance among you -- what he was doing -- where he came from -- and what seemed to have brought him into closer relationship with Smith?

Also, of *Rigdon* -- Gilbert says it is thought you saw him once at Smith's. Can you be sure of that? And whether it was *before* the B. of M. was printed? Did you know the 12 signers, certifying to the Divine origin of the B. of M. -- the Whitmers -- Harris -- Hiram Page -- and all the Smiths -- and were they ignorant or sensible -- learned or unlearned -- and did they or any of them, seem to adhere to Smith while he was digging for treasure, &c.?

You see I can *chalk out* a great variety of subjects or points on which I want information; but I might cut it short by asking, in general, for such information as you can give that will enlighten the public on the Origin of Mormonism and more especially its connection with the Rev. Spaulding's book. Of course you are an aged man -- I know what it is to be an old man, myself; but these cold winter days, we can do little else than sit in the house and read and write -- and perhaps you will be able to find time to reply to this, and thus oblige very much.

Your friend and obt. Ser.,   TH. GREGG.

P. S. -- More questions: Did you ever see, or try to see, the pretended plates, or how Smith acted in regard to them? Or did you ever see the *hole in the ground*, on Cumorah Hill, in which the plates were found -- or was there ever such a hole? *Please answer on, and return this sheet, and if* not enough of paper, add to it · I will pay postage,

In reply to Mr. Gregg's letter, Mr. Saunders wrote from Reading, Michigan, as follows:

January 28, 1885

Mister Gregg,

Dear Sir. I received your note ready at hand and will try answer the best I can and give all the information I can as respecting Mormonism and the first origin. As respecting Oliver Cowdery, he came from Kirtland in the summer of 1826 and was about there until fall and took a school in the district where the Smiths lived and the next summer he was missing and I didn't see him until fall and he came back and took school in the district where we lived and taught about a week and went to the school board and wanted the school board to let him off and they did and he went to Smith and went to writing the Book of Mormon and wrote all winter.

The Mormons say it wasn't wrote there but I say it was because I was there. I saw Sidney Rigdon in the spring of 1827, about the middle of March. I went to Smiths to eat maple sugar, and I saw five or six men standing in a group and there was one among them better dressed than the rest and I asked Harrison Smith who he was and he said his name was Sidney Rigdon, a friend of Joseph's from Pennsylvania. I saw him in the fall of 1827 on the road between where I lived and Palmyra, with Joseph. I was with a man by the name of Jugegsah, (sp.?). They talked together and when he went on I asked Jugegsah, (sp.?) who he was and he said it was Rigdon.

Then in the summer of 1828 I saw him at Samuel Lawrence's just before harvest. I was cutting corn for Lawrence and went to dinner and he took dinner with us and when dinner was over they went into another room and I didn't' see him again till he came to Palmyra to preach. You want to know how Smith acted about it. The next morning after he claimed to have got plates he came to our house and said he had got the plates and what a struggle he had in getting home with them.

Two men tackled him and he fought and knocked them both down and made his escape and secured the plates and had them safe and secure. He showed his thumb where he bruised it in fighting those men. After I went from the house, my mother says "What a liar Joseph Smith is; he lies every word he says; I know he lies because he looks so guilty; he can't see out of his eyes; how dare he tell such a lie as that." The time he claimed to have taken the plates from the hill was on 22 day of September, in 1827, and I went on the next Sunday following with five or six other ones and we hunted the side hill course and could not find no place where the ground had been broke.

There was large hole where the money diggers had dug a year or two before, but no fresh dirt. There never was such a hole; there never was any plates taken out of that hill nor any other hill in that country was in Wayne County. It is all a lie. No, sir, I never saw the plates nor no one else. He had an old glass box with a tile in it, about 7x 8 inches, and that was the gold plates and Martin Harris didn't know a gold plate from a brick at this time. Smith and Rigdon had an intimacy but it was very secret and still and there was a mediator between them and that was Cowdery.

The Manuscript was stolen by Rigdon and modelled over by him and then handed over to Cowdery and he copied them and Smith sat behind the curtain and handed them out to Cowdery and as fast as Cowdery copied them, they were handed over to Martin Harris and he took them to Egbert Grandin, the one who printed them, and Gilbert set the type. I never knew any of the twelve that claimed to have seen the plates except Martin Harris and the Smiths, I knew all the Smiths, they had not much learning, and they were poor scholars. The older ones did adhere to Joseph Smith. He had a peep stone he pretended to see in. He could see all the hidden treasures in the ground and all the stolen property. But that was all a lie, he couldn't see nothing. He was an impostor. I now will close. I don't know as you can read this. If you can, please excuse my bad spelling and mistakes.

Yours with Respect,
      From Lorenzo Saunders

Charles A. Shook, being duly sworn according to law, deposeth and saith that the foregoing letters of Thomas Gregg and Lorenzo Saunders are verbatim copies (excepting spelling, punctuation and capitalization) of the original, now in the possession of the American Anti-Mormon Association.

CHARLES A. SHOOK.

Subscribed to in my presence and sworn to before me, at Eddyville, Nebraska, this 13th day of February, 1913.

B. R. HEDGLIN, *Notary Public.*

Oliver Cowdery first came to Palmyra in the summer of 1826 instead of in the winter of 1828-9, as the Mormons claim.

Notes

1. The Salt Lake Daily Tribune Vol. XXXIIII. Salt Lake City, Utah, Sunday, April 15, 1888. No. 155.

2. Robert Patterson, Jr. *Who Wrote The Book of Mormon?* (Philadelphia: L. H. Everts & Co., 1882)

3. Charles A. Shook *True Origin of Book of Mormon Ibid p.119-120* (Cincinnati: Standard Pub. Co., 1914)

4. Robert Patterson, Jr. *Who Wrote The Book of Mormon?* P.434 REPRINTED FROM THE ILLUSTRATED HISTORY OF WASHINGTON COUNTY (Philadelphia: L. H. Everts & Co., 1882)

5. *Who Wrote the Book of Mormon?* Robert Patterson, Jr. (Philadelphia: L. H. Everts & Co., 1882) P.434

6. *REPRINTED FROM THE ILLUSTRATED HISTORY OF WASHINGTON COUNTY. PENNSYLVANIA. P434.*

7. *Who Wrote the Book of Mormon?* Robert Patterson, Jr. P.434 (Philadelphia: L. H. Everts & Co., 1882)

8. Arthur B. Deming NAKED TRUTHS ABOUT MORMONISM

9. Amos S. Hayden *History of the Disciples...P.239-241* (Cincinnati: Chase & Hall, 1875)

10. Rev. John A. Clark, D.D., *GLEANINGS BY WAY P315-317*

11. Charles A. Shook. The True Origins of the Book of Mormon P117-118 Rebecca Johnston Eichbaum Statement of September 18, 1879

12. Robert Patterson. Who wrote the Book of Mormon? 1882. Page 434

13. Mrs. Sophia Munson Witnessed by: A.B. Deming Mentor, Ohio, February, 1885. *Naked Truths About Mormonism.* (January, 1888)

14. Charles A. Shook (1876-1939) *True Origin of Book of Mormon* (Cincinnati: Standard Pub. Co., 1914)

CHAPTER FOUR

Dr. John C. Bennett

Dr. John Cook Bennett, Quartermaster General of the state of Illinois, became a convert to Mormonism in the summer of 1840 and soon after removed to the city of Nauvoo. Here he rapidly grew in favour with the prophet Joseph Smith and the Mormon people until he was elected to the position of "assistant president" of the Church during the illness of Sidney Rigdon. The intimacy between Smith and Bennett continued until the summer of 1842, when they quarrelled and Bennett left Nauvoo. Later, he published an *expose* of the conditions in that city through the columns of the Sangamo *Journal*, of Springfield, Illinois, and his book, "Mormonism Exposed."

On the origin of the Book of Mormon, Bennett says[1]

"I will remark here… that the Book of Mormon was originally written by the Rev. Solomon Spaulding, A.M., as a romance, and entitled the "Manuscript Found," and placed by him in the printing office of Patterson and Lambdin, in the city of Pittsburgh, from whence it was taken by a conspicuous Mormon divine, and re-modelled, by adding the religious portion, placed by him in Smith's possession, and then published to the world as the testimony exemplifies. This I have from the Confederation, (inner circle of Smith's friends) and its perfect correctness there is not a shadow of a doubt. There never were any plates of the Book of Mormon, excepting what were seen by the spiritual, and not the natural, eyes of the witnesses. The story of the plates is chimerical".

Dictionary definition:

Chimera *noun*

A hope or dream that is extremely unlikely ever to come true

Chimerical adjective

Governor Ford said of J.C. Bennett [2]

"This Bennett was probably the greatest scamp in the Western country. I have made particular enquiries concerning him, and have traced him in several places in which he had lived, before he joined the Mormons, in Ohio, Indiana, and Illinois, and he was everywhere accounted the same debauched, unprincipled, and profligate character."

Published in the Mormon owned newspaper The Wasp.

The Wasp
TRUTH CRUSHED TO EARTH WILL RISE AGAIN. -- BRYANT
Vol. I. - No. 6. Nauvoo, Hancock Co., Sat., May 21, 1842. Whole No. 6.

New election of Mayor and Vice Mayor, of the City of Nauvoo, on the resignation of General Bennett

On the 17th Instant General John C. Bennett resigned the office of Mayor of the City of Nauvoo, and on the 19th General Joseph Smith, the former Vice Mayor, was duly elected to fill the vacancy -- and on the same day General Hyrum Smith was elected Vice Mayor in place of General Joseph Smith elected Mayor.

The following vote of thanks was then unanimously voted to the Ex Mayor, General Bennett, by the City Council; to wit: Resolved by the City Council of the City of Nauvoo, that this Council tender a vote of thanks to General John C. Bennett, for his great zeal in having good and wholesome laws adopted for the Government of this city; and for the faithful discharge of his duty while Mayor of the same.

Passed May 10th 1842

JOSEPH SMITH, Mayor.

JAMES SLOAN, Recorder

Sarah M. Pratt, wife of Mormon leader Orson Pratt testified to the veracity of Bennett's statements in his book.

"This certifies that I was well acquainted with the Mormon Leaders and Church in general, and know that the principal statements in John C. Bennett's book on Mormonism are true".

Sarah M. Pratt.
Salt Lake City

The Author Wilhelm Ritter Von Wymetal interviewed Sarah M. Pratt And obtained the following[3]

May 21, 1886 I had a fresh interview with Mrs. Sarah M. Pratt, who had the kindness to give me the following testimony additional to the information given by her in our interviews in the spring of 1885. "I want you to have all my statements correct in your book," said the noble lady, "and put my name to them; I want the truth, the full truth, to be known, and bear the responsibility of it.

"I have told you that the prophet Joseph used to frequent houses of ill-fame. Mrs. White, a very pretty and attractive woman, once confessed to me that she made a business of it to be hospitable to the captains of the Mississippi steamboats. She told me that Joseph had made her acquaintance very soon after his arrival in Nauvoo, and that he had visited her dozens of times. My husband (Orson Pratt) could not be induced to believe such things of his prophet. Seeing his obstinate incredulity, Mrs. White proposed to Mr. Pratt and myself to put us in a position where we could observe what was going on between herself and Joseph the prophet.

We, however, declined this proposition. You have made a mistake in the table of contents of your book in calling this woman "Mrs. Harris." Mrs. [G. W.] Harris was a married lady, a very great friend of mine. When Joseph had made his dastardly attempt on me, I went to Mrs. Harris to unbosom my grief to her. To my utter astonishment, she said, laughing heartily: "How foolish you are! I don't see anything so horrible in it. Why, I AM HIS MISTRESS SINCE FOUR YEARS!"

"Next door to my house was a house of bad reputation. One single woman lived there, not very attractive. She used to be visited by people from Carthage whenever they came to Nauvoo. Joseph used to come on horseback, ride up to the house and tie his horse to a tree, many of which stood before the house. Then he would enter the house of the woman from the back. I have seen him do this repeatedly.

"Joseph Smith, the son of the prophet, and president of the re-organized Mormon Church, paid me a visit, and I had a long talk with him. I saw that he was not inclined to believe the truth about his father, so I said to him: 'You pretend to have revelations from the Lord. Why don't you ask the Lord to tell you *what kind of a man your father really was?*' He answered: 'If my father had so many connections with women, where is the progeny?' I said to him: 'Your father had mostly intercourse with married women, and as to single ones, Dr. Bennett was always on hand, when anything happened.'

It was in this way that I became acquainted with Dr. John C. Bennett. When my husband went to England as a missionary, he got the promise from Joseph that I should receive provisions from the tithing-house. Shortly afterward Joseph made his propositions to me and they enraged me so that I refused to accept any help from the tithing-house or from the bishop. Having been always very clever and very busy with my needle, I began to take in sewing for the support of myself and children, and succeeded soon in making myself independent. When Bennett came to Nauvoo, Joseph brought him to my house, stating that Bennett wanted some sewing done, and that I should do it for the doctor.

I assented and Bennett gave me a great deal of work to do. He knew that Joseph had his plans set on me; Joseph made no secret of them before Bennett, and went so far in his impudence as to make propositions to me in the presence of Bennett, his bosom friend. Bennett, who was of a sarcastic turn of mind, used to come and tell me about Joseph to tease and irritate me. One day they came both, Joseph and Bennett, on horseback to my house. Bennett dismounted, Joseph remained outside. Bennett wanted me to return to him a book I had borrowed from him.

It was a so-called doctor-book. I had a rapidly growing little family and wanted to inform myself about certain matters in regard to babies, etc., -- this explains my borrowing that book. While giving Bennett his book, I observed that he held something in the left sleeve of his coat. Bennett smiled and said: 'Oh, a little job for Joseph; one of his women is in trouble.' Saying this, he took the thing out of his left sleeve. It was a pretty long instrument of a kind I had never seen before. It seemed to be of steel and was crooked at one end. I heard afterwards that the operation had been performed; that the *woman* was very sick, and that Joseph was very much afraid that she might die, but she recovered.

"Bennett was the most intimate friend of Joseph for a time. He boarded with the prophet. He told me once that Joseph had been talking with him about his troubles with Emma, his wife. 'He asked me,' said Bennett, smilingly, 'what he should do to get out of the trouble?' I said, 'This is very simple. GET A REVELATION that polygamy is right, and all your troubles will be at an end.' "The only 'wives' of Joseph that lived in the Mansion House were the Partridge girls. This is explained by the fact that they were the servants in the hotel kept by the prophet. But when Emma found out that Joseph went to their room, they had to leave the house.

"I remember Emma's trip to St. Louis. I begged her to buy for me a piece of black silk there.

"You should bear in mind that Joseph did not think of a marriage or sealing ceremony for many years. He used to state to his intended victims, as he did to me: *'God does not care if we have a good time, if only other people do not know it.'* He only introduced as marriage ceremony when he had found out that he could not get certain women without it. I think Louisa Beeman was the first case of this kind. If any woman, like me, opposed his wishes, he used to say: 'Be silent, or I shall ruin your character. My character must be sustained in the interests of the Church.' When he had assailed me and saw that he could not seal my lips, he sent word to me that he would *work my salvation*, if I kept silent. I sent back that I would talk as much as I pleased and as much as I knew to be the truth, and as to my salvation, I would try and take care of that myself.

"In his endeavors to ruin my character Joseph went so far as to publish extra-sheet containing affidavits against my reputation. When this sheet was brought to me I discovered to my astonishment the names of two people on it, man and wife, with whom I had boarded for a certain time. I never thought much of the man, but the woman was an honest person, and I knew that she must have been *forced* to do such a thing against me. So I went to their house; the man left the house hurriedly when he saw me coming. I found the wife and said to her rather excitedly: 'What does it all mean?' She began to sob. 'It is not my fault,' said she. 'Hyrum Smith came to our house, with the affidavits all written out, and forced us to sign them. *'Joseph and the Church must be saved,'* said he. We saw that resistance was useless, they would have ruined us; so we signed the papers.'"

Let us now introduce a statement as to the reliability of Mrs. Pratt. She is well known in Salt Lake City and all over Utah as possessing all the virtues of an excellent wife and mother; but outsiders may wish to know of Mrs. Pratt's standing in this community, and I take pleasure in giving a testimonial.

Salt Lake City, May 1886.

We, the undersigned, cordially bear witness to the excellent reputation of Mrs. Sarah M. Pratt. We feel well assured that Mrs. Pratt is a lady whose statements are absolutely to be depended upon. Entire frankness and a high sense of honor and truth are regarded in this community, where she has dwelt since 1847, as her ruling characteristics.

> Charles S. Zane,
> *Chief Justice Utah Territory.*

> Arthur L, Thomas,
> *Secretary Utah Territory.*

> Rev. J. W. Jackson,
> *U. S. A. Chaplain, Fort Douglas.*

Sarah Pratt ended her marriage to husband Orson Pratt in 1868 because of his "obsession with marrying younger women and condemned polygamy because:

[Polygamy] completely demoralizes good men and makes bad men correspondingly worse. As for the women—well, God help them! First wives it renders desperate, or else heart-broken, mean-spirited creatures.

Pratt was one of the founders of the Anti-Polygamy Society in Salt Lake City. Pratt lashed out at Orson in an 1877 interview,

"Here was my husband, gray headed, taking to his bed young girls in mockery of marriage. Of course there could be no joy for him in such an intercourse except for the indulgence of his fanaticism and of something else, perhaps, which I hesitate to mention".

In 1874 she testified for Utah candidate Liberal Robert Baskin who accused his opponent George Q. Cannon of polygamy and said that his obligation to the Mormon hierarchy was superior to national law.

On her leaving the Church of Jesus Christ of Latter-Day Saints for which she was excommunicated on 4 October 1874, Pratt declared in 1875. "I am the wife of Orson Pratt...I was formerly a member of the Mormon Church...I have not been a believer in the Mormon doctrines for thirty years, and am now considered an apostate, I believe".

Van Wagoner concludes, "Polygamy made her a radical....By making public Joseph Smith's overtures and resisting what she considered to be collective infidelity, Sarah Pratt was judged a threat to the safety of the Church and considered to have committed apostasy."

Pratt, who resolved to "rear my children so that they should never espouse the Mormon faith while concealing from my neighbors and the Church authorities that I was thus rearing them," had twelve children by husband Orson Pratt:

Notes

1. John Cook Bennett. *A HISTORY OF THE SAINTS OR AN EXPOSE OF JOE SMITH AND MORMONISM. P123-4*
2. History of Illinois, p. 263
3. Wilhelm Ritter von Wymetal (under the pen-name of "W. Wyl") (1838-1896)
4. Mormon Portraits 1 Joseph Smith (SLC: Tribune Printing & Pub., 1886) P.60-63

CHAPTER FIVE

The Six Discussions

The Mormon Missionaries present six Discussions to those who are investigating the Church.

These discussions teach the Mormon "Plan of Salvation".

These young eager missionaries **DO NOT** know the real history of their own Church. Some of them were raised in that faith, some converted to it. There are also Senior Mission couples; they are usually married couples and usually over sixty years of age but not always.
The younger missionaries go out into the world two by two just like the Saviour commissioned His Twelve Apostles to do.

They do this at their own financial expense which is very considerable, some of them saving money from the time they are only children. They take time out from university or jobs for two whole years, (eighteen months for the female missionaries). The Elders (young male missionaries) are expected to serve a mission, women are not expected to do so.

While on their missions, the missionaries are counselled to listen to classical or 'uplifting' music or hymns. They are not permitted to listen to the radio or watch T.V. They may phone home on special occasions and write letters.

When they knock on doors they are earnestly trying to bring to you to what they believe is the truth. These days anyone can look up the Church history on the Internet and inform themselves about what really happened in the Church history. In the 1980s and before, there was no Internet, meaning information was less accessible.

The missionaries teach that the world is ripening in iniquity and this is marking the time for the Saviour's return to the Earth. They teach that this Earth is six thousand years old, that we are now in the seventh thousandth year and that the Saviour will soon come and reign on the earth. When Joseph Smith organized his Church he said the Second Coming was "even at the doors". When I questioned the missionaries about fossil finds and other archaeological and geological evidences attesting to the age of the Earth I was told that this Earth was not created out of nothing, but had been made with other materials, materials from other planets brought together to form this planet Earth.

Basically, ultimately, the missionaries job is to get baptisms, as many as possible and as soon as possible. The LDS Church will say that their Church is the fastest growing Church with x amount of new converts each year. What they don't divulge is the amount of people removing their names from the records of the Church.

The First Discussion

- ◆ The Plan of our Heavenly Father

- ◆ Introduction to prophets who reveal God's plan

Missionaries use these scriptures to confirm this.

New Testament, Acts chapter 3 verses 19-21:

19. Repent ye therefore, and be converted that your sins may be blotted out, when the times of refreshing shall come from the presence of the Lord.

20. and He shall send Jesus Christ, which before was preached unto you.

21. Whom the heavens must receive until the times of restitution of all things, which God hath spoken by the mouth of all His Holy Prophets since the world, began.

The Missionaries asked. If God spoke to Prophets anciently why would He cease to do so?

Joseph Smith and the "Restoration" of the Gospel of Jesus Christ

"The Restoration", they will state, occurred on a spring day in 1820 in Palmyra, New York, when a young fourteen year old boy named Joseph Smith received what is called "The First Vision". This is where he (Joseph Smith) claims God the Father and Jesus Christ appeared to him. Everything the Missionaries share with the investigator they will corroborate with scriptures from the Old and New Testament.

For example Joseph Smith claims that God the Father and Jesus are identical in image.

New Testament, Hebrews 1:1-3.

1. God who at sundry times and in divers manners spake in times past unto the fathers by the Prophets.

2. Hath in these last days spoke unto us by the Son, whom He hath appointed heir of all things, by whom also He made the worlds.

3. Who being the brightness of His glory and the express image of His person...

The First Vision

EXTRACTS FROM THE HISTORY OF JOSEPH SMITH, THE PROPHET
History of the Church, Vol. 1, Chapters 1-5
(As printed in "Dialogue: A Journal of Mormon Thought", Autumn 1966, page 35) [1]

So in accordance with my determination, to ask of God, I retired to the woods to make the attempt. It was on the morning of a beautiful clear day, early in the spring of eighteen hundred and twenty... I saw a pillar of light exactly over my head... When the light rested upon me I saw two personages (whose brightness and glory defy all description) standing above me in the air. One of them spoke unto me calling me by name,

and said (pointing to the other.) "This is my beloved Son, hear him."....
I asked the personages who stood above me in the light, which of all the
sects was right. I was answered that I must join none of them, for they
were all wrong, and the personage who addressed me said that all their
creeds were an abomination in his sight; that those professors were all
corrupt.... He again forbade me to join with any of them: and many other
things did he say unto me which I cannot write at this time.

The above account of the First Vision is the one given to investigators of
the Mormon Church.

Joseph Smith was said to have been fourteen years old when this
happened. There are conflicting written versions of the First Vision.

The following transcription is the earliest written account in Joseph
Smith's own hand. (Brigham Young University Studies, Spring 1969,
pages 277.78)[2]

Professor James B. Allen who was an Assistant Church Historian
admitted that the document was genuine. In an article published in 1966
he commented: "One of the most significant documents of that period yet
discovered was brought to light in 1965 by Paul. R. Cheesman, a graduate
student at Brigham Young University. This is a handwritten manuscript
apparently composed about 1833 and either written or dictated by Joseph
Smith. It contains an account of the early experiences of the Mormon
prophet and includes the story of the first vision. While the story varies
in some details from the version presently accepted, enough is there to
indicate that least as early as 1833 Joseph Smith contemplated writing
and perhaps publishing it. The manuscript has apparently lain in the
L.D.S. Church Historian's office for many years, and yet few if any who
saw it realised its profound historical significance."

The Mormon leaders suppressed this account of the First Vision for over
130 years, but after we (Mormonism-Shadow or Reality *by Jerald & Sandra*
Tanner)printed it thousands of copies were distributed throughout the
world. Finally four years after we published the document, the Church

Historian's Office made a public statement confirming the authenticity of the manuscript. Dean C. Jesse, a member of the staff at the LDS Church Historian's Office in Salt Lake City, claims that the document was written in 1831 or 1832.

"On at least three occasions prior to 1839 Joseph Smith began writing his history. The earliest of these is a six-page account recorded on three leaves of a ledger book, written between the summer of 1831 and November 1832....

"The 1831-32 history transliterated here contains the earliest known account of Joseph Smith's First Vision."

A photograph of Joseph Smith's first handwritten account of the first vision. This is the only account in Smith's own handwriting.

Handwritten letter of Joseph Smith

The First Vision is what the Mormon Church has as its foundation, if this is false then everything else that came after it is false also.

The important part of this document reads[3]
(Joseph Smith's Diary, 1835-36 p.24 as printed in Dialogue: A journal of Mormon Thought, spring 1971, p.87)

…. The Lord heard my cry in the wilderness and while in the attitude of calling upon the Lord in the 16th year of my age a pillar of light above the brightness of the sun at noonday came down from above and rested upon me and I was filled with the spirit of god and the Lord opened the heavens upon me and I saw and he spake unto me saying. Joseph my son they sins are forgiven thee, go thy way walk in my statutes and keep my commandments behold I am the Lord of glory. I was crucified for the world that all those who believe on my name may have Eternal life behold the world lieth in sin at this time and none doeth good no not one they have turned aside from the gospel and keep not my commandments they draw near unto me with their lips while their hearts are far from me and mine anger is kindling against the inhabitants of the earth to visit them according to this ungodliness and to bring to pass that which has been spoken of by the mouth of the prophets and Apostles behold and lo I come quickly as it was written of me in the cloud clothed in the glory of my Father….

Another account of the First vision

… I called upon the Lord in mighty prayer, a pillar of fire appeared above my head, it presently rested down upon me, and filled me with joy unspeakable, a personage appeared in the midst of this pillar of flame which was spread all around, and yet nothing consumed, another personage soon appeared like unto the first, he said unto me thy sins are forgiven thee, he testified unto me that Jesus Christ is the Son of God; and I saw many angels in communication…

Joseph Smith's Diary, 1835-36 p.24 Dialogue: A journal of Mormon Thought, spring 1971, p.87)
As quoted in Mormonism-Shadow or Reality. Jerald & Sandra Tanner

Brigham Young who became the second prophet of the Church said that "the Lord did not come" to Joseph Smith in the first vision, but instead He sent "His angel."

Brigham Young[4]

"The Lord did not come with the armies of heaven in power and great glory, nor send His messengers panoplied with aught else than the truth of heaven to communicate to the meek, the lowly, the youth of humble origin, the sincere enquirer after the knowledge of God. But He did send His angel to this same obscure person, Joseph Smith Jun., who afterwards became a Prophet, Seer, and Revelator, and informed him that he should not join any of the religious sects of the day, for they were all wrong; that He had a work for him to perform, inasmuch as he should prove faithful before Him."

At this point in the discussion the Missionaries will open the Old Testament to the Book of Ezekiel:

Ezekiel Chapter 37 verse 16-17.

16. Moreover, thou son of man, take thee one stick and write upon it, for Judah, and for the children of Israel his companions: then take another stick and write upon it for Joseph, the stick of Ephraim, and for all the house of Israel and his companions:

17. And join them one to another into one stick' and they shall become one in thine hand.

They will claim that the Holy Bible is the first stick, the stick of Judah, and the other stick is the Book of Mormon, the stick of Joseph. They explained that Lehi was of the tribe of Manasseh and the Jaredites who came to ancient America at the confounding of the tongues at Babel was of the tribe of Ephraim, both being from the tribe of Joseph. These, they claim, are the people of whom Jesus spoke when He said to His Apostles in Jerusalem:

"And other sheep I have which are not of this fold; them also I must bring, and they shall hear my voice; and there shall be one fold and one shepherd".

New Testament, John Chapter 10 verse 16

>M VA

According to an account, which Joseph Smith attributed to Harris, Anthon "stated that the translation was correct, more so than any he had before seen translated from the Egyptian". [Harris] then showed him those which were not yet translated, and he said that they were Egyptian, Chaldaic, Assyriac, and Arabic; and he said they were true characters." According to the same account, Anthon provided Harris with a certificate as to the veracity of the characters but tore it up after learning the characters were copied from a book said to have been delivered by an angel.

The missionaries will tell of the visit by Martin Harris to Professor Charles Anthon claiming that it was the fulfilment of a prophecy given in The Old Testament in the Book of Isaiah.
Joseph Smith stated that a portion of the brass plates was sealed. He gave some of the translated characters from the unsealed portion to Martin Harris (who was going to help to fund the publishing of the book) to take to a Professor Charles Anthon, in New York. Martin Harris was one of the witnesses of the divine authenticity of The Book of Mormon.

11. And the vision of all is become unto you as the words of a book that is sealed, which men deliver to one that is learned, saying, Read this, I pray thee: and he saith, I am not learned.

Old Testament, Book of Isaiah 29:11

What they do not tell the investigator is Mr. Charles Anthon's version of Martin Harris' visit, where he declared "Reformed Egyptian" to be a hoax. These young missionaries do not know of this account.

Professor Anthon's account of meeting with Harris

Professor Charles Anthon believed "Reformed Egyptian" was a hoax:

The following letter, written by Professor Charles Anthon, was published in E. D. Howe's Book entitled *Mormonism Unvailed*, (Painesville, OH. E.D.Howe, 1834), pp. 270-272.

Dr. Charles Anthon
Re: Authenticity of Writing Samples Allegedly Copied from the Golden Plates[5]

New York, Feb. 17, 1834.

Dear Sir -- I received this morning your favor of the 9th instant, and lose no time in making a reply. The whole story about my having pronouncd [sic] the Mormonite inscription to be "reformed Egyptian hieroglyphics" is *perfectly false*. Some years ago, a plain, and apparently simple-hearted farmer, called upon me with a note from Dr. Mitchell of our city, now deceased, requesting me to decypher [sic], if possible, a paper, which the farmer would hand me, and which Dr. M. confessed he had been unable to understand.

Upon examining the paper in question, I soon came to the conclusion that it was all a trick, perhaps a *hoax*. When I asked the person, who brought it, how he obtained the writing, he gave me, as far as I can now recollect, the following account: A "gold book," consisting of a number of plates of gold, fastened together in the shape of a book by wires of the same metal, had been dug up in the northern part of the state of New York, and along with the book an enormous pair of "*gold spectacles*"!

These spectacles were so large, that, if a person attempted to look through them, his two eyes would have to be turned towards *one* of the glasses merely, the spectacles in question being altogether too large for the breadth of the human face. Whoever examined the plates through the spectacles was enabled not only to *read* them, but fully to *understand* their meaning. All this knowledge, however, was confined at that time to a young man, who had the trunk containing the book and spectacles in his sole possession. This young man was placed behind a curtain, in the garret of a farm house, and being thus concealed from view, put on the spectacles occasionally, or rather, looked through one of the glasses, decyphered {*sic*} the characters in the book, and, having committed some of them to paper, handed copies from behind the curtain, to those who stood on the outside. Not a word, however, was said about the plates having been decyphered [sic] "by the gift of God." Everything, in this way, was effected by the large pair of spectacles.

The farmer added, that he had been requested to contribute a sum of money towards the publication of the *"golden book,"* the contents of which would, as he had been assured, produce an entire change in the world and save it from ruin. So urgent had been these solicitations that he intended selling his farm and handing over the amount received to those who wished to publish the plates. As a last precautionary step, however, he had resolved to come to New York, and obtain the opinion of the learned about the meaning of the paper which he brought with him, and which had been given him as a part of the contents of the book, although no translation had been furnished at the time by the young man with the spectacles. On hearing this odd story, I changed my opinion about the paper, and, instead of viewing it any longer as a hoax upon the learned, I began to regard it as part of a scheme to cheat the farmer of his money, and I communicated my suspicions to him, warning him to beware of rogues.

He requested an opinion from me in writing, which of course I declined giving, and he then took his leave carrying the paper with him. This paper was in fact a singular scrawl. It consisted of all kinds of crooked characters disposed in columns, and had evidently been prepared by some person who had before him at the time a book containing various alphabets, Greek and Hebrew letters, crosses and flourishes, Roman letters inverted or placed sideways, were arranged in perpendicular columns, and the whole ended in a rude delineation of a circle divided into various compartments, decked with various strange marks, and evidently copied after the Mexican Calendar given by Humboldt, but copied in such a way as not to betray the source whence it was derived. I am thus particular as to the contents of the paper, inasmuch as I have frequently conversed with my friends on the subject, since the Mormonite excitement began, and well remember that the paper contained any thing else but *"Egyptian Hieroglyphics."* Some time after, the same farmer paid me a second visit. He brought with him the golden book in print, and offered it to me for sale.

I declined purchasing. He then asked permission to leave the book with me for examination. I declined receiving it, although his manner was strangely urgent. I adverted once more to the roguery which had been in my opinion practised {sic} upon him, and asked him what had become of the gold plates. He informed me that they were in a trunk with the large pair of spectacles. I advised him to go to a magistrate and have the trunk examined. He said the "curse of God" would come upon him should he do this. On my pressing him, however, to pursue the course which I had recommended, he told me that he would open the trunk, if I would take the "curse of God" upon myself. I replied that I would do so with the greatest willingness, and would incur every risk of that nature, provided I could only extricate him from the grasp of rogues. He then left me.

I have thus given you a full statement of all that I know respecting the origin of Mormonism, and must beg you, as a personal favor, to publish this letter immediately, should you find my name mentioned again by these wretched fanatics.

Yours respectfully . . . CHAS. ANTHON

(Author's note: Alexander Humboldt in his travels throughout Mexico and South America was interested in and recorded all aspects of life. Included were the indigenous people of the New World, their history, culture, politics, and religions).

The Book of Mormon

32. And now, behold, we have written this record according to our knowledge, in the characters which are called among us the reformed Egyptian, being handed down and altered by us, according to our manner of speech.

33. And if our plates had been sufficiently large we should have written in Hebrew; but the Hebrew hath been altered by us also; and if we could have written in Hebrew, behold, ye would have had no imperfection in our record.

34. But the Lord knoweth the things which we have written, and also that none other people knoweth our language; and because that none other people knoweth our language, therefore he hath prepared means for the interpretation thereof.

The Book of Mormon: Book of Mormon, chapter 9 verses 32-34

If none other people knew the language, why were the written characters brought to Professor Anthon to decipher?

"And behold, when ye shall come unto me, ye shall write them and seal them up, that no one can interpret them; for ye shall write them in a language that they cannot be read."

The Book of Mormon: Book of Ether, chapter three verse 22

Caractors

Letter from Davis H. Bays[6]

"DEAR SIR: I herewith inclose {sic} what purports to be a fac-simile of the characters found upon the gold plates from which it is claimed the Book of Mormon was translated. The advocates of Mormonism maintain that these characters are 'Egyptian, Chaldaic, Assyrian and Arabic.'

"So far as I am informed, these characters have never been submitted to scholars of eminence for examination; and as the languages named fall within your province, including Egyptology and Archeology, your professional opinion as to their genuineness will be of great value to the general reader, in determining the exact truth with respect to this remarkable claim. I would also like your opinion upon the following questions? Namely:

1. Did Hebrew scholars at any time, either before or since Christ, keep their records on tablets, or plates of brass?"

2. If so, did they ever write in the Egyptian language?

3. Is there any evidence to show that the Pentateuch was ever written upon such plates of brass?

4. Is there any proof that the Law of Moses, or even the Decalogue, was ever written in the Egyptian language?"

In response to this communication, President James B. Angell, of the University of Michigan, at Ann Arbor, writes:

"REV. D. H. BAYS, *Dear Sir:* I have submitted your letter and inclosure {sic} to our Professor of Oriental languages, who is more familiar with the subjects raised by your questions than I am. He is a man of large learning in Semitic languages and archeology. The substance of what he has to say is:

1. The document which you enclose raises a moral rather than a *linguistic* problem. A few letters or signs are noticeable which correspond more

or less closely to the Aramaic, sometimes called Chaldee language; for example, s, h, g, t, l, b, n. There are no Assyrian characters in it, and the impression made is that *the document is fraudulent.*

2. There is no evidence that the Hebrews kept their records upon plates or tablets of brass; but the Assyrians, in the eighth century before Christ, did.

3. There is no evidence whatever to show that the Pentateuch was ever written on such plates of brass.'

> Yours Truly,
> "JAMES B. ANGELL"

The Doctrines and Dogmas of Mormonism
Davis H.Bays

The question raised by this document is not one of *language*, but of *morals*; and why of morals? The answer is obvious. If the characters were *Egyptian*, as claimed, the question would evidently be one of language rather than of morals. In the careful language of a scholar the writer says, "the impression made is *that the document is fraudulent.*"

A few of the letters, or signs, bear some resemblance to the Aramaic, or Chaldee, yet there is not a word of Egyptian in it. If the story told by these witnesses concerning the angel be true, the characters on these plates must be Egyptian; otherwise the witnesses are proved to be impostors.

Relative to the characters on the plates, Chas. H. S. Davis, M. D. Ph. D., of Meriden, Conn, author of "ANCIENT EGYPT *in the Light of Recent Discoveries,*" and a member of the American Oriental Society, American Philological Society, Society of Biblical Archeology of London, Royal Archeological Institute of Great Britain and Ireland, etc., etc., in answer to the letter of inquiry addressed to him, writes as follows:

"REV. D. H. BAYS, Dear Sir: I am familiar with Egyptian, Chaldaic, Assyrian and Arabic, and have considerable acquaintance with all of the

Oriental languages, and I can *positively assert* that there is not a letter to be found in the fac-simile {sic} submitted that can be found in the alphabet of any Oriental language, particularly of those you refer to -- namely, Egyptian, Chaldaic, Assyrian and Arabic.

"A careful study of the fac-simile shows that they are characters put down at random by an ignorant person -- with no resemblance to anything, not even shorthand.

"No record has ever shown that the Hebrews, or any other Eastern nation, kept their records upon plates or tablets of brass, but thousands upon thousands of tablets of baked clay have been brought to light, antedating two or three thousands years, before the time of Moses, while libraries of these baked clay tablets have been found, like those at Tell el Amara. At the time the Old Testament was written paper made from papyrus was in use, and as documents have been found in Egypt of the times of Moses, written on papyri, it is not unreasonable to suppose that we may find yet portions of the Old Testament.

"The treasures of Egypt and Palestine are only just being brought to light. Remarkable discoveries are yet to be made.

Respectfully,
"CHAS. H. S. DAVIS."

Rev. M.T. Lamb[7]

"(There are) sentences by the thousand, and whole chapters, whose very presence in the Book of Mormon, in the form in which they are found, settles the question of the modern origin of the book beyond the possibility of dispute."

In the discussions the missionaries will tell of the visit of the angel Moroni to Joseph Smith. In this visit Moroni told him where to go to find the brass/gold record which was to be translated into the Book of Mormon.

They will refer to a scripture from the Bible

New Testament
Book of Revelation

Chapter 14 verse 6.

6. and I saw another angel fly in the midst of heaven, having the everlasting gospel to preach to them that dwell on the Earth, and to every nation, and kindred and tongue, and people

The Book of Mormon claims to be a record of the Ancient Civilizations of the American continent who were descendants of an unknown people.

There is the legend in Mesoamerica of the bearded white God known as Quetzalcoatl, meaning The Feathered Serpent. The Feathers, symbolising Him coming from the sky, and serpent representing the type of Brazen Serpent lifted up by Moses in the wilderness which was said to have healed those who looked upon it, after they had been bitten by fiery serpents which were sent as a punishment from God.

The Missionaries claim this bearded white God (Quetzalcoatl) was in "fact" Jesus Christ, when He visited the Ancient American continent. They claim that when Jesus' was resurrected He went to the ancient inhabitants of America who were a remnant of the House of Israel.

The Golden Bible; or, The Book of Mormon Is It From God? M.T. Lamb[8]

That a Christian civilization has never existed in Central America, not even for a day. The people of Central America as far back as their record had been traced (and that is centuries earlier than the alleged beginning of the Nephite history), have always been an idolatrous people, as thoroughly heathen as any which the history of the world has described, worshipping idols the most hideous in form and feature that have ever been found upon earth, and accompanying that worship by human sacrifices as barbarous as the annals of history have recorded...

A sad fatality, is it not, dear reader, that in the very region of country where the Book of Mormon fixes magnificent temples and sanctuaries erected by a Christian people for the worship of the true God, there should be dug up out of the ruins of old temples and palaces such relics of the real religion of these ancient peoples? All the records that have come down to us make it certain that these horrid idols instead of the Lord Jesus were worshipped throughout Central America 2000 years ago.

It would indeed be a bright page in Central American history if the assertions of the Book of Mormon were true. But no such bright spot can be discovered in the Nahuan or the Mayan records. For more than three thousand years it was one unbroken record of superstition and human slaughter........... The entire civilization of the Book of Mormon, its whole record from beginning to end is flatly contradicted by the civilization and the history of Central America.

The Holy Ghost

The third member of the Godhead --- A personage of Spirit ---- Testifier of truth

The Missionaries will encourage the investigator to read the Book of Mormon and put Moroni's promise to the test. They claim that the Holy Ghost will testify of the truthfulness of its contents if one asks with a sincere heart and with faith.

3 Behold, I would exhort you that when ye shall read these things, if it be wisdom in God that ye should read them, that ye would remember how merciful the Lord hath been unto the children of men, from the creation of Adam even down until the time that ye shall receive these things, and ponder it in your hearts.

4 And when ye shall receive these things, I would exhort you that ye would ask God, the Eternal Father, in the name of Christ, if these things are not true; and if ye shall ask with a sincere heart, with real intent, having faith in Christ, he will manifest the truth of it unto you by the power of the Holy Ghost.

5 And by the power of the Holy Ghost ye may know the truth of all things.

The Book of Mormon: Moroni, Chapter 10 verses 3-5

The Second Discussion

The Gospel of Jesus Christ

1. Faith
Faith without works is dead.

2. Repentance
The sinner (investigator) needs to repent (for we have all sinned) and be baptised by full immersion for the remission of those sins. By doing so he/she can gain entry into God's kingdom. Baptism in the same manner as Jesus was baptised by John in the river Jordan.

3. The Gift of the Holy Ghost
Only those who hold the authority from God to perform this ordinance can bestow the Gift of The Holy Ghost. After the Apostles of Jesus Christ died, this authority had been lost from the earth. Joseph Smith the" Prophet of the Restoration" had this authority "restored" to him by the resurrected Peter, James and John (The keys of the ministering of Angels) on the banks of the Suseqhanna River. This power is called the Aaronic Priesthood or Lesser Priesthood referred to in the Old Testament as the Levitical Priesthood.

The Priesthood Authority or "Mormon" Priesthood... as some have referred to it as -- is the authority of God given to man by God - to act in His Name. Within the power of the priesthood, there are also inherent powers or rights of authority, which must be authorized for use -- in order to become functional. These rights or privileges that must be authorized for use -- are referred to as "The Keys of the Priesthood".

4. Obedience

Obedience to God and His laws bring blessings and Eternal Progression.

The Third Discussion

The Restoration of the gospel of Jesus Christ in these latter days

Apostasy

An Apostasy (or falling away) was prophesied.

1. Repent ye therefore, and be converted that your sins may be blotted out, when the times of refreshing shall come from the presence of the Lord.

2 And He shall send Jesus Christ, which before was preached unto you.

3 Whom the heavens must receive until the times of restitution of all things, which God hath spoken by the mouth of all His Holy Prophets since the world, began.

New Testament, Hebrews Chapter 1 verses 1- 3

The "True" Church

The Missionaries teach investigators that The Church of Jesus Christ of Latter-Day Saints is the "only true" Church on the face of the whole Earth and each person needs to be obedient to all God's commandments and become a member of His "only true" Church. They will encourage the investigator to continue reading the Book of Mormon and invite them to attend a Sacrament Meeting.

The Fourth Discussion

Eternal Progression - The Plan of Salvation

According to Mormon teachings, our pre-mortal existence is where we lived with our Heavenly Father before we came to this Earth. His name is Elohim. With visual aids and scriptures they will teach how Jesus, (whose name in the Pre-Mortal Existence was Jehovah) was our Elder Brother. Lucifer the devil was also our brother in the Pre-Mortal Existence. A Grand Council was held there to decide whether Jehovah or Lucifer should at some future time come to this Earth and be our Saviour.

Lucifer wanted all of Heavenly Father's children to come to Earth to receive a body of flesh and bone. We need a body of flesh and bone to be resurrected at the Last Day, but it would be quickened or powered by spirit and not by blood. Lucifer did not want us to have any free agency/free will.

Jehovah on the other hand wanted us to have our free-agency, the right to choose for ourselves whether to obey God's laws or not. He would be our Saviour and come to this Earth to show us what to do to get back to our Heavenly Father's presence. He would die for our sins and if we repented and lived a worthy life obeying His commandments, we could have the full benefit of His Atoning sacrifice. Those of us who voted for Jehovah in the Grand Council in the Pre-Mortal existence were sent, and are continuing to be sent to Earth to receive physical bodies. Those who voted for Lucifer (one third of the hosts of heaven) were denied this opportunity and are now spirits who tempt us to do evil through disobedience to keep us from going back to our Father in Heaven.

Old Testament: Isaiah Chapter 14 verse 12

12.How art thou fallen from heaven, O Lucifer, son of the morning! How art thou cut down to the ground, which didst weaken the nations!

Works for the dead

18. For Christ also hath once suffered for sins, the just for the unjust, that he might bring us to God, being put to death in the flesh, but quickened by the Spirit:

19. By which also he went and preached unto the spirits in prison.

New Testament: 1 Peter, Chapter 3 verses 18-19

The ordinances in behalf of the dead can only be performed in Mormon Temples, of which there are over one hundred worldwide.

According to the Book of Mormon, Nephi built a temple.

16. And I, Nephi, did build a temple; and I did construct it after the manner of the temple of Solomon save it were not built of so many precious things; for they were not to be found upon the land, wherefore, it could not be built like unto Solomon's temple. But the manner of the construction was like unto the temple of Solomon; and the workmanship thereof was exceedingly fine.

The Book of Mormon: 2nd Nephi, Chapter 5 verse 16

In earlier recordings he says otherwise.

25. And it came to pass that we did find upon the land of promise, as we journeyed in the wilderness, that there were beast in the forest of every kind, both the cow and the ox, and the ass and the horse, and the goat and the wild goat, and all manner of wild animals, which were for the use of men. And we did find all manner of ore, both of gold, and of silver, and of copper.

The Book of Mormon: 1st Nephi, Chapter 18 verse 25 (Emphasis added)

Works for the dead include the ordinances of baptism, anointing and washings, endowments and sealings. According to Mormon doctrine, when we depart this life we enter into the spirit world. There are two divisions in the spirit world, Paradise and Spirit prison. When Jesus was on the cross, one of the malefactors said unto him.

42. And he said unto Jesus, Lord remember me when thou comest into thy kingdom.

43. and Jesus unto him, Verily I say unto thee, today shalt thou be with me in paradise.

New Testament: Luke, Chapter 23 verses 42- 43

The Mormons claim that when Jesus was laid in the tomb, before He took up His body up again in the Resurrection, He went as a spirit to the spirits in spirit paradise and taught them His gospel. He taught about the saving ordinances of Baptism, the Sealing of families together forever, for the dead as well as the living. In Doctrine and Covenants (Mormon revelations revered as scripture) a vision given to Joseph F. Smith on October 3rd 1918 reads:

Doctrine and Covenants 138: 29-34

29. And as I wondered, my eyes were opened, and my understanding quickened, and I perceived that the Lord went not in person among the wicked and the disobedient who had rejected the truth, to teach them;

30. but behold, from among the righteous, he organised his forces and appointed messengers, clothed with power and authority, and commissioned them to go forth and carry the light of the gospel to them that were in darkness, even to all the spirits of men; and thus was the gospel preached to the dead.

31. And the chosen messengers went forth to declare the acceptable day of the Lord and proclaim liberty to the captives who were bound, even unto all who would repent of their sins and receive the gospel.

32. Thus was the gospel preached to those who had died in their sins, without knowledge of the truth, or in transgression, having rejected the prophets.

33. These were taught faith in God, repentance from sin, vicarious baptism for the remission of sins, the gift of the Holy Ghost by the laying on of hands,

34. And all other principles of the gospel that were necessary for them to know in order to qualify themselves that they might be judged according to men in the flesh, but live according to God in the spirit.

The Doctrine and Covenants Section 138 verses 29-34

"Scriptures" from the Book of Mormon are in direct contradiction to what "scriptures" in the Doctrine and Covenants state.

Book of Mormon

Chapter heading in the book of Alma

Mortality is a probationary time to enable men to repent and serve God.

Alma 42:4

4.And thus we see that there was a time granted unto man to repent, yea a probationary time, a time to repent and serve God".

Helaman 13:38

38. But behold, your days of probation are past; ye have procrastinated the day of your salvation until it is everlastingly too late, and your destruction is made sure; yea, for ye have sought for happiness in doing iniquity, which thing is contrary to the nature of that righteousness which is in our great and Eternal God.

Alma 34: 30-35

30. and now, my brethren, I would that, after ye have received so many witnesses, seeing that the holy Scriptures testify of these things, ye come forth and bring fruit meet for repentance.

31. Yea, I would that would come forth and harden not your heart any longer; for behold, now is the time and the day of your salvation; and therefore, if ye will repent and harden not your hearts, immediately shall the great plan of redemption be brought about unto you.

32. For behold this life is the time for men to prepare to meet god; yea, behold the day of this life is the day for men to perform their labours.

33. And now, as I said unto you before, as ye have had so many witnesses, therefore, I beseech of you that ye do not procrastinate the day of your repentance until the end; for after this day of life which is given us to prepare for eternity, behold if we do not improve our time while in this life, then cometh the night of darkness wherein no labour can be performed.

34. Ye cannot say that when ye are brought to that awful crisis that I will repent, that I will return to my God. Nay, ye cannot say this; for that same spirit which doth possess your bodies at the time that ye go out of this life, that same spirit will have power to possess your body in that eternal world.

35. For behold if ye have procrastinated the day of your repentance even until death, behold ye have become subjected to the devil, and he doth seal you his; therefore, the Spirit of the Lord hath withdrawn from you, and hath no place in you, and the devil hath all power over you; and this is the final state of the wicked.

These "scriptures" in the book of Mormon are shown to the investigator so they can ponder on the state of all those people who had never heard of the Gospel of Jesus Christ while they were on this Earth. The book of the Doctrine and Covenants is not usually given to investigators until after they are baptised.

According to Mormon teachings every person has a chance to learn of the Saviour and His Gospel even if they did not get the chance to do so in this life. In the Spirit world they can accept or reject what they are taught while there. Who teaches them? The spirits of the departed faithful saints will carry out this work. The term "saint" here means a faithful follower of Jesus Christ and not the canonised saints in the Roman Catholic Church.

For example: "John" dies without hearing the gospel, if he was a good person in this life, he will go to paradise. If he was a bad person and lived a bad life he will go to spirit prison. Regardless of which he goes to, he will be taught the gospel while there.

If he believes the Principles and Ordinances of the gospel and sincerely repents of any sins he has committed while on this Earth, then a faithful temple going worthy Mormon can stand as a proxy for him and have the ordinances of Baptism, Endowment and other necessary ordinances performed in his behalf. These ordinances have to be done by proxy because he does not have his body to perform them himself. These ordinances are necessary for him to receive salvation and exaltation to enable him to return to the presence of God the Father and His Son Jesus Christ.

These are the called the vicarious works for the dead

Else what shall they do which are baptised for the dead, if the dead rise not at all: why are they then baptised for the dead?
1ˢᵗ Corinthians Chapter 15 verse 29

Brigham Young who succeeded Joseph Smith as the Prophet of The Mormon Church explains.

> "Your endowment is, to receive all those ordinances in the house of the Lord, which are necessary for you, after you have departed this life, to enable you to walk back to the presence of the Father, passing the angels who stand as sentinels, being enabled to give them the key words, the signs and tokens, pertaining to the holy Priesthood, and gain your eternal exaltation in spite of Earth and Hell"

Book of Mormon

Helaman 6 verse 26

26. Now behold, those secret oaths and covenants did not come forth unto Gadianton from the records which were delivered unto Helaman; but behold, they were put into the heart of Gadianton by that same being who did entice our first parents to partake of the forbidden fruit—

Joseph Smith stated[9]

"God made Aaron to be the mouth piece for the children of Israel, and He will make me be **god** to you in His stead, and the elders to be mouth for me; and if you don't like it, you must lump it".

Brigham Young said about Joseph Smith[10] "Well, now examine the character of the Savior, and examine the character of those who have written the Old and New Testaments; and then compare them with the character of Joseph Smith, the founder of this word... and you will find that his character stands as fair as that of any man's mentioned in the bible. We can find no person who presents a better character to the world when the facts are know than Joseph Smith, Jun., the prophet and his brother Hyrum Smith, who was murdered with him."

Brigham Young said[11]

No one can get to the highest heaven without Joseph Smith's consent
"...no man or woman in this dispensation will ever enter into the celestial kingdom of God without the consent of Joseph Smith,"

Brigham Young also said God was progressing in knowledge[12]

"God himself is increasing and progressing in knowledge, power, and dominion, and will do so, worlds without end,"

The Book of Mormon

29. He commandeth that there shall be no priestcrafts; for, behold, priestcrafts are that men preach and set themselves up for a light unto the world, that they may get gain and praise of the world; but they seek not the welfare of Zion.
2nd Nephi chapter 26 verse 29

Any Mormon member who is worthy to go to the temple can perform this work, males for males, and females for females. How do Church members know about "John" to do this work in his behalf? Names are gathered by faithful Latter-Day Saints from Registry Offices, Church Records, Census records, and gravestones. The Mormon Church has the world's largest genealogical collection of records. They are documented and processed so the faithful temple goers can go to the temple and do the work for those who have departed this life, no matter what religious persuasion they may have been while they were alive on this Earth.

But it is not only the religiously ignorant who get this work done for them, as far as the Mormon Church is concerned the whole world is in error and they (the Mormons) claim are the only ones that have all the truth and the authority. This work will have to be done for everyone. This is what they claim "The Millennium" is for. One thousand years when The Saviour will be here to oversee and complete the work for the dead. Names and birth dates of those who pre-date records will be provided by the angels, everyone will have their work done, whether they accept it or not in the Spirit world is up to them.

In the temples married couples can be sealed forever to each other. In most Churches the marriage ceremony states. Till death us do part. In the Mormon Church couples can be sealed to each other and have their children sealed to them, so that they can become a sealed Eternal family unit in the Celestial kingdom of God.

This they claim is the Sealing power that Jesus gave to Peter.

New Testament, Matthew Verse 16:19

19. And I will give unto thee the keys of the kingdom of heaven: and whatsoever thou shall bind on earth shall be bound in heaven and whatsoever thou shalt loose on earth shall be loosed in heaven.

The Mormons claim that that their Prophet holds the keys of the Kingdom of God on the earth and not the Pope who claims succession from Peter.

Chastity
The missionaries teach the law of Chastity.
Abstaining from sexual relations before marriage and fidelity within marriage

The Word of Wisdom

This is essentially the Church's health code. It involves abstaining from smoking, consumption of alcohol, tea, coffee and other harmful drugs.

It was given in a 'revelation' to Joseph Smith and became known as The Word of Wisdom:

Doctrine and Covenants Section 89

1. A word of wisdom, for the benefit of the council of high priests, assembled in Kirtland, and the Church, and also the saints in Zion.

2. To be sent greeting; not by commandment or constraint, but by revelation and the word of wisdom, showing forth the order and will of God in the temporal salvation of all saints in the last days.

3. Given for a principle with promise, adapted to the capacity of the weak and the weakest of all saints, who are or can be called saints.

4. Behold, verily, thus saith the Lord unto you: In consequence of evils and designs which do and will exist in the hearts of conspiring men in the last days, I have warned you, and forewarn you, by giving unto you this word of wisdom by revelation—

5. That inasmuch as any man drinketh wine or strong drink among you, behold it is not good, neither meet in the sight of your Father, only in assembling yourselves together to offer up your sacraments before him.

6. and, behold, this should be wine, yea, pure wine of the grape of the vine, of your own make.

7. *And again, strong drinks are not for the body, neither for the belly, but for the washing of your bodies.*

8. *And again tobacco is not for the body, neither for the belly, and is not good for man, but is an herb for bruises and all sick cattle, to be used with judgement and skill.*

9. *And again hot drinks are not for the body or the belly.*
Yea flesh of the beasts and the fowls of the air, I, the Lord have ordained for the use of man with thanksgiving; nevertheless they are to be used sparingly;

10. *and again, verily I say unto you, all wholesome herbs God hath ordained for the constitution, nature, and use of man—*

11. *Every herb in the season thereof, and every fruit in the season thereof; all these to be used with prudence and thanksgiving.*

12. *Yea, flesh also of beasts and of the fowls of the air, I, the Lord, has ordained for the use of man with thanksgiving; nevertheless they are to be used sparingly.*

13. *and it is pleasing unto me that they should not be used only in times of winter, or of cold, or famine.*

14. *All grain is ordained for the use of man and of beasts, to be the staff of life, not only for man but for the beasts of the field, and the fowls of heaven, and all wild animals that run or creep on the earth;*

15. *And these hath God made for the use of man only in times of famine and excess of hunger.*

16. *All grain is good for the food of man; as also the fruit of the vine; that which yieldeth fruit, whether in the ground or above the ground—*

17. *Nevertheless, wheat for man, and corn for the ox, and oats for the horse, and rye for the fowls and for swine, and for all beasts of the field, and barley for all useful animals, and for mild drinks, as also other grain.*

18. And all saints who remember to keep and do these sayings, walking in obedience to the commandments, shall receive health in their navel and marrow to their bones;

19. And shall find wisdom and great treasures of knowledge, even hidden treasures;

20. And shall run and not be weary and shall walk and not faint.

21. And I, the Lord, give unto them a promise, that the destroying angel shall pass by them, as the children of Israel, and not slay them. Amen.

How the Word of Wisdom "revelation" came about according to an account given by Brigham Young, the second prophet of the Church of Jesus Christ of Latter-day Saints.

Remarks, delivered at Provo, Saturday, February 8th 1868 by President Brigham Young[13]

"When the school of the prophets was inaugurated one of the first revelations given by the Lord to His servant Joseph Smith was the Word of Wisdom. The members of that school were but a few at first, and the prophet commenced to teach them in doctrine to prepare them to go out into the world to preach the gospel unto all people, and gather the elect from the four quarters of the earth, as the prophets anciently have spoken. While the instruction prepared the Elders to administer in word, it did not supply the teachings necessary to govern their private or temporal lives: it did not say whether they should be merchants, farmers, mechanics, or money changers. The prophet began to instruct them how to live that they might be better prepared to perform the great work they are called to accomplish.

I think I am well acquainted with the circumstances which led to the giving of the Word of wisdom as any man in the Church, although I was not present at the time to witness them. The first school of the prophets was held in a small room situated over the prophet Joseph's kitchen, in a house which belonged to Bishop Whitney, and which was attached to his store, which store might be about fifteen feet square. In the rear of this building was a kitchen probably ten by fourteen feet containing rooms and pantries. Over this kitchen was situated the room in which the prophet received revelations in which he instructed his brethren.

The brethren came to that place for hundreds of miles to attend school in a little room probably no larger than eleven by fourteen. When they assembled together in this room after breakfast, the first they did was to light their pipes and while smoking, talk about the great things of the kingdom, and spit all over the room, and as soon as the pipe was out of their mouths a large chew of tobacco would then be taken. Often when the Prophet entered the room to give the school instructions he would find himself in a cloud of tobacco smoke. This and the complaints of his wife at having to clean so filthy a floor, made the Prophet to think upon the matter, and he enquired of the Lord relating to the conduct of the Elders in using tobacco, and the revelation known as the Word of Wisdom was the result of his enquiry".

President Brigham Young, April 7th 1861 Salt Lake City[14]

"You know that we all profess to believe the "Word of Wisdom". There has been a great deal said about it, more in former than in latter years. We as Latter-day Saints care but little about tobacco' but as "Mormons", we use a vast quantity of it. As Saints, we use but little; but as "Mormons", we use a great deal. How much do you suppose goes annually from this territory and has for ten or twelve years past, in gold and silver to supply the people with tobacco? I will say $60,000.

Brother William H. Hooper, our Delegate in Congress came here in 1849, and during about eight years he was selling goods his sales for tobacco alone amounted to $28,000 a year at the same time there were other stores that sold their share and drew their share of the money expended yearly besides what has been brought in by the keg and by the half keg. The traders and passing emigration have sold tons of tobacco, beside what is sold here regularly.

I say that $60,000 annually is the smallest figure I can estimate the sales at. Tobacco can be raised here as well as it can be any other place. It wants attention and care. If we use it, let us raise it here. I recommend for some man to go raising tobacco. One man who came her last fall is going to do so; and if he is diligent, he will raise a quantity. I want to see some man go and make a business of raising tobacco and stop sending money out the territory for that article".

It is claimed that Joseph Smith observed the Word of Wisdom. In Church history it states otherwise.

May 2nd 1843 Called at the office and drank a glass of wine with Sister Jenetta Richards, made by her mother in England, and reviewed a portion of the conference minutes.[15]
(History of the Church, vol.2, p.378)

January 1836. We then partook of some refreshments, and our hearts were made glad with the fruit of the vine.[16]
(History of the Church, vol. 2, p369)

Elders Orson Hyde, Luke S. Johnson, and Warren Parrish, then presented the Presidency with three servers of glasses filled with wine to bless. And it fell to my lot to attend to this duty, which I cheerfully discharged. It was then passed around in order, then the cake in the same order; and suffice it to say, our hearts were made glad while partaking of the bounty of earth which was presented, until we had taken our fill...[17]
(History of the Church, vol.2, p.378)

Joseph Smith continued to disobey the Word of Wisdom until the day of his death. The History of the Church records the following incident in Carthage jail... "The guard wanted some wine, Joseph gave Dr. Richards two dollars to give the guard; The guard immediately sent for a bottle of wine, pipes, and two small papers of tobacco; ...... Dr. Richards uncorked the bottle, and presented a glass to Joseph, who tasted, as Brother Taylor and the doctor, and the bottle was then given to the guard, who turned to go out".[18]
(History of the Church, vol. 6, p 616)
As quoted in *The Changing World of Mormonism* by Jerald & Sandra Tanner

The Chicago Times contained the following article about the history of the church, including extensive excerpts from B. W. Richmond's eyewitness account of events leading up to and immediately following the martyrdom of Joseph and Hyrum Smith.

Excerpt from that account [19]

Half a century ago there lived in New York, in the vicinity of where Joseph Smith first became known to fame, a young man named B. W. Richmond, who afterward studied medicine and acquired the title of doctor. He formed Joseph's acquaintance there, and was familiar with the denomination attending his self-announcement as a prophet. In later years he saw him in Ohio, and observed his course with interest.

"I was travelling in the west, and reached Nauvoo, June 24, and with friends, went to the Nauvoo House, kept by Joseph Smith. As I entered the hall I saw a well dressed individual sated {sic} on a trunk at the further end of the hall, quietly smoking a cigar who was pointed out to me as Joseph Smith. He was over six feet tall, of heavy build, with broad shoulders, light hair and complexion, light blue eyes, a long nose, a retreating forehead, large brain and short neck. It was the first time I had [-] seen him, and the impression was a [-] one. He was easy in his manners, and seemed sure of an acquittal if he could get a fair hearing.

Presently he mounted a beautiful chestnut horse, and with [-] others rode up Main Street to Masonic hall, where the state arms were delivered up".

The Chicago Times 1875.
Mormon leaders have made three important changes concerning the Word of Wisdom in Joseph Smith's History of the Church. On one occasion Joseph Smith asked "Brother Markham" to get a pipe and some tobacco" for Apostle Willard Richards. These words have been replaced with the word "medicine" in recent printings of the History of the Church.

Another time Joseph Smith related that he gave some of the "brethren" a "couple of dollars, with directions to replenish" their supply of "whiskey."

In modern editions of the History of the Church, twenty-three words have been deleted from this reference to cover up the fact that Joseph Smith encouraged "the brethren" to disobey the Word of Wisdom.

Another time Joseph Smith frankly admitted that he "drank a beer at Moessers." These words have been omitted in recent Church history printings.

Two entries in Joseph Smiths' diary were omitted from the History of the Church when it was compiled. March 11 1843 Joseph Smith told of having "tea with his breakfast." When his wife asked him how he liked it, he replied "if it was a little stronger he should like it better."
On another occasion "Joseph prophesied in the name of the Lord that he would drink wine" with Orson Hyde "in the east".

(Joseph Smith Diary, January 20, 1843)

The Fifth Discussion
Keeping the Commandments

Fasting

Church members fast on the first Sunday of every month and at other times if they feel the need to do so to obtain special help from the Lord.

Tithing

Old Testament, Malachi 3:10

10. Bring ye all the tithes into the storehouse, that there may be meat in my storehouse, and prove me now herewith, saith the Lord of Hosts, if I will not open the windows of heaven, and pour you a blessing, that there shall not be room enough to receive it.

Church members pay one tenth of their income to the Church. When asked if one should pay one tenth of gross or net income one is asked "How do you want your blessings?"

The Sixth Discussion

Becoming a member in the Lord's Kingdom, through baptism into the "True Church" by those holding the authority to do so.

Exaltation. To go where God resides, this is the Highest Degree/Level in the Celestial Kingdom. There are lesser Kingdoms called the Terrestrial and the Telestial.

New Testament, *1 Corinthians 15: 40-41*

40. There are also Celestial bodies, and bodies' terrestrial; but the glory of the celestial is one, and the glory of the terrestrial is another.

41. There is one glory of the sun, and another glory of the moon, and another glory of the stars; for one star differeth from another in glory.

Exaltation can only come by becoming a member of the L.D.S Church and obeying the laws and ordinances of their gospel, except for those who do not have the mental or physical capacities to do so.

The Three-fold Mission of the Church

- **Perfecting the Saints**
- **Proclaiming the gospel**
- **Redeeming the Dead**

During the discussions an investigator may feel something that they have never felt before; therefore they may think they (the Mormons) must be telling the truth. This feeling however can be felt in any setting of the same spirit. Jesus said.

New Testament, *Matthew 18 verse 20*

"Where two or three are gathered in my name, there will I be in the midst of them"

The missionaries will say it is because the Mormon Church is the only true Church and the Holy Spirit is in it along with all authority from God. Having been raised as a Roman Catholic I told them about the Catholic Pope and his claim to be the successor of Peter. The Missionaries then showed me the scripture.

New Testament, *Matthew 16:13-19*

13. When Jesus came into the coasts of Caesarea Philippi, he asked his disciples, saying, whom do men say that I the Son of man am?

14. And they said, some day that thou are John the Baptist: some Elias; and others, Jeremias, or one of the prophets.

15. He saith unto them, but whom say ye that I am?

16. And Simon Peter answered and said, Thou are the Christ, the Son of the living God.

17. And Jesus answered and said unto him, blessed art thou Simon Bar-jona: for flesh and blood hath not revealed it unto thee, but my Father which is in heaven.

18. And I say also unto thee, that thou art Peter, and upon this rock I will build my Church; and the gates of hell shall not prevail against it.

19. And I will give unto thee the keys of the kingdom of heaven: and whatsoever thou shall bind on earth shall be bound in heaven and whatsoever thou shalt loose on earth shall be loosed in heaven.

The missionaries taught that Peter himself was not the rock; the rock that Jesus referred to was the rock of revelation, the revelation that flowed into Peter from God the Father, telling him who Jesus really was. The Mormon Church claims to be built on revelation. "The First Vision" revealed from the heavens and Moroni the angel revealing where to find the "buried" record.

Old Testament, *Amos Chapter 3 verse 7*

7. Surely the Lord God will do nothing, but he revealeth his secret unto his servants the prophets.

The **Wentworth letter** was a letter written in 1842 by Joseph Smith Jnr. to John Wentworth, editor and proprietor of the Chicago Democrat. It outlined the history of the Latter Day Saint Movement up to that time, and included Mormonism's Articles of Faith.

The Articles of Faith (of the Church of Jesus Christ of Latter-day Saints)

1. We believe in God the Eternal Father and in His Son, Jesus Christ, and in the Holy Ghost.

2. We believe that men will be punished for their own sins, and not for Adam's transgression.

3 We believe that through the Atonement of Christ, all mankind may be saved, by obedience to the laws and ordinances of the Gospel.

4. We believe that the first principles and ordinances of the Gospel are: first, Faith in the Lord Jesus Christ; second, Repentance; third, Baptism by immersion for the remission of sins; fourth, laying on of hands for the gift of the Holy Ghost.

5. We believe that a man must be called of God, by prophecy, and by the laying on of hands by those who are in authority, to preach the Gospel and administer in the ordinances thereof.

6. We believe in the same organisation that existed in the Primitive Church, namely, apostles, prophets, pastors, teachers, evangelists and so forth.

7. We believe in the gift of tongues, prophecy, revelation, visions, healing, interpretation of tongues, and so forth.

8. We believe the Bible to be the word of God as far as it is translated correctly; we also believe the Book of Mormon to be the word of God.

9. We believe all that God has revealed, all that He does now reveal, and we believe that He will yet reveal many great and important things pertaining to the Kingdom of God.

10. We believe in the literal gathering of Israel and in the restoration of the Ten tribes; that Zion (the New Jerusalem) will be built upon the American continent; that Christ will reign personally upon the earth; and, that the earth will be renewed and receive its paradisiacal glory.

11. We claim the privilege of worshipping Almighty God according to the dictates of our own conscience, and allow all men the same privilege, let them worship how, where, or what they may.

12. We believe in being subject to kings, presidents, rulers, and magistrates, in obeying, honouring, and sustaining the law.

13. We believe in being honest, true, chaste, benevolent, virtuous, and in doing good to all men: indeed, we may say that we follow the admonition of Paul--- We believe all things, we hope all things, we have endured many things, and hope to be able to endure all things. If there is anything virtuous, lovely, or of good report or praiseworthy, we seek after these things.

Joseph Smith

B.H Roberts said of the Articles of Faith[20]

"These Articles of Faith were not produced by the labored efforts and harmonized contentions of scholastics, but were struck off by one inspired mind at a single effort to make a declaration of that which is most assuredly believed by the church, for one making earnest inquiry about the truth."

"The combined directness, perspicuity, simplicity and comprehensiveness of this statement of the principles of our religion may be relied upon as strong evidence of a divine inspiration resting upon the Prophet, Joseph Smith."

The Articles of Faith are similar to, and may have been partially derived from, an earlier creed written by Oliver Cowdery in the *Messenger and Advocate* 1, October 1834, p.2. [21]

to *correct* others upon the principles of salvation, not knowing firstly that our foundation is sure.

That our principles may be fully known we here state them briefly:

We believe in God, and his Son Jesus Christ. We believe that God, from the beginning, revealed himself to man; and that whenever he has had a people on earth, he always has revealed himself to them by the Holy Ghost, the ministering of angels, or his own voice. We do not believe that he ever had a church on earth without revealing himself to that church: consequently, there were apostles, prophets, evangelists, pastors, and teachers, in the same.— We believe that God is the same in all ages; and that it requires the same holiness, purity, and religion, to save a man *now*, as it did anciently; and that, as he is no respecter of persons, always has, and always will re-veal himself to men when they call upon him.

We believe that God has revealed himself to men in this age, and commenced to raise up a church preparatory to his second advent, when he will come in the clouds of heaven with power and great glory.

We believe that the popular religious theories of the day are incorrect; that they are without parallel in the revelations of God, as sanctioned by him; and that however faithfully they may be adhered to, or however zealously and warmly they may be defended, they will never stand the strict scrutiny of the word of life.

We believe that all men are born free and equal; that no man, combination of men, or government of men, have power or authority to compel or force others to embrace any system of religion, or religious creed, or to use force or violence to prevent others from enjoying their own opinions, or practicing the same, so long as they do not molest or disturb others in theirs, in a manner to deprive them of their privileges as free citizens—or of worshiping God as they choose, and that any attempt to the contrary is an assumption unwarrantable in the revelations of heaven, and strikes at the root of civil liberty, and is a subversion of all equitable principles between man and man.

We believe that God has set his hand the second time to recover the remnant of his people, Israel; and that the time is near when he will bring them from the four winds, with songs of everlasting joy, and reinstate them upon their own lands which he gave their fathers by covenant.

And further: We believe in embracing good wherever it may be found; of proving all things, and holding fast that which is righteous.

This, in short, is our belief, and we stand ready to defend it upon its own foundation when ever it is assailed by men of character and respectability.— And while we act upon these broad principles, we trust in God that we shall never be confounded!

Neither shall we wait for opposition; but with a firm reliance upon the justice of such a course, and the propriety of disseminating a knowledge of the same, we shall endeavor to persuade men to turn from error and vain speculation; investigate the plan which heaven has devised for our salvation; prepare for the year of recompense, and the day of vengeance which are near, and thereby be ready to meet the Bridegroom!

OLIVER COWDERY.
Kirtland, Ohio, October, 1834.

Spain.—It is said that Spain contains eleven millions of inhabitants—on an average, 27 to a square mile. And when it is recollected that a considerable part of the kingdom is rendered incapable of cultivation in consequence of its lofty mountains, it must be certain that the population is quite dense. It is also said that there are 28,242 houses appropriated to

Notes

1. (As printed in "Dialogue: A Journal of Mormon Thought", Autumn 1966, page 35) As quoted in *Mormonism-Shadow or Reality. Page 145-146.* Jerald & Sandra Tanner
2. As quoted in Mormonism-Shadow or Reality. *Page 145-146.* Jerald & Sandra Tanner.
3. As quoted in Mormonism-Shadow or Reality. Jerald & Sandra Tanner.
4. *Journal of Discourses*, vol.2:171. February 18th 1855
5. E. D. Howe. *Mormonism Unvailed.* 1834, pp. 270-272
6. *THE DOCTRINES AND DOGMAS OF MORMONISM P.261-265 Davis H. Bays* (St. Louis: Christian Pub. Co., 1897)
7. *M.T. Lamb. The Golden Bible 1887*
8. *The Golden Bible; or, The Book of Mormon Is It From God?* M.T. Lamb
9. Joseph Smith, *History of the Church*, vol. 6, pp. 319-320
10. *Journal of Discourses*, vol. 14, p. 203
11. *Journal of Discourses*, vol. 7, p. 289
12. *Journal of Discourses*, vol. 6, p. 120
13. Journal of Discourses, vol.12, p.158) February 8th 1868
14. Journal of Discourses Vol. 9, Page 36. April 7th. 1861
15. (History of the Church, vol.2, p.378) As quoted in The Changing World of Mormonism by Jerald & Sandra Tanner
16. (History of the Church, vol. 2, p369) As quoted in The Changing World of Mormonism by Jerald & Sandra Tanner.
17. (History of the Church, vol.2, p.378)As quoted in The Changing World of Mormonism by Jerald & Sandra Tanner.
18. (History of the Church, vol. 6, p 616) As quoted in The Changing World of Mormonism by Jerald & Sandra Tanner
19. (Joseph Smith Diary, January 20, 1843)As quoted in The Changing World of Mormonism by Jerald & Sandra Tanner.
20. B. H. Roberts, Comprehensive History of the Church, Vol.2, Ch.47, p.131
21. Page of the *Messenger and Advocate* 1(1), October 1834, p.2.

Chapter Six

Witnesses to the Book of Mormon

Testimony of Three Witnesses

Be it known unto all nations, kindreds, tongues, and people, unto whom this work shall come: That we, through the grace of God the Father, and our Lord Jesus Christ, have seen the plates which contain this record, which is a record of the people of Nephi, and also of the Lamanites, their brethren, and also of the people of Jared, who came from the Tower of which hath been spoken. And we also know that they have been translated by the gift and power of God, for his hath declared it unto us; wherefore we know of a surety that the work is true. And we also testify that we have seen the engravings, which are upon the plates; and they have been shown unto us by the power of God, and not of man. And we declare with words of soberness, that an angel of God came down from heaven, and he brought and laid before our eyes, that we beheld and saw the plates, and the engravings thereon; and we know that it is by the grace of God the Father, and our Lord Jesus Christ, that we beheld and bear record that these things are true. And it is marvellous in our eyes. Nevertheless, the voice of the Lord commanded us that we should bear record of it; wherefore to be obedient unto the commandments of God, we bear testimony of these things. And we know that if we are faithful in Christ, we shall rid our garments of the blood of all men, and be found spotless before the judgement seat of Christ, and shall dwell with him eternally in the heavens. And the honour be to the Father, and to the Son, and to the Holy Ghost, which is one God. Amen.

Oliver Cowdery
David Whitmer
Martin Harris
The Book of Mormon

Oliver Cowdery

By early 1838 conflicts had arisen between Smith and Cowdery.

Leadership
Cowdery competed with Smith for leadership of the new Church and disagreed with the Prophet's economic and political programme and sought a personal financial independence [from the] Zion society that Joseph Smith envisioned.

Church and State
In March 1838, Smith and Rigdon moved to Far West, which had been under the presidency of Cowdery's brothers-in-law, David and John Whitmer. There they took charge of the Missouri Church and initiated a number of policies that Cowdery and the Whitmers believed violated separation of Church and state.

Personal Behaviour
In January 1838, Cowdery wrote to his brother Warren that he and Joseph Smith had "had some conversation in which in every instance I did not fail to affirm that which I had said was strictly true. A dirty, nasty, filthy affair of his and Fanny Alger's was talked over in which I strictly declared that I had never deserted from the truth in the matter, and as I supposed was admitted by himself."

Fanny Alger, was a teenage maid living with the Smiths, and may have been Joseph Smith's first plural wife, a practice that Cowdery opposed.

On April 12th 1838 a Church court excommunicated Cowdery after he failed to appear at a hearing on his membership and sent a letter resigning from the Church instead. The Whitmer brothers, William Wines Phelps and Book of Mormon witness Hiram Page were also excommunicated from the Church at the same time.

Cowdery and the Whitmers' became known as "the dissenters," but they continued to live in and around Far West, where they owned a great deal of property. On June 17th 1838 President Sidney Rigdon announced to a large Mormon congregation that the dissenters were "as salt that had lost its savor" and that it was the duty of the faithful to cast the dissenters out "to be trodden beneath the feet of men." Oliver Cowdery and the Whitmer's took this Salt Sermon as a threat against their lives, and as an implicit instruction to the Danites, (who were a secret Mormon vigilante group), and fled the county. Stories about their treatment circulated in nearby non-Mormon communities and increased the tension that led to the Mormon War.

After separating himself from the Mormons, Oliver Cowdery became a member of the Methodist Protestant Church of Tiffin, Seneca County, Ohio.

****

From Charles A. Shook The True Origin of the Book of Mormon[1]

I now introduce the affidavit of C. J. Keen, a highly respected citizen of Tiffin, as proof that Cowdery renounced Mormonism and united with the Methodist Protestant Church:

Personally appeared before me, the undersigned, a Notary Public within and for said county, G. J. Keen, a resident of said county, to me well known, and being sworn according to law makes oath and says:

I was well acquainted with Oliver Cowdery who formerly resided in this city, that sometime in the year 1840 Henry Cronise, Samuel Waggoner and myself, with other Democrats of this county, determined to establish a Democratic newspaper in this city to aid in the election of Martin Van Buren to the Presidency, and we authorized Henry Cronise, Esq., to go East and purchase a suitable press for that purpose. Mr. Cronise went east, purchased a press and engaged Oliver Cowdery to edit the paper. Mr. Cowdery arrived in Tiffin (O.) some time before the press arrived. Some time after Mr. Cowdery's arrival in Tiffin, we became acquainted with his (Cowdery's) connection with Mormonism.

We immediately called a meeting of our Democratic friends, and having the Book of Mormon with us, it was unanimously agreed that

Mr. Cowdery could not he permitted to edit said paper. Mr. Cowdery opened a law office in Tiffin, and soon effected a partnership with Joel W. Wilson. In a few years Mr. Cowdery expressed a desire to associate himself with a Methodist Protestant Church of this city.

Rev. John Souder and myself were appointed a committee to wait on Mr. Cowdery and confer with him respecting his connection with Mormonism and the Book of Mormon. We accordingly waited on Mr. Cowdery at his residence in Tiffin, and there learned his connection, from him, with that order, and his full and final renunciation thereof. We then inquired of him if he had any objection to making a public recantation. He replied that he had objections; that, in the first place, it could do no good; that he had known several to do so and they always regretted it. And, in the second place, it would have a tendency to draw public attention, invite criticism, and bring him into contempt.

"But," said he, "nevertheless, if the Church requires it, I will submit to it, but I authorize and desire you and the Church to publish and make known my recantation." We did not demand it, but submitted his name to the Church, and he was unanimously admitted a member thereof. At that time he arose and addressed the audience present, admitted his error and implored forgiveness, and said he was sorry and ashamed of his connection with Mormonism. He continued his membership while he resided in Tiffin, and became superintendent of the Sabbath-school, and led an exemplary life the while he resided with us. I have lived in this city upwards of fifty-three years, was auditor of this county, was elected to that office in 1840. I am now in my eighty-third year, and well remember the facts above related.

(Signed) G. J. KEEN

Sworn to before me and subscribed in my presence, this 14th day of April, A. D. 1885

FRANK L. EMICH,

Notary Public in Seneca, O.

In the year 1848 Cowdery traveled to meet with followers of Brigham Young and the Quorum of the Twelve who were camped at Winter Quarters, Nebraska. He was re-baptized into the Church that same year. Two years later he developed a respiratory illness, and died on March 3, 1850 in the home of David Whitmer in Richmond, Missouri. David Whitmer claimed that Cowdery died believing Joseph Smith was a fallen prophet and that his revelations in the Doctrine & Covenants must be rejected.

David Whitmer
President of the Church of Christ (Whitmerite)

Although the main body of the Latter Day Saints eventually relocated to Nauvoo, Illinois. David Whitmer continued to live in Richmond, where he operated a livery stable and became a prominent and respected citizen.

After the assassination of Joseph Smith in 1844, several rival leaders claimed to be Joseph Smith's successor, including Brigham Young, Sidney Rigdon, and James J. Strang. Many of Rigdon's followers became disillusioned by 1847 and some, including Apostle William E. McLellin and Benjamin Winchester, remembered David Whitmer's 1834 ordination to be Smith's successor. At McLellin's urging, Whitmer exercised his claim to be Smith's successor and the (Whitmerite Church) was formed in Kirtland, Ohio.

However, Whitmer never joined the body of the new Church and it dissolved relatively quickly.

Around this time, fellow Book of Mormon witness Oliver Cowdery, began to correspond with Whitmer. After travelling from Ohio to Kanesville (Council Bluffs), Cowdery met in the Kanesville Tabernacle meeting, called to sustain Brigham Young as the new President of the Church. Cowdery bore his testimony with a conviction to the truthfulness of everything that had happened spiritually with Joseph Smith and the Book of Mormon. Meeting with Young at Winter Quarters, Nebraska, he requested readmission into the Church, where he was re-baptised. Cowdery then travelled to meet with Whitmer in Richmond, to persuade David Whitmer to move west with him to rejoin the Saints in Utah. While staying with Whitmer, however, Cowdery succumbed to consumption and died.

Whitmer continued to live in Richmond and in 1867; he was elected to fill an unexpired term as mayor (1867–1868). In 1876, Whitmer again asserted his claim to be the successor of Joseph Smith and organized a second Church of Christ (Whitmerite). In 1887, he published a pamphlet entitled *An Address to All Believers in Christ*, in which he affirmed his testimony of the Book of Mormon, but denounced The Church of Jesus Christ of Latter day Saints in Utah. At the end of his life, Whitmer ordained a nephew to be his successor. David Whitmer died January 25th 1888 in Richmond. The Whitmerite Church survived until the 1960s.

Printed in (Dialogue: A Journal of Mormon Thought, Winter, 1972, pp.83-84)[2]

…There is a possibility that the witnesses saw the plates in vision only… There is testimony from several independent interviewers, all non-Mormon, that Martin Harris and David Whitmer said they saw the plates with their "spiritual eyes" only…. This is contradicted, however, by statements like that of David Whitmer in the Saints Herald in 1882, "these hands handled the plates, these eyes saw the angel." But Z.H. Gurley elicited from Whitmer a not so positive response to the question, "did you touch them?" His answer was, "We did not touch nor handle the plates."…. So far as the eight witnesses go, William Smith said his father never saw the plates except under a frock. And Stephen Burnett quotes Martin Harris that "the eight witnesses never saw them…." Yet John Whitmer told Wilhelm Poulson… that he saw the plates when they were not covered, and he turned the leaves.

David Whitmer's account taken from his own book
An Address to All Believers in Christ[3]   Richmond, Missouri 1887

I will now give you a description of the manner in which the Book of Mormon was translated. Joseph Smith would put the seer stone into a hat, and put his face in the hat, drawing it closely around his face to exclude the light; and in the darkness the spiritual light would shine. A piece of something resembling parchment would appear, and on that appeared the writing. One character at a time would appear, and under it was the interpretation in English. Brother Joseph would read off the English to Oliver Cowdery, who was his principal scribe, and when it was written down and repeated to Brother Joseph to see if it was correct, then it would disappear, and another character with the interpretation would appear. Thus the Book of Mormon was translated by the gift and power of God, and not by any power of man.

Brigham Young[4]
June 5th 1859

"Some of the witnesses of the Book of Mormon, who handled the plates and conversed with the angels of God, were afterwards left to doubt and to disbelieve that they had ever seen an angel.

One of the Quorum of the Twelve-a young man full of faith and good works, prayed, and the vision of his mind was opened, and the angel of God came and laid the plates before him, and he saw and handled them, and saw the angel, and conversed with him as he would with one of his friends; but after all this, he was left to doubt, and plunged into apostacy [sic], and has continued to contend against this work. There are hundreds in a similar condition".

Martin Harris

Statement from Lucy Harris on her husband[5] *Palmyra, Nov. 29, 1833.*

Being called upon to give a statement to the world of what I know respecting the Gold Bible speculation, and also of the conduct of Martin Harris, my husband, who is a leading character among the Mormons, I do it free from prejudice, realizing that I must give an account at the bar of God for what I say. Martin Harris was once industrious attentive to his domestic concerns, and thought to be worth about ten thousand dollars. He is naturally quick in his temper and his mad-fits frequently abuses all who may dare to oppose him in his wishes. However strange it may seem, I have been a great sufferer by his unreasonable conduct. At different times while I lived with him, he has whipped, kicked, and turned me out of the house.

About a year previous to the report being raised that Smith had found gold plates, he became very intimate with the Smith family, and said he believed Joseph could see in his stone any thing he wished. After this he apparently became very sanguine in his belief, and frequently said he would have no one in his house that did not believe in Mormonism; and because I would not give credit to the report he made about the gold plates, he became more austere towards me. In one of his fits of rage he struck me with the but end of a whip, which I think had been used for driving oxen, and was about the size of my thumb, and three or four feet long. He beat me on the head four or five times, and the next day turned me out of doors twice, and beat me in a shameful manner. -- The next day I went to the town of Marion, and while there my flesh was black and blue in many places. His main complaint against me was that I was always trying to hinder his making money.

When he found out that I was going to Mr. Putnam's, in Marion, he said he was going too, but they had sent for him to pay them a visit. On arriving at Mr. Putnam's, I asked them if they had sent for Mr. Harris; they replied they knew nothing about it; he, however, came in the evening. Mrs. Putnam told him never to strike or abuse me any more; he then denied ever striking me; she was however convinced that he lied, as the marks of his beating me were plain to be seen, and remained more than two weeks. Whether the Mormon religion be true or false, I leave the world to judge, for its effects upon Martin Harris have been to make him more cross, turbulent and abusive to me. His whole object was to make money by it. I will give one circumstance in proof of it. One day, while at Peter Harris' house, I told him he had better leave the company of the Smiths, as their religion was false; to which he replied, if you would let me alone, I could make money by it.

It is in vain for the Mormons to deny these facts; for they are all well known to most of his former neighbors. The man has now become rather an object of pity; he has spent most of his property, and lost the confidence of his former friends. If he had labored as hard on his farm as he has to make Mormons, he might now be one of the wealthiest farmers in the country. He now spends his time in traveling through the country spreading the delusion of Mormonism, and has no regard whatever for his family.

With regard to Mr. Harris' being intimate with Mrs. Haggard, as has been reported, it is but justice to myself to state what facts have come within my own observation, to show whether I had any grounds for jealousy or not. Mr. Harris was very intimate with this family, for some time previous to their going to Ohio. They lived a while in a house which he had built for their accommodation, and here he spent the most of his leisure hours; and made her presents of articles from the store and house. He carried these presents in a private manner, and frequently when he went there, he would pretend to be going to some of the neighbors, on an errand, or to be going into the fields. -- After getting out of sight of the house, he would steer a straight course for Haggard's house, especially if Haggard was from home. At times when Haggard was from home, he would go there in the manner above described, and stay till twelve or one o'clock at night, and sometimes until day light. If his intentions were evil, the Lord will judge him accordingly, but if good, he did not mean to let his left hand know what his right hand did. The above statement of facts, I affirm to be true.

LUCY HARRIS

Lucy Harris died in the summer of 1836, and on November 1, 1836, Harris married Carol Young.

MORMONISM[6]

Abigail Harris   *Palmyra, Wayne Co. N. Y. 11th mo, 28th, 1833*

In the early part of the winter in 1828, I made a visit to Martin Harris' and was joined in company by Jos. Smith, Sen. and his wife. The Gold Bible business, so called, was the topic of conversation, to which I paid particular attention that I might learn the truth of the whole matter. -- They told me that the report that Joseph, jun. had found golden plates, was true, and that he was in Harmony, Pa. translating them -- that such plates were in existence, and that Joseph, jun. was to obtain them, was revealed to him by the spirit of one of the Saints that was on this continent, previous to its being discovered by Columbus.

Old Mrs. Smith observed that she thought he must be a Quaker, as he was dressed very plain. They said that the plates he then had in possession were but an introduction to the Gold Bible -- that all of them upon which the bible was written, were so heavy that it would take four stout men to load them into a cart -- that Joseph had also discovered by looking through his stone, the vessel in which the gold was melted from which the plates were made, and also the machine with which they were rolled; he also discovered in the bottom of the vessel three balls of gold, each as large as his fist. The old lady said also, that after the book was translated, the plates were to be publicly exhibited -- admitance {sic} 25 cents.

She calculated it would bring in annually an enormous sum of money -- that money would then be very plenty, and the book would also sell for a great price, as it was something entirely new -- that they had been commanded to obtain all the money they could borrow for present necessity, and to repay with gold. The remainder was to be kept in store for the benefit of their family and children. This and the like conversation detained me until about 11 o'clock. Early the next morning, the mystery of the Spirit being like myself (one of the order called Friends) was revealed by the following circumstance:

The old lady took me into another room, and after closing the door, she said, "have you four or five dollars in money that you can lend until our business is brought to a close? the spirit has said you shall receive four fold." I told her that when I gave, I did it not expecting to receive again -- as for money I had none to lend. I then asked her what her particular want of money was; to which she replied, "Joseph wants to take the stage and come home from Pennsylvania to see what we are all about." To which I replied, he might look in his stone and save his time and money. The old lady seemed confused, and left the room, and thus ended the visit.

In the second month following, Martin Harris and his wife were at my house. In conversation about Mormonites, she observed, that she wished her husband would quit them, as she believed it was all false and delusion. To which I head {sic} Mr. Harris reply: *"What if it is a lie; if you will let me alone I will make money out of it!"* I was both an eye and an ear witness of what has been stated above, which is now fresh in my memory, and I give it to the world for the good of mankind. I speak the truth and lie not, God bearing me witness.   ABIGAIL HARRIS.

MORMONISM [7]

MARTIN HARRIS is the next personage of note in the Golden Bible speculation. He is one of the *three witnesses* to the truth of the book, having been shown the plates through the agency of an Angel, instead of the Prophet Joseph, who always had them in possession. Before his acquaintance with the Smith family, he was considered an honest, industrious citizen, by his neighbors. His residence was in the town of Palmyra, where he had accumulated a handsome property. He was naturally of a very visionary turn of mind on the subject of religion, holding one sentiment but a short time.

He engaged in the new Bible business with a view of making a handsome sum of money from the sale of the books, as he was frequently heard to say. The whole expense of publishing an edition of 5000 copies, which was borne by Martin, to secure the payment of which, he mortgaged his farm for $3000. Having failed in his anticipations about the sale of the books, (the retail price of which they said was fixed by an Angel at $1.75, but afterwards reduced to $1.25, and from that down to any price they could obtain) he adopted Smith as his Prophet, Priest and King. Since that time, the frequent demands upon Martin's purse have reduced it to a very low state.

He seems to have been the soul and body of the whole imposition, and now carries the most incontestible {sic} proofs of a religious maniac. He frequently declares that he has conversed with Jesus Christ, Angels and the Devil. Christ he says is the handsomest man he ever saw; and the Devil looks very much like a jack-ass, with very short, smooth hair, similar to that of a mouse. He says he wrote a considerable part of the book, as Smith dictated, and at one time the presence of the Lord was so great, that a screen was hung up between him and the Prophet; at other times the Prophet would sit in a different room, or up stairs, while the Lord was communicating to him the contents of the plates.

He does not pretend that he ever saw the wonderful plates but once, although he and Smith were engaged for months in deciphering their contents. He has left his wife to follow the fortunes of Smith. He has frequent fits of phrophecying, {sic} although they are not held in very high repute among his brethren. A specimen of his prophetic powers we subjoin. They were written for the special information of a friend of his who placed them upon the wall of his office, and are in these words:

Within four years from September 1832, there will not be one wicked person left in the United States; that the righteous will be gathered to Zion, (Missouri) and that there will be no President over these United States after that time.

MARTIN HARRIS.

I do hereby assert and declare that in four years from the date hereof, every sectarian and religious denomination in the United States shall be broken down, and every Christian shall be gathered unto the Mormonites, and the rest of the human race shall perish. If these things do not take place, I will hereby consent to have my hand separated from my body.

MARTIN HARRIS.

Martin is an exceedingly fast talker. He frequently gathers a crowd around him in bar-rooms and in the streets. -- Here he appears to be in his element, answering and explaining all manner of dark and abstruse theological questions, from Genesis to Revelations; declaring that every thing has been revealed to him by the "power of God." During these flights of fancy, he frequently prophecies the coming of Christ, the destruction of the world, and the damnation of certain individuals.

At one time he declared that Christ would be on earth within fifteen years, and all who did not believe in the book of Mormon would be destroyed.

He is the source of much trouble and perplexity to the honest portion of his brethren, and would undoubtedly long since have been cast off by Smith, were it not for his money, and the fact that he is one of the main pillars of the Mormon fabric. Martin is generally believed, by intelligent people, to be laboring under a partial derangement; and that any respectable jury would receive his testimony, in any case, of ever so trifling a nature, we do not believe; yet, the subjects of the delusion think him a competent witness to establish miracles of the most unreasonable kind. But we leave him for the present.

MORMONISM [8]

Martin Harris was first a Quaker, then a Universalist, next a Restorationist, then a Baptist, next a Presbyterian, and then a Mormon.

Even before he had become a Mormon, Harris had changed his religion at least five times. After Smith's death, Harris continued this earlier pattern, remaining in Kirtland and accepting James J. Strang as Mormonism's new prophet, a prophet with his own set of supernatural plates and witnesses to authenticate them. By 1847, Harris had broken with Strang and accepted the leadership claims of fellow Book of Mormon witness, David Whitmer. Mormon Apostle William E. Mc Lellin organized a Whitmerite congregation in Kirtland, and Harris became a member. By 1851 Harris accepted another Latter Day Saint factional leader, Gladden Bishop as prophet and joined Bishop's Kirtland-based organization. In 1855 Harris joined with the last surviving brother of Joseph Smith, William Smith and declared that William was Joseph's true successor.

Harris was also briefly intrigued by the "Roll and Book," a supernatural scripture delivered to the Shakers. The Shakers felt that Christ had made his second appearance on earth, in a chosen female known by the name of Ann Lee. The Shakers did not believe the Book of Mormon, but they had their own book entitled A Holy, Sacred and Divine Roll and Book;

From the Lord God of Heaven, to the Inhabitants of Earth. More than sixty individuals gave testimony to the Sacred Roll and Book, which was published in 1843. Not all, but some of them mention angels appearing.

In this book appears the testimony of eight witnesses:
We, the undersigned, hereby testify that we saw the holy Angel standing upon the housetops, as mentioned in the foregoing declaration, holding the Roll and Book.

Betsey Boothe.	Sarah Maria Lewis
Louisa Chamberlain.	Sarah Ann Spencer
Caty De Witt.	Lucinda Mc Daniels
Laura Ann Jacobs.	Maria Hedrick.

By the 1860s, all of these organizations had either dissolved or declined. In 1856, Harris's wife Caroline left him to gather with the Mormons in Utah.

The Testimony of Eight Witnesses of the Book of Mormon

Be it known unto all nations, kindreds, tongues, and people, unto whom this work shall come: That Joseph Smith, Jun., the translator of this work, has shown unto us the plates of which hath been spoken, which have the appearance of gold; and as many of the leaves as the said Smith has translated we did handle with our hands; and we also saw the engravings thereon, all of which has the appearance of ancient work, and of curious workmanship. And this we bear record with words of soberness that the said Smith has shown unto us, for we have hefted, and know of a surety that the said Smith has got the plates of which we have spoken. And we give our names unto the world, to witness unto the world that which we have seen. And we lie not, God bearing witness of it.

Christian Whitmer,	Hiram Page
Jacob Whitmer,	Joseph Smith. Sen.
Peter Whitmer, Jun.	Hyrum Smith
John Whitmer,	Samuel H. Smith

Christian Whitmer

Born January 18, 1798 in Dauphin, Pennsylvania, USA. Whitmer moved with his parents' family to New York in 1809. On February 22, 1825, he married Ann Schott (1801–1866) in Fayette, New York. In June of 1829, Christian Whitmer, along with several of his brothers became a special witness of the Book of Mormon. On April 11, 1830, he and Ann were baptized into the newly organized "Church of Christ" as this was original name of the "Church of Jesus Christ of Latter Day Saints." They subsequently moved to Jackson County, Missouri, where Whitmer was appointed a leading elder of the Church.

By 1835, Whitmer and his family had relocated to the new latter day Saint settlement of Far West, Missouri, where Whitmer sat on the "High Council". He died there in 1835.

Jacob Whitmer

Born January 27, 1800 Jacob Whitmer moved with his parents' family to New York, where he married Elizabeth Schott on September 29, 1825. Jacob and Elizabeth had nine children together, only three of which survived to adulthood.

Whitmer's younger brother David became a close associate of Joseph Smith Jnr. In June 1829, Jacob Whitmer joined his brothers in signing a statement testifying that he personally saw and handled the Golden Plates said to be in Smith's possession. On April 11, 1830, he was baptized into the newly organized "Church of Christ" as this was original name of the "Church of Jesus Christ of Latter Day Saints."

He gathered with early Church members to Jackson County, Missouri, USA, but was driven by non-Mormon vigilantes from his home there and later from his home in Clay County, Missouri, as well. He then settled in Caldwell County Missouri where he served on Far West's High Council. He was excommunicated from the Church of Jesus Christ of Latter Day Saints in 1838 along with the rest of the living members of the Whitmer family, and driven again from his home. He settled finally near Richmond in neighbouring Ray County where he worked as a shoemaker and farmer. He died on April 21ˢᵗ, 1856 still affirming his testimony of the Book of Mormon.

Peter Whitmer, Jr.

Born September 27ᵗʰ 1809 in Fayette, New York. Peter Whitmer Jr. and several of his brothers became special witnesses of the Book of Mormon in June of 1829. Soon after the organization of the Latter Day Saint Church on April 6, 1830, Whitmer was called to travel with Oliver Cowdery, Parley P. Pratt and Ziba Peterson on a special mission to preach the faith to the Native Americans. This mission led to the conversion of former Campbellite minister Sidney Rigdon.

Whitmer subsequently moved to Jackson County Missouri, where he married Vashti Higley on October 14ᵗʰ 1832, with whom he had three children. He was excommunicated from the Church of Jesus Christ of Latter Day Saints in 1838 along with the rest of the living members of the Whitmer family, and driven again from his home. By 1835, Whitmer and his family had relocated to the new Latter Day Saint settlement of Far West, Missouri where he sat on the Church's High Council. He died of tuberculosis on September 22, 1836 in Liberty, Missouri.

John Whitmer

Member of the presidency of the Church and first official Church Historian

Later in 1831, Whitmer joined the growing number of Latter Day Saints in Jackson County, Missouri. Problems at Church headquarters in Kirtland relating to the Kirtland Safety Society Bank, caused Joseph Smith, Jr., and Sidney Rigdon to relocate to Far West in early 1838. A brief leadership struggle ensued, which led to the excommunication of the John Whitmer and the entire Whitmer family as well as Oliver Cowdery, W.W. Phelps and others. These men continued to live in Far West for a time and became known as the "dissenters". Sidney Rigdon, in his Salt Sermon, warned the dissenters to leave the county and his words were soon followed up by perceived threats from the newly formed Mormon confraternity known as the Danites.

John Whitmer's parents and his brother David remained in Richmond for the rest of their lives, but John and his own family returned to Far West. Emptied of the Latter Day Saints, Far West became something of a ghost town. Many of its houses were moved off to other settlements, and Far West lost the county seat to nearby Kingston. Whitmer continued to live in Far West, buying up land (including the temple site) and eventually amassing a large farm. He occasionally gave visitors tours of the former settlement.

After Joseph Smith's assassination in 1844, several leaders asserted their claims to be his rightful successor. Among these was Whitmer's brother David. In 1847, Whitmer was briefly part of a renewed Church of Christ (Whitmerite).

Whitmer died on July 11, 1878 in Far West. He is buried in Kingston Cemetery Kingston.

After his call as Church Historian, Whitmer began to write a record entitled, *The Book of John Whitmer, Kept by Commandment*. His book begins with an account of events leading up to the relocation of the Church's headquarters from New York to Kirtland, Ohio. He discusses many of the troubles experienced by the Latter Day Saints in Missouri and ends the work with an account of his own excommunication in March of 1838. Afterwards, a continuation tells of the mistreatment he felt he and the other "dissenters" had received at the hands of Joseph Smith and Sidney Rigdon. Whitmer's manuscript is now in the archives of the Community of Christ, the second largest denomination of the Latter-day Saint movement.

Hiram Page

While Page was living with the Whitmers in Fayette, New York, Joseph Smith Jnr.arrived in August of 1830 to discover Hiram using a "seer stone" to receive revelations for the Church. The only available detail about the stone was that it was black. The revelations were regarding the organization and location of Zion. Oliver Cowdery and the Whitmer family believed the revelations Page had received were true. In response, Joseph Smith received a revelation during the conference in September of that year to have Oliver Cowdery go to Hiram and convince him that his revelations are of the devil.

Doctrine and Covenants, section 28 verse 11

11. And again, thou shalt take thy brother, Hiram Page, between him and thee alone, and tell him that those things which he hat written from that stone are not of me and that Satan deceiveth him;

At the conference, there was considerable discussion on the topic. Hiram agreed to discard the stone and the revelations he received and join in following Joseph Smith as the sole revelator for the Church. The members present confirmed this unanimously with a vote. Later the stone was ground to powder and the revelations purportedly received through it were burned.

In May of 1831 Page moved his family to Thompson, Ohio under Lucy Mack Smith's direction. He again moved his family to Jackson County, Missouri in 1832 and joined the Latter Day Saints gathering there. With the other Whitmers, they formed a cluster of ten or twelve homes called the "Whitmer Settlement". Hiram owned 120 acres of land in the area.

During the growing anti-Mormon hostilities in Jackson County, Page was severely beaten by a group of non-Mormon vigilantes on October 31, 1833. On July 31 and August 6, 1834 he testified to the facts of the beatings. By 1834 he and his family were expelled along with the other Latter Day Saints and lived for a time in neighbouring Clay County, before moving to Far West. Page and other members of the Whitmer family were excommunicated from the Latter Day Saint Church in 1838. He later bought a farm in Excelsior Springs back in Clay County.

William E. McLellin baptized Hiram Page, David Whitmer, John Whitmer and Jacob Whitmer on September 6, 1847 into his newly formed Church of Christ. William ordained Hiram a high priest in the Church. Hiram participated in the subsequent ordinations of the others. He died on his farm in Excelsior Springs on August 12, 1852, still affirming his testimony of the Book of Mormon.

Joseph Smith, Sr.

Father of Joseph Smith Jnr., who founded the Latter Day Saint movement. Joseph Sr. was the first Presiding Patriarch of the Latter Day Saint Church, a member of the First Presidency of the Church, and a Master Freemason of the Ontario Lodge No. 23 of Canandaigua, New York. In January 1831, Joseph Smith, Sr. and his family moved to the Church's new headquarters in Kirtland, Ohio. He was ordained to be the Church's first Presiding Patriarch on 18th December 1833.

Likening his father to Adam, Joseph Smith Jnr. said, "So shall it be with my father; he shall be called a prince over his posterity, holding the keys of the Patriarchal priesthood over the kingdom of God on earth, even the Church of the Latter Day Saints"
Quoted in Bates and Smith, page 34

As part of his new role, Joseph Smith Sr. presided in council meetings, ordained other patriarchs and administered Patriarchal blessings.

On September 3, 1837 Smith was also made an Assistant Counsellor in the First Presidency of the Church. Smith moved with his family to Far West, Missouri in 1838 and from there to the Church's new headquarters at Nauvoo, Illinois in 1839. Old age and illnesses had taken their toll and by the end of summer 1840, Smith realized he was dying. He called his family around him to administer Patriarchal blessings.

He blessed his wife: "Mother, do you not know that you are the mother of as great a family as ever lived upon the earth ... They are raised up to do the Lord's work" He blessed and ordained his eldest surviving son,

Hyrum to succeed to the office of Presiding Patriarch by right of lineage. Joseph Smith Sr. died on 14th September 1840

Hyrum Smith

Older brother of Joseph Smith Jnr. and also a leader in the early Latter Day Saint Movement.

In1831 as the Church headquarters and membership moved West, Hyrum and his family established a home in Kirtland, Ohio. During his residence there he served as foreman of the quarry providing stone for the Kirtland temple.

Between 1831 and 1833 he served proselyting missions to Missouri and Ohio. In 1834, under the direction of Joseph Smith, he recruited members for a militia; (Zion's Camp) and travelled with the group to the aid of the Latter Day Saints in Missouri. He was appointed Second Counsellor in the Church's First Presidency in November 1837. In 1838/1839 Hyrum, Joseph and three other Church leaders shared a jail cell in Liberty, Missouri while awaiting trial.

After relocating to Nauvoo, Illinois Hyrum was ordained as Presiding Patriarch of the Church, a position formerly held by his deceased father, Joseph Smith, Snr. He also was ordained by Joseph to the priesthood office of Apostle and replaced Oliver Cowdery as Assistant President of the Church. In this capacity, Hyrum acted as President of the Church in Joseph's absence and was designated to be Joseph's successor if he were killed or incapacitated.

When warned of possible danger, Joseph urged Hyrum and his family to flee to Cincinnati, Ohio, Hyrum refused and, in 1844, travelled with Joseph to Carthage, Illinois where both were charged with riot and treason. Joseph, Hyrum, John Taylor and Willard Richards were held awaiting trial in a jail in Carthage. On June 27th 1844, the building was attacked by a mob of between sixty to two hundred men.

While attempting to barricade the door to prevent the mob from entering, Hyrum was shot in the face and killed instantly. Taylor was struck by several bullets but survived with the help of Richards. Joseph was killed by at least two shots and fell through a second story window to the ground where he was shot again.

Samuel Harrison Smith

One of the younger brothers of Joseph Smith Jnr. Samuel Smith remained devoted to his brother and his brother's Church throughout his life.

Born in Turnbridge, Vermont Samuel had moved with his family to western New York by the 1820s. When Smith's father missed a mortgage payment on the family farm on the outskirts of Manchester Township, near Palmyra, a local Quaker named Lemuel Durfee purchased the land and allowed the Smith family to continue to live there in exchange for Samuel's labour at Mr. Durfee's store.

At the end of June 1829 Samuel, along with his brother Hyrum, his father, and several men of the Peter Whitmer, Snr. family, signed a joint statement declaring their testimony of the golden plates that Joseph Smith claimed to have translated into the Book of Mormon.

Samuel Smith's brothers, Joseph and Hyrum were assassinated in 1844 while being held in Carthage jail, in Illinois. Samuel, risking attack by a mob, travelled to the jail and retrieved his brothers' bodies. Some Church members assumed that Samuel would succeed his brother Joseph as the president of the Latter Day Saint Church.

However, Samuel fell ill shortly after their deaths and died just one month later. The sole remaining Smith brother, William, charged that Brigham Young had arranged for Samuel to be poisoned to prevent his accession to the presidency. Others attributed Samuel's death to an internal injury sustained during his retrieval of the bodies or to illness. William Smith's charges were neither proven nor disproven.

Four witnesses were Whitmers and three were members of Joseph Smith's own family. The eighth witness, Hiram Page was married to a Whitmer daughter.

Mark Twain was later to observe on the Book of Mormon witnesses. "I could not feel more satisfied and at rest if the entire Whitmer family had testified."

The following account given by more than one of Joseph Smith's key men to Thomas Ford who was governor of Illinois.

They (Smith's key men) told Ford, that the witnesses were "set to continual prayer, and other spiritual exercises. "Then at last "he assembled them in a room, and produced a box which he said contained the precious treasure. The lid was opened; the witnesses peeped into it, but making no discovery, for the box was empty, they said, "Brother Joseph, we do not see the plates." The prophet answered them, "O ye of little faith! How long will God bear with this wicked and perverse generation? Down on your knees, brethren every one of you, and pray God for the forgiveness of your sins and for a holy and living faith which cometh down from heaven." The disciples dropped to their knees, and began to pray in the fervency of their spirit, supplicating God for more than two hours with fanatical earnestness; at the end of which time, looking again into the box, they were now persuaded that they saw the plates".

Newspaper reports at that time said that all three witnesses told different versions.

The written witness account was apparently written first by Joseph Smith and then he got them to sign it.

The missionaries will push the investigator towards having baptism performed by one holding the authority to perform this ordinance and claim that John the Baptist had this special Priesthood, which can be traced back to Aaron (Moses' brother).

This priesthood is called the Lesser Priesthood or Aaronic Priesthood. Jesus sought out John (they say) because John was the only one who had the authority to baptize Him by the power of that Lesser or Aaronic Priesthood. The other Priesthood in the Church is called the Higher Priesthood, which is referred to as the Melchisidek Priesthood *(called after Melchisidek who was the great High Priest of Salem). Old Testament*. Within this Priesthood are the offices of elder, seventy, high priest, patriarch and apostle and this priesthood must be present and functional whenever the kingdom of God is on the earth in its fullness. This Priesthood confers the Gift of The Holy Ghost which means after baptism a confirmation then takes place and within this ordinance the Holy Ghost is then conferred. The missionaries will say 'receive the Holy Ghost'.

John the Baptist said

New Testament, *Matthew Chapter 3 verse 11*

11. I indeed baptise you with water unto repentance: but he that cometh after me is mightier than I, whose shoes I am not worthy to bear: he shall baptize you with the Holy Ghost and with fire:

The Missionaries will reveal other "books of Scripture". The Doctrine & Covenants and the Pearl of Great Price. The Book of Mormon is handed out to anyone who will take it. The Doctrine & Covenants and the Pearl of Great Price is given to those who are baptised or seriously preparing for baptism. These are like the pearls that are not to be "cast before the swine".

When some people are baptised into the Church it causes a lot of problems within their families. The scripture to cover this particular challenge would be:

The New Testament, *Matthew Chapter 10 verses 35-38*

34. *Think not that I am come to send peace on earth: I came not to send peace, but a sword.*

35. *For I am come to set a man at variance against his father, and the daughter against her mother, and the daughter in law against her mother in law.*

36. *And a man's foes shall be they of his own household.*

37. *He that loveth father or mother more than me is not worthy of me: and he that loveth son or daughter more than me is not worthy of me.*

38. *And he that taketh not his cross, and followeth after me, is not worthy of me.*

Notes

1. Charles A. Shook. *The True Origin of the Book of Mormon*
2. (Dialogue: A Journal of Mormon Thought, Winter, 1972, pp.83-84) As quoted in Mormonism-Shadow or Reality. Jerald & Sandra Tanner
3. *An Address to All Believers in Christ* Page 12
4. *Journal of Discourses*, Vol. 7, p. 164
5. *Mormonism Unvailed.* Eber Dudley Howe 1834
6. *Mormonism Unvailed.* Eber Dudley Howe 1834
7. *Mormonism Unvailed.* E.D. Howe p.13-15
8. *Mormonism Unveiled* E. D. Howe, 1834, pp. 260-261

Chapter Seven

The Doctrine & Covenants

The Doctrine & Covenants is a collection of divine revelations and inspired declarations given for the establishment and regulation of the kingdom of God on the earth in the last days. Although most of the sections are directed to members of The Church of Jesus Christ of Latter-Day Saints, the messages, warnings, and exhortations are for the benefit of all mankind, and contain an invitation to all people everywhere to hear the voice of the Lord Jesus Christ, speaking to them for their temporal well-being and their everlasting salvation. Most of the revelations in this compilation were received through Joseph Smith, Jun., the first prophet and President of The Church of Jesus Christ of Latter-Day Saints. Others were issued through some of his successors in the Presidency.

The following appeared in Tiffany's monthly in 1859[1]

People sometimes wonder that the Mormons can revere Joseph Smith, that they can by any means make a Saint of him. But they must remember that the Joseph Smith preached in England, and the one shot at Carthage, Illinois, are not the same. The ideal prophet differs widely from the real person. To one, ignorant of his character, he may be idealized and be made the impersonation of every virtue. He may be associated in the mind with all that is pure, true, lovely and divine. Art may make him, indeed, an object of religious veneration. But remember, the Joseph Smith thus venerated, is not the real, actual Joseph Smith.... But one that art has created.

****

Mormon writers state that Joseph Smith's claim to be a prophet is established by the fulfilment of his prophecies. A careful examination of the evidence seems to prove just the opposite.

138

The Canadian Revelation[2]

David Whitmer, a Book of Mormon witness tells, of a false revelation that Joseph Smith gave when the Book of Mormon was in the hands of the printer:

When the Book of Mormon was in the hands of the printer, more money was needed to finish the printing of it. We were waiting on Martin Harris who was doing his best to sell part of his farm, in order to raise the necessary funds. After a time Hyrum Smith and others began to get impatient, thinking that Martin Harris was too slow and under transgression for not selling his land at once, even if at a great sacrifice. Brother Hyrum thought they should not wait any longer on Martin Harris, and that the money should be raised in some other way.

Brother Hyrum was vexed with Brother Martin, and thought that they should get money by some means outside of him, and not let him have anything to do with the publication of the Book, or receiving any of the profits thereof if any profits should accrue... Brother Hyrum said it had been suggested to him that some of the brethren might go to Toronto Canada, and sell the copy-right of the Book of Mormon for considerable money: and he persuaded Joseph to enquire of the Lord about it. Joseph concluded to do so. He had not yet given up the stone. Joseph looked into the hat in which he placed the stone, and received a revelation that some of the brethren should go to Toronto, Canada, and that they would sell the copy-right of the Book of Mormon. Hiram Page and Oliver Cowdery went on this mission, but they failed entirely to sell the copyright, returning without any money. Joseph was at my father's house when they returned.

I was there also, and am eye witness to these facts... Well, we were all in great trouble, and we asked Joseph how it was that he had received a revelation from the Lord for some brethren to go to Toronto and sell the copy-right, and the brethren had utterly failed in their undertaking. Joseph did not know how it was, so he enquired of the Lord about it, and behold the following revelation came through the stone. "Some revelations are of God: some revelations are of man: and some revelations are of the devil." So we see that the revelation to go to Toronto and sell the copyright was not of God, but was of the devil or the heart of man.

David Whitmer states that there were "other false revelations that came through Brother Joseph as mouthpiece.... Many of Brother Joseph's revelations were never printed. The revelation to go to Canada was written down on paper, but was never printed"

William Harris[3]
Mormonism Portrayed (1803-aft. 1841)

On page 112, Book of Covenants, he (Smith) claims exemption from temporal labour. "And in temporal labour thou shalt not have strength, for this is not thy calling; attend to thy calling, and thou shalt have wherewith to magnify thy office. And again I say unto you that if ye desire the mysteries of the kingdom, provide for him food and raiment, and whatsoever thing he needeth, to accomplish the work." Now, every one who has any knowledge of Smith knows that the averment in this revelation is not true; for he is a large, portly man, remarkable for his physical strength.

It was, then, evidently designed merely to excuse his laziness, and enable him to suck a livelihood from his followers.

By reference to page 181, Book of Covenants, it will appear that Smith is at the head of the Mormon Church. "And thou shalt not command him who is at the *head of the Church.*" And, in the Book of Mormon, page 66: "And he shall be great, like unto Moses."

Search the annals of infallible Rome! Read the history of her most aspiring pretenders, and when was there ever-assumed higher titles, greater authority, or more immaculate holiness, than is now assumed by this image of the beast, arisen in these latter days!

In reviewing these claims of Smith, what a striking contrast is presented between him and the Apostles! They acknowledged no head but Christ; they sought no titles but those of Apostles, servants, or ministers of the New Covenant. -- All were permitted to receive revelations for the Church -- all were on a level, as regards their authority. But Smith, not satisfied with calling himself a seer, a prophet, and a revelator, claims to be "great like unto Moses." It almost seems like blasphemy, but, as thousands profess to believe in the claims of this empty pretender, it becomes a duty to expose their weakness in the most effectual manner possible.

Let us, then, ask, where is the least point of analogy between these men? We read of Moses being sent by God, from the burning bush to deliver the Israelites from under the tyranny of Pharaoh, of the signs and wonders that attested his mission, of his leading the people out, of their journeying through the wilderness, of the division of the Red Sea, of the cloudy and fiery pillar that went before to guide them in the way, of angel's food and quails for their subsistence, of rivers of water flowing from the flinty rock to satiate their thirst, of the miraculous durability of their clothing, of their glorious reception of the lively oracles, the cloud overshadowing, the mountain shaking, the trump of God waxing louder and louder, the voice of Nature's Author heard, his glory manifested, the people quaking, and all this in attestation of the divinity of the mission of Moses, and the laws of Jehovah.

Now, what is there in the history of your Latter Day Prophet that can compare with this? Where was the power of this pretender to work miracles, when his followers, fainting with hunger, were famished on the way? Where was he, when their enemies pressed sore upon them, threatening destruction? Did he then give even the slightest assistance to his people? No! On the contrary, he led the flight. Give us, then, at least, one well authenticated and incontestable instance of the miraculous power of this man, before he is claimed to be great like unto Moses.

But where is there any analogy in the character of the two men? Moses was said to be the meekest and one of the most benevolent and upright of men. Now, is there any of this meekness in the character of Smith? Let his harangues to his people speak, let his own writings speak, and they will show him to be one of the most vindictive men that can be produced. And what evidence is there of his benevolence? At the very time that the widows of the Church, and, indeed, the poorer class, were suffering for want of the common necessaries of life, Smith, and his co-adjutor, S. Rigdon, demanded at the hands of the people, twelve hundred dollars per year, in order to aggrandize himself, and enable him to live in luxury.

And when some complained that this would be a violation of the rules of the Church, he remarked, that if he could not obtain his demand, his people might go to hell, and he would go to the Rocky Mountains! And this, too, when the Bishop is appointed by revelation, to deal out to every man according to his wants. Here, then, is a beautiful specimen of his benevolence -- he must have his enormous demands satisfied, though his people starve, even by breaking through the laws of the Church. Where was there any thing like Moses in this? But look at his example before his people. At the very time that their enemies were pressing them, he was found, like a giddy boy, or an abandoned renegade, wrestling for amusement, on the Sabbath day; and when reproved, said, "Never mind, it is a time of war."

The Lords Coming

"In 1835 Joseph Smith prophesied that the coming of the Lord was near and that fifty-six years should wind up the scene".

"President Smith then stated... it was the will of God that those who went to Zion, with a determination to lay down their lives, if necessary, should be ordained to the ministry and go forth to prune the vineyard for the last time, or the coming of the Lord, which was nigh-- even fifty-six years, should wind up the scene."

From Joseph Smith's diary, March 10, 1843: "... I prophesy in the name of the Lord God-- & let it be written: that the Son of Man will not come in the heavens until I am 85 years old 48 years hence or about 1890. "

Joseph Smith said that a voice once told him the following. "My son, if thou livest until thou art eighty-five years of age, thou shalt see the coming of the Son of Man." I was left to draw my own conclusions concerning this; and I took the liberty to conclude that if I did not live to that time, He would make His appearance. But I do not say whether He will make his appearance or I shall go where He is "

January 23, 1833, Joseph Smith recorded the following in his History of the Church[4]
" ... My father presented himself.... I asked of him a father's blessing, which he granted by laying his hands upon my head, in the name of Jesus Christ, and declaring that I should continue in the priest's office until Christ comes."

Some of the Twelve Apostles in the Mormon Church were told similar things.
Lyman E. Johnson was.... That he shall live until the gathering is accomplished ... and that shall see the Saviour come and stand upon the earth with power and great glory "

History of the Church), vol 2, page 182 The Changing World of Mormonism Jerald & Sandra Tanner

A Temple in Zion

Revelation given to Joseph Smith September 22 and 23, 1832

Yea, the word of the Lord concerning his Church, established in the last days for the restoration of his people... For the gathering of his saints to stand upon mount Zion, which shall be the city of New Jerusalem.

Which city shall be built, beginning at the temple lot, which is appointed by the finger of the Lord, in the western boundaries of the state of Missouri, and dedicated by the hand of Joseph Smith, Jun., and others....

Verily this is the word of the Lord that the city New Jerusalem shall be built by the gathering of the saints, beginning at this place, even the place of the temple, which temple shall be reared in this generation.

For verily this generation shall not all pass away until an house shall be built unto the Lord, and a cloud shall rest upon it...?

Therefore, as I said concerning the sons of Moses-- for the sons of Moses and also the sons of Aaron shall offer an acceptable offering and sacrifice in the house of the Lord, which house shall be built unto the Lord in this generation, upon the consecrated spot as I have appointed.

Doctrine and Covenants 84: 2-5, 31

To date no temple has ever been built on that lot.

The Civil War

On 25th December 1832 Joseph Smith gave his revelation concerning the Civil War.

Doctrine and Covenants, 87: 1-5

1. *Verily, thus saith the Lord concerning the wars that will shortly come to pass, beginning at the rebellion of South Carolina, which will eventually terminate in the death of and misery of many souls;*

2. *And the time will come that war will be poured out upon all nations, beginning at this place.*

3. *For behold the Southern States shall be divided against the Northern States, and the Southern States will call on other nations, even the nation of Great Britain, as it is called, and they shall also call upon other nations, in order to defend themselves against other nations; and then war will be poured out upon all nations.*

4. *and it shall come to pass, after many days, slaves shall rise up against their masters, who shall be marshalled and disciplined for war.*

5. *And it shall come to pass that the remnants who are left of the land will marshal themselves, and shall become exceedingly angry, and shall vex the Gentiles with a sore vexation.*

The American Civil War (1861–1865) which is also known by several other names, was a civil war between the United States of America (the "Union") and the Southern slave states of the newly formed Confederate States of America under Jefferson Davis.

The Union included all of the Free States and the five-slaveholding Border States and was led by Abraham Lincoln and the Republican Party. Republicans opposed the expansion of slavery into territories owned by the United States, and their victory in the presidential election of 1860 resulted in seven Southern states declaring their secession from the Union even before Lincoln took office. The Union rejected secession, regarding it as rebellion.

Mormons believe this revelation proves Joseph Smith to be a prophet. The revelation was given in 1832 and the Civil War did not begin until 1861. Larry Jonas shows that Joseph Smith could have easily have received the idea for this revelation from the views of his time.

Larry Jonas[5]
"On July 14, 1832, Congress passed a tariff act, which South Carolina thought, was so bad; she declared the tariff null and void. President Andrew Jackson alerted the nation's troops. At the time Smith made his prophecy, the nation expected a war between North and South to begin at the rebellion of South Carolina. This can be confirmed in a U.S. history book. Better yet, let me confirm it from a Latter-day Saints Church publication, Evening and Morning Star... the issue which came out for January 1833. The news of South Carolina's rebellion was known before January 1833. It was known before December 25, 1832 but it was not available in time for the December issue.

It takes quite a while for news to be set up even today in our dailies. We would expect it to wait for a month to come out in a monthly. The example contains the information available to the Church before the paper hit the street... The example and the prophecy are strangely similar... Both consider the pending war a sign of the end--- which it was not. In fact the war expected in 1832 did not come to pass..."

The Pearl of Great Price

Is a selection of materials touching many significant aspects of the faith and doctrine of the Church of Jesus Christ of Latter-day Saints. These items were produced by the prophet Joseph Smith and were published in the Church periodicals of his day.
It contains:

+ Selections from the Book of Moses

+ The Book of Abraham written on papyri

+ Joseph Smith ---- Matthew, An extract from the testimony of Matthew in Joseph Smith's translation of the Bible.

+ Joseph Smith ---- History

+ The Articles of Faith of the Church of Jesus Christ of Latter-day Saints

The Book of Abraham

Joseph Smith's own history tells of the discovery of the Papyri [6]

"The records were obtained from one of the catacombs of Egypt, by the celebrated French traveller, Antonio Sebolo.... He made a will of the whole, to Mr. Michael Chandler.... On opening the coffins, he discovered two rolls of papyrus...
History of the Church, vol.2, pp. 348-49

Michael Chandler received mummies along with the papyri and went around exhibiting them. He arrived into Kirtland, Ohio, where Joseph Smith became very interested in them. The Church purchased the mummies and the papyri. Joseph Smith examined the papyri and declared that they were the writings of Abraham and Joseph of Egypt.

Josiah Quincy, who met with Joseph Smith at Nauvoo, gave the following account of his visit: [7]

The prophet referred to his miraculous gift of understanding all languages.... "And now come with me," said the prophet, "and I will show you the curiosities, ".... "These are mummies "said the exhibitor. " I want you to look at that little runt of a fellow over there. He was a great man in his day. Why that was Pharaoh Necho, King of Egypt!" Some parchments with hieroglyphics were then offered to us...

"That is the handwriting of Abraham, the Father of the Faithful, "said the prophet. "This is the autograph of Moses, and these lines were written by his brother Aaron. Here we have the earliest account of the Creation, from which Moses composed the First Book of Genesis."

We were further assured that the prophet was the only mortal who could translate these mysterious writings, and that his power was given by direct inspiration.

Very few scholars at that time understood anything about the Egyptian language; there was no one to refute Joseph Smith's claims.

In 1860 the science of Egyptology had advanced to the point where some people felt that it could be used to test Joseph Smith's ability as a translator. One Egyptologist, M. Theodule Deveria, not only accused Joseph Smith of making a false translation but also of altering the scene shown in the facsimiles in The Book of Abraham.

Facsimle No 1

A FACSIMILE FROM THE BOOK OF ABRAHAM No.1

Later in 1912 Rt. Rev. F.S. Spalding published a brochure. The Reverend had submitted the facsimiles of some of the parchment pages from which the Book of Abraham had been translated... to a number of eminent Egyptian scholars.

Dr. A.H. Sayce of Oxford, England: "It is difficult to deal seriously with Joseph Smith's impudent fraud.... Smith has turned the Goddess into a king and Osiris into Abraham".

James H. Breasted, Ph.D., Haskell Oriental Museum, University of Chicago and first American citizen to obtain a PhD in Egyptology.

"These three facsimiles of Egyptian documents in the "Pearl of Great Price" depict the most common objects in the mortuary religion of Egypt.

Joseph Smith's interpretations of them as part of a unique revelation through, Abraham, therefore, very clearly demonstrate that he was totally unacquainted with the significance of these documents and absolutely ignorant of the simplest facts of Egyptian writing and civilization".

Facsimle No 2

A FACSIMILE FROM THE BOOK OF ABRAHAM No.2

Joseph Smith's papyri were subsequently lost.

However on November 27th, 1967, the Deseret News (Mormon owned publication)

Announced: [8]
New York -- A collection of papyrus manuscripts, long believed to have been destroyed in the Chicago Fire of 1871 was presented to The Church

of Jesus Christ of Latter-Day Saints here Monday by the Metropolitan Museum of Art...

Included in the papyri is a manuscript identified as the original document from which Joseph Smith had copied the drawing, which he called "Facsimile No 1", and published with the Book of Abraham.

The Joseph Smith Papyri have been dated to the late Ptolemaic or early Roman period.

PTOLEMY I (SOTER I)

323-285 B.C.

PTOLEMAIC DYNASTY

Upon the death of Alexander the Great in 323 BC, the throne of Egypt fell to Ptolemy I, the son of Lagus. He was a veteran soldier and trusted commander who had served Alexander. He started the Ptolemaic Dynasty, which lasted about 300 years.

The Ptolemaic period is so-called because at this time Egypt was ruled by a series of kings all named Ptolemy. The period began with the conquest of Egypt by Alexander the Great. On Alexander's death in 323 BC his empire was divided among his generals; Egypt fell to one named Ptolemy, who later declared himself king.

Ptolemaic Dynasty (O.C. 305 - 30 B.C)

Ptolemy I Soter (Meryamun Setepenre)

Ptolemy II Philadelphus (Userkaenre Meryamun)

Ptolemy III Euergetes (Iwaennetjerwysenwy Sekhemankhre Setepenamun)

Ptolemy IV Philopater (Iwaennetjerwymenkhwy Setepptah Userkare Sekhemankhamun)

Ptolemy V Epiphanes (Iwaennetjerwymerwyitu Setepptah Userkare Sekhemankhamun)

Ptolemy VI Philomentor (Iwaennetjerwyper Setepptahkhepri Irmaatenamunre)

Ptolemy VII Neos Philopater

Ptolemy VIII Euergetes

The Book of Abraham Chapter 1 verses 6, 7 & 8

6 *For their hearts were set to do evil and were wholly turned to the god of Elkenah and the god of Libnah, and the god of Mahmackrah, and the god of Korash, and the god of Pharaoh, king of Egypt;*

7 *Therefore they turned their hearts to the sacrifice of the heathen in offering up their children unto these dumb idols, and hearkened not unto my voice, but endeavored to take away my life by the hand of the priest of Elkenah. The priest of Elkenah was also the priest of Pharaoh.*

8 *Now, at this time it was the custom of the priest of Pharaoh, the king of Egypt, to offer up upon the altar which was built in the land of Chaldea, for the offering unto these strange gods, men, women, and children.*

The title of Pharaoh started being used for the king during the New Kingdom, specifically during the middle of the eighteenth dynasty.

The eighteenth dynasty of ancient Egypt XVIII (c.1550-c.1292 (BCE) is perhaps the best known of all the dynasties of ancient Egypt.

Dynasty XVIII is often combined with Dynasties XIX and XX to form the New Kingdom period of ancient Egyptian history.

The **New Kingdom of Egypt**, also referred to as the **Egyptian Empire**, is the period in ancient Egyptian history between the 16th century BC and the covering the Eighteenth, Nineteenth, and Twentieth Dynasties of Egypt. The New Kingdom followed the Second Intermediate Period and was succeeded by the Third Intermediate Period.

Three groups of names have applied to Egypt. In the early period of Egypt, during the Old Kingdom, Egypt was referred to as Kemet (Kermit), or Kmt, which means the Black land. They called themselves "Remetch en Kermet", which means the "People of the Black Land". The term refers to the rich soil found in the Nile Valley and Delta. But it was also sometimes referred to as Deshret, or dshrt, which refers to the "Red Land", or deserts of which Egypt is mostly comprised.

Later, Egyptians referred to their country as "Hwt-ka-Ptah" (Ht-ka-Ptah, or Hout-ak Ptah), which means "Temple for Ka or Ptah", or "House of the Ka of Ptah". Ptah was one of Egypt's earliest Gods.

Egypt, as people of the world refer to the country today, is a derivative of this ancient name. In pronouncing Hwt-ka-Ptah, the Greeks changed this word to Aegyptus (Aigyptos).

Theodule Deveria was a prominent French Egyptologist. 1831- 1871.

Deveria studied the collection of Egyptian papyri at the Louvre for many years, and was considered in his day an expert on Ancient Egyptian funery texts.

The renowned Sir E. A. Wallis Budge said of him." No other scholar had such a wide and competent knowledge of the Book of the Dead", and that his death was a "great loss" to Egyptology.

Theodule Deveria's translations of the facsimiles in the Book of Abraham are published in *The Rocky Mountain Saints: A Full and Complete History of the Mormons* by T. B. Stenhouse written in 1873.

The Book of Abraham is in fact a funery text called "The Book of Breathings". Even though it has been proven to be false, the Mormon Church still holds it up as scripture.

Notes

1. *Tiffany's monthly*, published by Joel Tiffany 1859, p.170
2. David Whitmer. *An Address To All Believers In Christ*, 1887, pp. 30-31
3. William Harris, Mormonism Portrayed (Warsaw: Sharp & Gamble, 1841)
4. (History of the Church, vol. 2, p.188) *The Changing World of Mormonism Jerald & Sandra Tanner*
5. *Mormon Claims Examined*, by Larry S. Jonas, p.52)
6. *History of the Church, vol.2, pp. 348-49*
7. Josiah Quincy, *Figures of the Past From the Leaves of Old Journals*, 3rded (Boston, 1883),
8. *The Deseret News 1967 As quoted in The Changing World of Mormonism. Jerald & Sandra Tanner*

Chapter Eight

The Sacrament in the Mormon Church

Sacrament Meeting is held most Sundays with few exceptions for Church conferences. The meeting consists of Opening prayer and an opening hymn. The Sacrament is then blessed and passed to the congregation. Plain bread is used and water to represent the emblems of Jesus Christ's body and blood. The water is distributed in tiny plastic cups.

Mormons do not believe in Transubstantiation.

(Transubstantiation: The change of the substance of bread and wine into the Body and Blood of Christ occurring in the Eucharist according to the teaching of some Churches including the Roman Catholic Church.)

After Sacrament there are talks given by members of the congregation, followed by a closing hymn and a closing prayer. Then the members of the congregation disperse to their different classes for Sunday school. New members or investigators attend Gospel Essentials class. The more seasoned members attend Gospel Doctrine class. When Gospel Essentials and Gospel Doctrine class end the members then disperse to their final class in Sunday school. Young adults attend Young Women and Young Men classes. Women over a certain age attend Relief Society. Young men over a certain age attend Priesthood class. There exists in the Church an organization called Primary, and this is like a Church playschool with a spiritual theme for children.

After becoming a member one would soon be issued with a calling.

What is a calling? They will tell you that a calling comes from God through the Branch President or Bishop (shepherd of the flock) to a particular individual. To refuse the calling is to refuse God. A branch president presides over a small congregation called a Branch, whereas a Bishop presides over a larger one, it is called a Ward.

In areas where congregations are small the missionaries will cite the following scriptures
Matthew 7: 13-14

13. Enter ye in at the strait gate: for wide is the gate, and broad is the way that leadeth to destruction, and many there be that go in thereat:

14. Because strait is the gate, and narrow is the way, which leadeth unto life, and few there be that find it.

In the Book of Mormon 1 Nephi 14: 7-12 an angel speaks to Nephi:

7.For the time cometh, saith the Lamb of God, that I will work a great and a marvellous work among the children of men; a work which shall be everlasting, either on the one hand or on the other--- either to the convincing of them unto peace and life eternal, or unto the deliverance of them to the hardness of their hearts and the blindness of their minds unto their being brought down into captivity, and also into destruction, both temporally and spiritually, according to the captivity of the devil, of which I have spoken.

8. and it came to pass that when the angel had spoken these words, he said unto me: Rememberest thou the covenants of the Father unto the house of Israel? I said unto him, yea.

9. and it came to pass that he said unto me: Look, and behold that great and abominable Church, which is the mother of abominations, whose founder is the devil,

10. And he said unto me: Behold there are save two Churches only; the one is the Church of the Lamb of God, and the other is the Church of the devil; wherefore whoso belonged not to the Church of the Lamb of God belonged to that great Church, which is the mother of abominations; and she is the whore of all the earth.

11. And it came to pass, that I looked and beheld the whore of all the earth, and she sat upon many waters; and she had dominion over all the earth, among all nations, kindred's, tongues, and people.

12. And it came to pass that I beheld the Church of the Lamb of God, and it's numbers were few, because of the wickedness and abominations of the whore who sat upon many water; nevertheless, I beheld that the Church of the Lamb, who were the saints of God, were also upon all face of the earth; and their dominions upon the face of the earth were small, because of the wickedness of the great whore whom I saw.

Chapter Nine

Polygamy/Plural Marriage

Joseph Smith gave the revelation concerning polygamy/plural marriage on July 12, 1843

The Doctrine and Covenants. Section 132: 1-4, 19, 34, 35, 38, 39, 52, 60-62

1.Verily thus saith the Lord into you my servant Joseph, that inasmuch as you have enquired of my hand to know and understand wherein I, the Lord, justified my servants Abraham, Isaac and Jacob, as also Moses, David and Solomon, my servants, as touching the principle and doctrine of their having many wives and concubines---

2. Behold and lo, I am the Lord thy God, and will answer thee as touching this matter.

3. Therefore, prepare thy heart to receive and obey the instructions, which I am about to give unto you; for all those who have this law revealed unto them must obey the same.

4. for behold, I reveal unto you a new and an everlasting covenant; and if ye abide not that covenant, then ye are damned; for no one can reject this covenant and be permitted to enter into my glory.

19. And again, verily I say unto you, if a man marry a wife by my word, which is my law, and by the new and everlasting covenant, and it is sealed unto them by the Holy Spirit of promise, by him who is anointed, unto whom I have appointed this power and the keys of this priesthood; and it shall be said unto them—Ye shall come forth in the first resurrection; and if it be after the first resurrection, in the next resurrection; and shall inherit thrones, kingdoms, principalities, and powers, dominions, all heights and depths—then shall it be written in the Lamb's Book of Life, that he shall commit no murder whereby to shed innocent blood, and if ye abide in my covenant, and commit no murder whereby to shed innocent blood, it shall be done unto them in all things whatsoever my servant hath put upon them, in time, and through all eternity; and shall be of full force when they are out of the world; and they shall pass by the angels, and the gods, which are set there, to their exaltation and glory in all things, as hath been sealed upon their heads, which glory shall be a fulness and a continuation of the seeds forever and ever.

34 God commanded Abraham, and Sarah gave Hagar to Abraham to wife. And why did she do it? Because this was the law; and from Hagar sprang many people. This, therefore, was fulfilling, among other things, the promises.

35 Was Abraham, therefore, under condemnation? Verily I say unto you, nay; for I, the Lord, commanded it.

38 David also received many wives and concubines, and also Solomon and Moses my servants, as also many others of my servants, from the beginning of creation until this time; and in nothing did they sin save in those things which they received not of me.

39 David's wives and concubines were given unto him of me, by the hand of Nathan, my servant, and others of the prophets who had the keys of this power; and in none of these things did he sin against me save in the case of Uriah and his wife; and, therefore he hath fallen from his exaltation, and received his portion; and he shall not inherit them out of the world, for I gave them unto another, saith the Lord.

52 And let mine handmaid, Emma Smith, receive all those that have been given unto my servant Joseph, and who are virtuous and pure before me; and those who are not pure, and have said they were pure, shall be destroyed, saith the Lord God.

60 Let no one, therefore, set on my servant Joseph; for I will justify him; for he shall do the sacrifice which I require at his hands for his transgressions, saith the Lord your God.

61 And again, as pertaining to the law of the priesthood—if any man espouse a virgin, and desire to espouse another, and the first give her consent, and if he espouse the second, and they are virgins, and have vowed to no other man, then is he justified; he cannot commit adultery for they are given unto him; for he cannot commit adultery with that that belongeth unto him and to no one else.

62 And if he have ten virgins given unto him by this law, he cannot commit adultery, for they belong to him, and they are given unto him; therefore is he justified.

This 1843 revelation was apparently given to convince Emma Smith (Joseph's wife) that polygamy was right. William Clayton, who wrote the revelation as Smith dictated it, provides the following information[1]

On the morning of 12th of July 1843; Joseph and Hyrum came into the office… They were talking on the subject of plural marriage. Hyrum said to Joseph, "if you will write the revelation on celestial marriage, I will take it and read it to Emma, and I believe I can convince her of its truth, and you will hereafter have peace." Joseph smiled and remarked, "You do not know Emma as well as I do."… Joseph then said, "Well, I will write the revelation and we shall see." …. Hyrum then took the revelation to read to Emma. Joseph remained with me in the office until Hyrum returned. When he came back, Joseph asked him how he had succeeded. Hyrum replied that he had never received a more severe talking to in his life.…

Joseph quietly remarked, "I told you, you did not know Emma as well as I did. " Joseph then put the revelation in his pocket… Two or three days after the revelation was written Joseph related to me and several others that Emma had so teased, and urgently entreated him for the privilege of destroying it, that he became so weary of her teasing, and to get rid of her annoyance, he told her that she might destroy it and she had done so, but he had consented to her wish in this matter to pacify her, realizing that he could rewrite it at any time if necessary.

Brigham Young said[2]

Emma took that revelation, supposing she had all there was; but Joseph had wisdom enough to take care of it, and he had handed the revelation to Bishop Whitney, and he wrote it all off.... She went to the fireplace and put it in, and put the candle under it and burnt it, and she thought that was the end of it, and she will be damned as sure as she is a living woman. Joseph used to say that he would have her hereafter, if he had to go to hell for her, and he will have to go to hell for her as sure as he ever gets her.
(Journal of Discourses, vol. 17, p.159)

Doctrine and Covenants

54. And I command mine handmaid, Emma Smith, to abide and cleave unto my servant Joseph, and to none else. But if she will not abide this commandment she shall be destroyed, saith the Lord; for I am the Lord thy God, and will destroy her if she abide not in my law.
                    Doctrine and Covenants, Section 132:54

Emma was not destroyed and less than a year after this revelation was written Joseph Smith was killed. Emma lived until 1879.

In section 101, verse 4 of the 1835 Doctrine and Covenants it states:

4. " Inasmuch as this Church of Christ has been reproached with the crime of fornication, and polygamy: we declare that we believe, that one man should have one wife; and one woman, but one husband, except in the case of death, when either is at liberty to marry again."

Why was the above doctrine removed and not found in the current Doctrine and Covenants?

Mormon Apologists claim: "The answer is simple. It wasn't a revelation. It was written by Oliver Cowdery, not Joseph Smith. That particular Section written by Oliver Cowdery was approved by the membership of the Church while Smith was out of town."

This section was printed in every edition of the Doctrine and Covenants until the year 1876. At that time the Mormon leaders' inserted section 132, which permits a plurality of wives. The section condemning polygamy was therefore removed.

Doctrine and Covenants Section 132: 38-39

38 David also received many wives and concubines, and also Solomon and Moses my servants, as also many others of my servants, from the beginning of creation until this time; and in nothing did they sin save in those things which they received not of me.

39 David's wives and concubines were given unto him of me, by the hand of Nathan, my servant, and others of the prophets who had the keys of this power; and in none of these things did he sin against me save in the case of Uriah and his wife; and, therefore he hath fallen from his exaltation, and received his portion; and he shall not inherit them out of the world, for I gave them unto another, saith the Lord.

Book of Mormon "scriptures" contradict this.

23 But the word of God burdens me because of your grosser crimes. For behold, thus saith the Lord: This people begin to wax in iniquity; they understand not the scriptures, for they seek to excuse themselves in committing whoredoms because of the things which were written concerning David, and Solomon his son.

24 Behold, David and Solomon truly had many wives and concubines, which thing was abominable before me, saith the Lord.

25 Wherefore, thus saith the Lord, I have led this people forth out of the land of Jerusalem, by the power of mine arm that I might raise up unto me a righteous branch from the fruit of the loins of Joseph.

26 Wherefore, I the Lord God will not suffer that this people shall do like unto them of old.

27 Wherefore, my brethren, hear me, and hearken to the word of the Lord: For there shall not any man among you have save it be one wife; and concubines he shall have none;

The Book of Mormon, the book of Jacob chapter 2:23-27

Eleven of Joseph Smith's wives were between ages 14 and 20, nine were in their 20s, eight were in Smith's own peer group of 31 to 40, and two were in their 40s and three in their 50s. Brigham Young married a total of 55 wives, 54 of them after becoming a Latter Day Saint. He stated that upon being taught about plural marriage "It was the first time in my life that I desired the grave." By the time of his death, Young had 57 children by 16 of his wives; 46 of his children reached adulthood.

The Mormon leaders[3]

The Mormon leaders were worried that the missionaries would take the best women converts for themselves. Heber C. Kimball a member of the First Presidency, admonished: "I say to those elected to go on missions, remember they are not your sheep: they belong to Him that sends you. Then do not make a choice of any of those sheep; do not make selections before they are brought home and put into the fold. You understand that. Amen".

Heber C. Kimball instructed some departing missionaries[4]

"I want you to understand that it is not to be as it has been heretofore. The brother missionaries have been in the habit of picking out the prettiest women for themselves before they get here, and bringing on the ugly ones for us: hereafter you have to bring them all here before taking any of them, and let us all have a fair shake "

Apostle Orson Pratt published certain rules governing the practise of Polygamy. One of those rules was that a man must obtain the consent of the first wife before entering into the practice of plural marriage, yet Pratt himself married two of his wives without the knowledge or consent of any of his other wives.

Joseph Smith was already in the practice of plural marriage before he ever enquired of the Lord to see if it was right. Doctrine and Covenants section 132 verse one tells that Joseph Smith enquired of the Lord to see if plural marriage was right, but verse 52 shows that he had already taken wives before the revelation was given, for it commanded Emma his wife to receive the other women that had already been given to Joseph.

In Mormon Portraits 1866. Dr. Wyl gave the following information[5]

"Joseph Smith finally demanded the WIVES OF ALL THE TWELVE APOSTLES that were at home then in Nauvoo....Vilate Kimball, the first wife of Heber C. Kimball, loved her husband, and he loved her, hence a reluctance to comply with the Lord's demand that Vilate should be CONSECRATED... They thought the command of the Lord must be obeyed in some way, and a 'proxy' way suggested itself to their minds. They had a young daughter only getting out of girlhood, and the father apologizing to the prophet for his wife's RELUCTANCE to comply with HIS DESIRES, stating, however, that the act must be right or it would not be counseled - the abject slave of a father asked Joe IF HIS DAUGHTER WOULDN'T DO AS WELL AS HIS WIFE. Joe replied that she would do just as well, and The Lord would accept her instead. The half-ripe bud of womanhood was DELIVERED over to the PROPHET".

In 1850 John Taylor, who became the third President of the Church, denied that the Church believed in the practice of plural marriage, when he himself at the time had six living wives. In 1852, after years of deception, the Mormons publicly admitted that they were practicing polygamy.

According to Stanley S. Ivins[6]

According to Stanley S. Ivins, the Endowment House Records reveal that on November 22, 1870, Mormon Apostle Orson Pratt had himself sealed (married for eternity) to 101 dead women. On November 29, 1870 he was sealed to 109 dead women. On the same day Orson's brother Parley P. Pratt who was dead had 91 dead women sealed to him.

Wilford Woodruff who became the fourth President of the Church was sealed to 189 dead women.

Moses Franklin Farnsworth was sealed to 345 dead women.

Abraham Cannon was sealed to 400 dead women.

1890 Manifesto

The **"1890 Manifesto"**, sometimes simply called **"The Manifesto"**, is a statement, which officially ceased the practice of plural marriage in The Church of Jesus Christ of Latter-Day Saints (LDS Church), signed by Church President Wilford Woodruff in September 1890. The Manifesto was a dramatic turning point in the history of the Church of Jesus Christ of Latter-day Saints. It has been canonized in the LDS Church Standard Works as **Official Declaration—1**.

The Manifesto prohibited Church members from entering into any marriage prohibited by the law of the land, but did not require the dissolution of existing plural marriages.

Aftermath and post-Manifesto plural marriage

Within six years of the announcement of the Manifesto, Utah had become a state, and federal prosecution of Mormon polygamists subsided. However, Congress still refused to seat representatives-elect who were polygamists, including B.H. Roberts.

Some Mormon historians have documented that some Church apostles covertly sanctioned plural marriages after the Manifesto. This practice was especially prevalent in Mexico and Canada because of an erroneous belief that such marriages were legal in those jurisdictions.

However, a significant minority were performed in Utah and other western American states and territories. The estimates of the number of post-Manifesto plural marriages performed range from scores to thousands, with the actual figure probably close to 250. Today, the LDS

Church officially acknowledges that although the Manifesto "officially ceased" the practice of plural marriage in the Church, "the ending of the practice after the Manifesto was ... gradual."

The twelfth Article of Faith of the Church states

12. *We believe in being subject to kings, presidents, rulers, and magistrates, in obeying, honouring, and sustaining the law.*

Appointed Surveyor General of Utah in 1855, David H. Burr[7]

"The fact is, these people repudiate the authority of the United States in this country and are in open rebellion against the general government."

Brigham Young[8]

He openly declared that he would not surrender the actual government of the territory to any man. In a discourse in the Tabernacle, on June 19, 1853, he said, "We have got a territorial government, and I am and will be governor, and no power can hinder it, until the Lord Almighty says, 'Brigham, you need not be governor any longer.'

The twelfth Article of Faith:

12. *We believe in being subject to kings, presidents, rulers, and magistrates, in obeying, honouring, and sustaining the law.*

Rumours of post-Manifesto marriages surfaced and began to be examined by Congress in the Reed Smoot hearings. In response, Church president Joseph F. Smith issued a "Second Manifesto" in 1904, which reaffirmed the Church's opposition to the creation of new plural marriages and threatened excommunication for Latter-day Saints who continued to enter into or solemnize new plural marriages. Apostles John W. Taylor and Matthias F. Cowley each resigned from the Quorum of the Twelve Apostles due to disagreement with the Church's position on plural marriage. Plural marriage continues to be grounds for excommunication from the LDS Church.

The cessation of plural marriage within the LDS Church gave rise to the Mormon fundamentalist movement.

Heber C. Kimball, first Counsellor to Brigham Young, commented:[9]

The principle of plurality of wives will never be done away.
(*Deseret News, November 7, 1855*)

President Heber C. Kimball also stated[10]

Tabernacle, Great Salt Lake City, April 4, 1866

I speak of plurality of wives as one of the most holy principles that God ever revealed to man, and all those who exercise an influence against it, unto whom it is taught, man or woman, will be damned, and they, and all who will be influenced by them, will suffer the buffetings of Satan in the flesh; for the curse of God will be upon them, and poverty, and distress, and vexation of spirit will be their portion; while those who honor this and every sacred institution of heaven will shine forth as the stars in the firmament of heaven, and of the increase of their kingdom and glory there shall be no end.

Heber C. Kimball [11]
It would be as easy for the United States to build a tower to remove the sun, as to remove polygamy, or the Church and kingdom of God.
Millennial Star, vol. 28, p. 190.

The U.S. Supreme Court ruled in 1878 that plurality of wives (polygamy), as originally permitted by the Mormon religion, violated criminal law and was not defensible as an exercise of religious liberty. The Latter-day Saints renounced polygamy in 1890, but the practice has persisted among some, although it has been rarely prosecuted.

George Reynolds a member of the church was charged with bigamy under the Morrill Anti-Bigamy Act after marrying Amelia Jane Schofield while still married to Mary Ann Tuddenham in Utah Territory.

In *Reynolds v. United States*, 98 U.S. 145 (U.S. 1878), the defendant pleaded before court that the doctrines of the church compelled him to marry twice and he acted only according to his religious belief. The defendant sought protection under First Amendment as he was practicing the doctrines in his religion. The court opined that, the defendant's practice of bigamy was just a religious practice and not a religious belief. The court held that although the First Amendment of the U.S. constitution dictates that government cannot interfere with religious beliefs, religious practices do not merit same constitutional protection.

Bigamy conducted on the basis of religious faith cannot be accepted as a defense by courts. If a religion allows polygamy, a person who is a believer of the religion cannot claim protection under the First Amendment. Bigamy is a statutory crime. The intention of a person is not an element to charge the offense. When a second marriage is committed without termination of the first one, a person can be charged of bigamy without getting into the intention of the person. (Utah 1877)

Bigamy is a Class C Felony.

The First Amendment to the US Constitution

"Congress shall make no law respecting an establishment of religion, or prohibiting the free exercise thereof; or abridging the freedom of speech, or of the press; or the right of the people peaceably to assemble, and to petition the Government for a redress of grievances."

Twelfth Article of Faith

12. *We believe in being subject to kings, presidents, rulers, and magistrates, in obeying, honouring, and sustaining the law.*

Various meetings held in the Mormon Church

Held once a month is Branch or Ward Council and Welfare meeting, if a person serves as a leader/teacher in any of the organizations in the Church they are expected to attend these meetings.

There is a Home-making meeting every month for the women in the Church to attend. This has since been re-named to Home, family, & Personal Enrichment meeting. This is held in the evening. There is a programme in the Church called visiting teaching, where two sisters are assigned to visit three other sisters in their respective homes and help them with anything they need help with, be it temporally or spiritually. A message from the monthly Church publication, The Ensign is shared.

Home teaching is where the Priesthood (men) go out to families and bring them a message from the same Church publication "The Ensign" wherein each month is a spiritual message from the President (Prophet) of the Church. Not everyone carries out their visiting or home teaching, but most do. Activities for young men or young women are held on an evening or weekend day.

For those preparing to go to the Temple, a Temple preparation class would be held on a weekday evening. Family History Centres open for members to do their genealogical research. Sometimes there would be a baptism to attend. Social evenings are held where all the members of the Branch/Ward would get together and have a nice evening playing games or having a barbeque. These are great events for the missionaries to bring investigators to. Firesides (spiritual meetings to bring investigators to) are usually held on a weekday evening.

Monday nights are left free for Family home evening. F.H.E. is where the family is to have a night in free from other Church meetings and everything else to be together, to have a spiritual lesson, games and refreshments.

Notes

1. *History of the Church, by Joseph Smith, Introduction to vol. 5*
2. *Journal of Discourses, vol. 17, p.159*
3. Journal of Discourses, vol. 6, p. 256
4. *The Lion of the Lord*, New York, 1969, pp. 129-30
5. Mormon Portraits. 1886, pp. 70-72
6. The Changing World of Mormonism, Jerald & Sandra Tanner p.234
7. *MORMONISM The Islam of America* By BRUCE KINNEY, D. D. P39
8. *Journal of Discourses*, Vol.1, p 188
9. *Deseret News, November 7, 1855*
10. *Journal of Discourses, vol. 11, p.211*
11. *Millennial Star, vol. 28, p. 190*

CHAPTER TEN

Blessings within the Mormon Church

What is a blessing? A male who has been ordained an Elder and holds the Melchizidek Priesthood can administer a blessing. His hands are laid upon the recipient's head and a blessing, which is "supposed" to come from the Lord, is revealed. One or more Elders can assist in giving this "blessing".

Members who have been in the Church nearly a year are encouraged to prepare for the temple and to receive a Patriarchal Blessing. A Patriarch is an ordained office in the Melchizidek Priesthood. What is a Patriarchal Blessing?

Patriarchal blessings in The Church of Jesus Christ of Latter-day Saints

In The Church of Jesus Christ of Latter day Saints a Patriarchal Blessing is given when an authorized Patriarch (a man ordained to the priesthood office of Patriarch) places his hands on the head of the recipient and pronounces the said blessing. The recipient must have previously received permission for the blessing from their bishop or branch president, this permission is only given after an interview to determine the recipient's worthiness. The purpose of a Patriarchal blessing is to.

(1) Identify the tribe of Israel (if any) to which the Latter-day Saint member belongs.

(2) To bless the member with knowledge and spiritual gifts.

(3) To give advice or help to the individual (often this includes foretelling of possible future events, opportunities, and temptations).

Within the L.D.S. Church, a Patriarchal blessing is considered to be an actual revelation for the recipient, with the promises made in the blessing considered conditional upon the recipient's obedience to gospel principles.

The recipient is informed "through revelation" to which of the tribes of Israel they belong. This is done to acknowledge the fulfilment of the Church doctrine that through baptism members become part of the House of Israel. The vast majority of members will have been declared to come from the tribe of Ephraim (son of Joseph) as it is from this tribe that the restored gospel would be taken to the rest of the World.

Additionally, it is believed that each tribe differs slightly and a person may come to understand the unique circumstances of his or her life better by knowing to which tribe they belong. The differences between the tribes are generally acknowledged to arise from the differences in the blessings Jacob pronounced upon his sons and his sons Joseph's sons, Ephraim and Manasseh. A Patriarchal blessing is usually pronounced upon a member only once. In certain rare circumstances, a person may receive permission from the Church Presidency to receive an additional Patriarchal blessing.

In general the only other people present are very close family members such as parents or the person's spouse, but they would have to be members of the Church also. The Patriarch places his hands on the seated person's head and speaks the blessing aloud. A recording of the blessing is made at the same time. Transcribed copies of all blessings are stored in Church records and are considered by the Church to be revelation.

Members receive a copy of their blessing, and are advised to consult it throughout their life. Since members of the Church consider the blessings to be direct revelation from God, they are advised to treat their blessing as sacred and only share them with family members who are also members of the Church.

Any Church member found worthy and spiritually mature by their priesthood leader may receive a Patriarchal blessing. Individuals who have been members from childhood generally ask to receive their Patriarchal blessing as adolescents.

Former Church President, Ezra Taft Benson stated

"A Patriarchal blessing is the inspired and prophetic statement of your life's mission together with blessings, cautions, and admonitions as the patriarch may be prompted to give."
(Ezra Taft Benson, *Ensign*, May 1986, p 43-44)

Patriarchal blessings during the life of Joseph Smith

The first Latter Day Saint Patriarchal blessings were performed by Joseph Smith Senior., the father of Mormon Church founder Joseph Smith Junior. Joseph Smith Junior first ordained his father to the role of patriarch on December 18, 1833 with a mission to provide "father's blessings" to those without fathers in the Priesthood. Smith senior gave his son Joseph Smith, a blessing on December 9th 1834 prophesying that the younger Smith would establish Zion, subdue his enemies, enjoy his posterity to the latest generation, and "stand on the earth" to witness the Second Coming.

Before Joseph Sr. died, he ordained his eldest living son Hyrum Smith to the role of Patriarch and he continued to give Patriarchal blessings.

Church members receiving their Patriarchal blessings are advised to fast on the day. In Patriarchal blessings the member's lineage is declared (what tribe of Israel he/she comes from). If a member is not declared to be from a tribe of Israel then he/she becomes such through baptism, through what is called The Abrahamic Covenant.

Scriptures in the Old Testament state otherwise.

Micah, Chapter 5 verse 12

12. *And I will cut off witchcrafts out of thine hand: and thou shalt have <u>no more soothsayers.</u>*

Soothsayer:

One who claims to be able to foretell events or predict the future; a seer

Isaiah, Chapter 47 verse 13

13. Thou art wearied in the multitude of thy counsels. Let now the astrologers, the stargazers, and the monthly prognosticators, stand up, and save thee from these things that shall come upon thee.

CHAPTER ELEVEN

The Temple

A place where a worthy Church member can receive his/her "Endowment". When they are endowed then they can have the Endowment performed for a deceased individual.

There are over one hundred temples around the world. Church members perform the ordinances for the dead.

The vicarious ordinances have been performed for many millions at this stage. Where did these ordinances originate?

Joseph Smith was a Mason; he progressed to the Sublime Degree of Master Mason in a very short time. A few weeks after doing so, he claimed he received a revelation pertaining to the Pure Endowment, which he would soon reveal to the Saints.

Benjamin F. Johnson (1818-1905)[1]

Benjamin F. Johnson, an intimate friend and associate of Joseph Smith recalls in his Autobiography.

"In lighting him to bed one night he showed me his garments and explained that they were such as the Lord made for Adam from skins, and gave me such ideas pertaining to endowments as he thought proper. He told me Freemasonry, as at present, was the apostate endowments, as sectarian religion was the apostate religion".

Autobiography (1818-1846) Benjamin F. Johnson, My Life's Review chapter six

Elder Heber C. Kimball, who had been a Mason for many years, related that after Joseph Smith became a Mason, he explained to his brethren that Masonry had been taken from the priesthood."

In 1919 Salt Lake Herald, Latter-Day Apostle Melvin J. Ballard has been quoted as saying the following[2]

"Modern Masonry is a fragmentary presentation of the ancient order established by King Solomon. From whom it is said to have been handed down through the centuries".

Frequent assertion that some details of the Mormon Temple ordinances resemble Masonic rites, led him to refer to this subject, the speaker declared, and he added, "that he was not sorry there was such a similarity, because of the fact that the ordinances and rites revealed to Joseph Smith constituted a reintroduction upon the earth of the divine plan inaugurated in the Temple of Solomon in ancient days".

Neither the Masonic or Mormon rituals can be shown to date to King Solomon's temple. In fact, most historians place the beginning of Freemasonry in the 1700s.

Prior to 1860 most Masonic writers accepted the legends of Freemasonry which claimed that it originated in antiquity. Although these claims were challenged by most anti-Masonic writers in the United States... most Masonic writers refused to discount these claims until a school of English investigators began to evaluate lodge minutes, ancient rituals, and municipal records. Eventually this movement...debunked the notion that the rituals practiced in Speculative Freemasonry originated before the sixteenth century.

Robert Freke Gould and others argued that the best evidence indicated that Operative Freemasonry originated with trade guilds in the Middle Ages and that the development of Speculative Freemasonry, with ceremonies and rituals similar to those practiced today, began in the seventeenth century.... the rituals of Freemasonry have never been static, but have evolved both in time and place. For example, only post-1760 rituals included separate obligations for degrees in conjunction with signs, penalties, tokens, and words, the form found in most subsequent rituals and the same format followed in the Mormon temple endowment.

("Similarity of Priesthood in Masonry," *Dialogue: A Journal of Mormon Thought*, vol.27, no.3, fall 1994, pp.103-104) (As quoted in *Mormonism— Shadow or Reality?* by Jerald & Sandra Tanner

Robert Freke Gould (1836-1915)

A founding member and the second Master of Quatuor Coronati Lodge No. 2076, London, Robert Freke Gould contributed twenty-five papers and many notes to *Ars Quatuor Coronatorum*. A lieutenant in the 31st Regiment, English Army and later a barrister from 1868, he is best remembered as an early proponent of the authentic school of masonic research and for his three-volume *History of Freemasonry* (1883-1887).

Masonic Legend of Enoch

Enoch is shown the hill Moriah in a vision.
Enoch is shown a hidden treasure.
Enoch's treasure includes a gold plate with
engravings
Enoch's marble pillar is carved with Egyptian
Hieroglyphics.
Enoch's marble pillar tells the story of the treasure.
Enoch erects a brass pillar that tells the story of the
creation.
Enoch writes the history of the Tower of Babel on
the marble pillar.
Enoch's brass pillar has a metal ball on top that
has the power to direct.
Enoch predicts that after the Flood, an Israelitish
descendent will find the treasure.
Three Masons find the treasure after three attempts.
Three Masons are witnesses to the treasure.
Solomon's treasure contained the gold plate,
a brass pillar/record, the high priests breastplate,

The urim and thummin and a metal ball. It also contained the Tetragrammaton, the name of God.

The three Masons note that the gold plate gives off enough light to illuminate the cavern.

Enoch's treasure is first hidden in his own cavern, then later transferred to the hill Moriah.

King Solomon allows only a few to see the treasure.

Enoch's cavern is covered by a large stone with an iron ring.

Enoch is called by God to preserve the knowledge of the treasure.

King Solomon changes the status of his underground cavern from secret to sacred.

Joseph Smith's Story

Smith shown the hill Cumorah in a vision.

Smith is shown the gold plates.

Smith's gold plates are engraved.

Smith's plates are engraved in Reformed Egyptian.

Smith's Book of Mormon tells the story of the gold plates.

The Book of Mormon includes brass plates containing the first five books of Moses.

The Book of Mormon contains the book of Ether, a history of a migration from the Tower of Babel.

The Book of Mormon tells of a brass ball, the Liahona that acts as a compass.

The Book of Mormon foretells an Israeltish descendent, having the same name as Joseph of Egypt.

Smith tries to take the plates and is only successful after three attempts.

Smith also arranges for three witnesses: Martin Harris, Oliver Cowdery, and David Whitmer.

Smith's treasure consisted of the brass plates, the Urim and Thummim, the breastplate, and a metal ball called the Liahona.

The Book of Mormon plates are kept first in a hill called Shim, and then transferred to the hill Cumorah.

Smith allows only a few to see the plates.

Smith earlier claimed the plates were in an iron box, but later said it was stone.

Smith is called by God to preserve the knowledge of his treasure.

Mormon leaders claim the temple ceremony is not secret but sacred.

Symbols in the architecture Salt Lake City Temple

Masonic symbols in the architecture of the Salt Lake Temple include the sun, moon, stars, all-seeing eye, hand grip, and the beehive.

One of the more familiar symbols of Mormonism is the beehive. Examples of Mormon pioneer use of the hive can be seen on Brigham Young's home (known as the Beehive House) in Salt Lake City. However, most people are not aware that the beehive was a symbol of Masonry years before Joseph Smith started his Church. The Beehive, Masonically, is an emblem of industry. While many people are aware of the symbols used on the Salt Lake temple, they were also used on other LDS buildings in Utah. Mormon use of Masonic symbols has also been publicly acknowledged.

More symbols used by the Mormons that are associated with Freemasonry. The compass, the square, ritualistic handgrips, two interlaced traingles forming a six pointed star. The new Nauvoo Temple has numerous windows with the up-side down, five pointed star which is used in Masonry, however Satanists also use it. The five-pointed star was used in the Nauvoo Temple and other early temples, but its meaning was wholesome. Inverted stars did not generally become associated with the occult until after the time of Joseph Smith.

The symbol of the star - whether it has five or six points - and the pentagram can be used for good or evil purposes. The fact that Satan worshippers have given evil meanings to the star, the broken cross, the goat, the moon, or whatever does not make the symbols inherently evil. Mormon apologists have quickly come to their Church's defence by insisting that pentagrams have historically been a positive symbol and only recently have become a symbol of evil, therefore concluding that any comparison to the Nauvoo pentagrams is nothing more than sensationalism.

It may be argued that this symbol was not meant by Joseph Smith to have *"occult or satanic"* meanings. Several books on the subject, sympathetic to Wicca and Witchcraft, insist that the occult association of the inverted pentagram goes back much further than the 1850s.

The All-Seeing Eye / The Eye of Horus

On the Salt Lake City Temple, above a window of the east central tower is the All-Seeing-Eye. The All-Seeing-Eye is taken from the left eye, the "moon" or "sound" eye of the pagan god Horus, the son of Osiris and Isis.

The ancient Egyptian Eye of Horus or *wedjat* ('Whole One') is a powerful symbol of protection and is also considered to confer wisdom, health and prosperity. Horus was one of the most important Egyptian gods a sun god represented as a falcon or with the head of a hawk, whose right eye was the sun and whose left eye was the moon.

He was the son of Osiris (god of the underworld) and Isis (mother goddess). Osiris was slain by his own brother, the evil Set (jackal-headed god of night), and Horus fought Set to avenge his father's death, winning the battle but losing an eye in the process. The eye was restored by the magic of Thoth, the god of wisdom and the moon, which allowed Horus to grant Osiris rebirth in the underworld. The Eye of Horus symbol was used in funerary rites and decoration, as instructed in the Egyptian *Book of the Dead*. After 1200 BC it was also used by the Egyptians to represent fractions, based on repeated division by two.

The ancient Egyptians depicted both the right and the left eyes of Horus. The wounding of the left eye served as a mythical explanation of the phases of the moon, and its magical restoration meant that the left was usually the one used as an amulet and considered to be the 'Eye of Horus'. The right eye is sometimes referred to as the 'Eye of Ra', the sun god, though often little distinction is made between the two eyes.

The all-seeing eye of Horus has connections to the ancient Egyptian god of the underworld, mystical creatures born of gods and reborn through magic. It states repeatedly in the Bible how He (God) hates other gods, magic, paganism, witchcraft and communication with the dead.

The Beehive

While there is little doubt that the bee has long been a symbol of industry and work ethic, it has unassailable ties to pagan religions.

A bee surmounting a triangle has depicted the Hindu God Shiva and Krishna often had a blue bee on his forehead. Yogic writings liken the hum emitted by the lowest 'chakra' (energy centre in the body) to the sound made by the bumblebee. The second temple built at Delphi was said to be built by bees.

Coins from Ephesus in Greece dating from the 5th century B.C. depict a queen bee as a symbol of the Great Mother. (Ephesus was known throughout the ancient world for its temple to the Great Mother Goddess). The mystery Rites of Eleusis, centred around the goddess Demeter, were widely regarded as the high point of Greek religion and were conducted by (among others) the Panageis Priestesses or Milissae - meaning bees.

The beehive is a symbol steeped in paganism and mystery religions with no connections to traditional Christianity.

Notes

1. Autobiography (1818-1846) Benjamin F. Johnson, *My Life's Review.* Chapter six
2. ("Similarity of Priesthood in Masonry," *Dialogue: A Journal of Mormon Thought*, vol.27, no.3, fall 1994, pp.103-104) (As quoted in *Mormonism—Shadow or Reality?* by Jerald & Sandra Tanner

CHAPTER TWELVE

Blood Atonement[1]

Joseph Smith said

"I [am] opposed to hanging, even if a man kill another, I will shoot him, or cut off his head, spill his blood on the ground, and let the smoke thereof ascend up to God; and if ever I have the privilege of making a law on that subject, I will have it so."

On another occasion Joseph stated, "Hanging is the popular method of execution among the Gentiles in all countries professing Christianity, instead of blood for blood according to the law of heaven."

Although the doctrine was taught, or at least suggested before the Saints went to Utah, blood atonement was fully developed by Brigham Young:

Apostle William Smith, brother of Joseph Smith, Junior[2]

"[My life was in danger] if I remained there, because of my protest against the doctrine of Blood Atonement and other new doctrines that were brought into the Church."

Brigham Young[3]

"Will you love your brothers and sisters likewise, when they have committed a sin that cannot be atoned for without the shedding of their blood? Will you love that man or woman well enough to shed their blood? That is what Jesus Christ meant."

Brigham Young[4]

"Suppose you found your brother in bed with your wife, and put a javelin through both of them. You would be justified, and they would atone for their sins, and be received into the Kingdom of God. I would at once do so, in such a case; and under the circumstances, I have no wife whom I love so well that I would not put a javelin through her heart, and I would do it with clean hands.... There is not a man or woman, who violates the covenants made with their God that will not be required to pay the debt. The blood of Christ will never wipe that out; your own blood must atone for it."

"If you want to know what to do with a thief that you may find stealing, I say kill him on the spot, and never suffer him to commit another iniquity. I will prove by my works whether I can mete out justice to such persons, or not. I would consider it just as much my duty to do that, as to baptize a man for the remission of his sins."

Brigham Young[5]

"It is true that the blood of the Son of God was shed for sins through the fall and those committed by men, yet men can commit sins which it [the blood of Christ] can never remit."

Brigham Young[6]

"This is loving your neighbour as ourselves; if he needs help, help him; and if he wants salvation and it is necessary to spill his blood on the earth in order that he may be saved, spill it."

Apostle Orson Pratt[7]

"The people of Utah are the only ones in this nation who have taken effectual measures... to prevent adulteries and criminal connections between the sexes. The punishment, for these crimes is death to both male and female. And this law is written on the hearts and printed in the thoughts of the whole people."

Apostle Jebediah M. Grant[8]

"I say, there are men and women that I would advise to go to the Presidency immediately, and ask him to appoint a committee to attend to their care; and then let a place be selected, and let that committee shed their blood. We have amongst us that are full of all manner of abominations, those who need to have their blood shed, for water will not do, their sins are too deep a dye...

I believe that there are a great many; and if they are covenant breakers we need a place designated, where we can shed their blood... Brethren and sisters, we want you to repent and forsake your sins. And you who have committed sins that cannot be forgiven through baptism, let your blood be shed, and let the smoke ascend, that the incense thereof may come up before God as an atonement for your sins, and that the sinners in Zion may be afraid."

Apostle George A. Smith[9]

"The principle, the only one that beats and throbs through the heart of the entire inhabitants of this Territory, is simply this: The man who seduces his neighbors wife must die, and her nearest relative must kill him!"

Joseph Fielding Smith[10]

"Joseph Smith taught that there were certain sins so grievous that man may commit that they will place the transgressors beyond the power of the atonement of Christ. If these offences are committed, then the blood of Christ will not cleanse them from their sins even though they repent. Therefore their only hope is to have their blood shed to atone, as far as possible, in their behalf. This is scriptural doctrine, and is taught in all the standard works of the Church."

Miss Bullock of Provo, Utah[11]

"I married Jesse Hartly, knowing he was a 'Gentile' in fact, but he passed for a Mormon, but that made no difference with me, although I was a Mormon, because he was a noble man, and sought only the right. By being my husband, he was brought into closer contact with the members of the Church, and was thus soon enabled to learn many things about us, and about the Heads of the Church, that he did not approve, and of which I was ignorant, although I had been brought up among the Saints; and which, if known among the Gentiles, would have greatly damaged us. I do not understand all he discovered, or all he did; but they found he had written against the Church, and he was cut off, and the Prophet required as atonement for his sins, that he should lay down his life. That he should be sacrificed in the endowment rooms; where human sacrifices are sometimes made in this way.

This I never knew until my husband told me, but it is true. They kill those there who have committed sins too great to be atoned for in any other way. The Prophet says, if they submit to this he can save them; otherwise they are lost. Oh! That is horrible. But my husband refused to be sacrificed, and so set out alone for the United States: thinking there might be at least a hope of success. I told him when he left me, and left his child, that he would be killed, and so he was.

William Hickman and another Danite, shot him in the canyons; and I have often since been obliged to cook for this man, when he passed this way, knowing all the while, he had killed my husband. My child soon followed after its father, and I hope to die also; for why should I live? They have brought me here, where I wish to remain, rather than to return to Salt Lake where the murderers of my husband curse the earth, and roll in affluence unpunished."

R.N. Baskin[12]
"In the excavations made within the limits of Salt Lake City during the time I have resided there, many human skeletons have been exhumed in various parts of the city.... I have never heard that it was ever the custom to bury the dead promiscuously throughout the city; and as no coffins were ever found in connection with any of these skeletons, it is evident that the death of the persons to whom they once belonged did not result from natural causes, but from the use of criminal means."

Danite William Hickman[13]

"It was one of the hot-beds of fanaticism, and I expect that more men were killed there, in proportion to population, than in any other part of

Utah. In that settlement it was certain death to say a word against the authorities, high or low."

Apostle Bruce R. McConkie[14]

"From the days of Joseph Smith to the present, wicked and evilly-disposed persons have fabricated false and slanderous stories to the effect that the Church, in the early days of this dispensation, engaged in a practice of blood atonement where under the blood of apostates and others was shed by the Church as an atonement for their sins... there is not one historical instance of so-called blood atonement in this dispensation, nor has there been one event or occurrence whatever, of any nature, from which the slightest inference arises that any such practice either existed or was taught....

"But under certain circumstances there are some serious sins for which the cleansing of Christ does not operate, and the law of God is that men must then have their own blood shed to atone for their sins."

Bruce R. McConkie, Mormon Doctrine

Apostle Bruce R. McConkie[15] once explained: "As a mode of capital punishment, hanging or execution on a gallows does not comply with the law of blood atonement, for the blood is not shed"

Bruce R. McConkie, Mormon Doctrine

Mormon writer Klaus J. Hansen noted[16]

In 1888, apostle Charles W. Penrose observed that "Because of the laws of the land and the prejudices of the nation, and the ignorance of the world, this law cannot be carried out, but when the time comes that the law of God shall be in full force upon the earth, then this penalty will be inflicted for those crimes committed by persons under covenant not to commit them." However, shortly after the Mormons established the government of God in Utah on what they believed to be a permanent basis, they attempted to enforce the doctrine. Brigham Young insisted that there were "plenty of instances where men have been righteously slain in order to atone for their sins"

J. M. Grant who was a member of the First Presidency under Brigham Young, made the following statements concerning blood atonement[17]

Some have received the Priesthood and knowledge of the things of God, and still they dishonour the cause of truth, commit adultery, and every other abomination beneath the heavens... They will seek unto wizards that peep... get drunk and wallow in the mire and filth, and yet they call themselves Saints... There are men and women that I would advise to go to the President immediately, and ask him to appoint a committee to attend to their case; and then let a place be selected, and let that committee shed their blood.

We have those amongst us that are full of all manner of abominations, those who need to have their blood shed, for water will not do, their sins are of too deep a dye.

You may think that I am not teaching you Bible doctrine, but what says the apostle Paul? I would ask how many covenant breakers there are in this city and in this kingdom. I believe there are a great many; and if they are covenant breakers we need a place designated, where we can shed their blood.

Taken from the confessions of John D. Lee[18]

The sinful member was to be slain for the remission of his sins, it being taught by the leaders and believed by the people that the right thing to do with the sinner who did not repent and obey the council, was to take the life of the offending party, and thus save his everlasting soul. This was called "Blood Atonement "....

The most deadly sin among the people was adultery, and many men were killed in Utah for that crime.

Rosmos Anderson was a Danish man... He had married a widow lady somewhat older than himself, and she had a daughter that was fully grown at the time of the reformation. The girl was very anxious to be sealed to her stepfather, and Anderson was equally anxious to take her for a second wife, but as she was a fine looking girl, Klingensmith desired her to marry him, and she refused. At one of the meetings during the reformation Anderson and his stepdaughter confessed that they had committed adultery, believing when they did so that Brigham Young would allow them to marry when he learned the facts. Their confession being full, they were re-baptised and received into full membership.

They were then placed under covenant that if they committed adultery again, Anderson should suffer death. Soon after this a charge was laid against before the council, accusing him of adultery with his stepdaughter. This Council was composed of Klingensmith and his two counsellors; it was the Bishop's Council. Without giving Anderson any chance to defend himself or make a statement, the Council voted that Anderson must die for violating his covenants. Klingensmith went to Anderson and notified him that the orders were that he must die by having his throat cut, so that the running of his blood atones for his sins.

Anderson being a firm believer in the doctrines and teachings of the Mormon Church, made no objections, but asked for half a day to prepare for death. His request was granted. His wife was ordered to prepare a suit of clean clothing, in which to have her husband buried, and was informed that he was to be killed for his sins, she being directed to tell those who should enquire after her husband that he had gone to California.

Klingensmith, James Haslam, Daniel Mc Farland and John M. Higbee dug a grave in a field near Cedar City, and that night, about 12 o clock, went to Anderson's house and ordered him to make ready to obey the Council. Anderson got up, dressed himself, bid his family good-bye, and without a word of remonstrance accompanied those that he believed were carrying out the will of "Almighty God." They went to the place were the grave was prepared; Anderson knelt down upon the side of the grave and prayed, Klingensmith and his company then cut Anderson's throat from ear to ear and held him so that his blood ran into the grave.

As soon as he was dead they dressed him in his clean clothes, threw him into the grave and buried him.

They then carried his bloody clothing back to his family, and gave them to his wife to wash, when she was again instructed to say that her husband was in California. She obeyed their orders.

No move of that kind was made in Cedar City, unless it was done by order of the "Council" or "High Council."

I was at once informed of Anderson's death... The killing of Anderson was then considered a religious duty and a just act. It was justified by all the people, for they were bound by the same covenants, and the least word of objection to thus treating the man who had broken his covenant would have brought the same fate upon the person who was so foolish as to raise his voice against any act committed by order of the Church authorities.

Notes

1. Prophet Joseph Smith, Jr., *History of the Church*, v. 5, p. 296
2. William Smith Temple Lot Case p.98
3. Deseret News, April 16, 1856
4. Brigham Young, Journal of Discourses, v. 1, pp. 108-109
5. Brigham Young, Journal of Discourses, v. 4, p. 54
6. Brigham Young, Journal of Discourses, v. 4, p. 220
7. Apostle Orson Pratt, The Seer, p. 223
8. Journal of Discourses, v. 4, pp. 49-51
9. Journal of Discourses, v. 4, pp. 49-51
10. Prophet Joseph Fielding Smith, Doctrines of Salvation, v. 1, pp. 135-136, 1954
11. Miss Bullock of Provo, Utah, quoted by Mary Ettie V. Smith, in Nelson Winch Green, *Mormonism its rise, progress, and present condition… 1858, 1870 ed., p. 273*
12. R.N. Baskin, *Reminiscences of Early Utah, 1914, pp. 154-155*
13. Danite William Hickman, *Brigham Young's Destroying Angel, 1964, p. 284*
14. Bruce R. McConkie, *Mormon Doctrine, p. 92*
15. *Mormon Doctrine, 1958, p. 314*
16. *Quest for Empire, p.70 (As quoted in The Changing World of Mormonism. Jerald & Sandra Tanner)*
17. *Journal of Discourses, vol. 4, pp. 49-50; also published in Deseret News, Oct. 1, 1856*
18. *Confessions of John D. Lee, 1880, pp. 282-83*

CHAPTER THIRTEEN

JOSEPH SMITH MOVE TO FAR WEST MISSOURI 1838

The Church had already been forcibly removed from Independence, Missouri in 1833. Many forceful revelations had ensured the safety of "Zion" in those years but the citizens chose to evict their Mormon neighbours. What added more to the Mormon disappointment was the failure of Zion's camp between 1833 to 1834 to fulfil what Joseph Smith had predicted. Not only did the camp not end as predicted, it suffered a deadly outbreak of cholera. Back in Kirtland Ohio Joseph Smith was not finding success either.

Joseph started his own Bank there, which he called the Kirtland Safety Society in 1836. With no federal or state approval they began printing their own currency. In 1837 this bank failed and with it the remaining good feelings of the other citizens in Ohio. In a cloud of legal difficulties Joseph travelled to Far West Missouri in January 1838 in what Church historian and prophet Joseph Fielding Smith called a "flight."

William Harris said of this period[1]

"I now return to Missouri. The Mormons who had settled in and about Independence, having become very arrogant, claiming the land as their own, -- saying, the Lord had given it to them -- and making the most haughty assumptions, so exasperated the old citizens, that a mob was raised in 1833, and expelled the whole Mormon body from the county. They fled to Clay county, where the citizens permitted them to live in quiet till 1836, when a mob spirit began to manifest itself, and the Mormons retired to a very thinly settled district of the country, where they began to make improvements. -- This district was, at the session of 1836-7 of the Missouri Legislature, erected into a county, by the name of Caldwell, with Far West for its county seat. Here the Mormons remained in quiet, until after the Bank explosion in Kirtland, in 1838, when Smith, Rigdon, &c. arrived. Shortly after this, the Danite Society was organized, -- the object of which, at first, was to drive the dissenters out of the county.

The members of this society were bound together by an oath and covenant, with the penalty of death attached to a breach, to defend the Presidency, and each other, unto death -- right or wrong. They had their secret signs, by which they knew each other, either by day or night; and were divided into bands of tens and fifties, with a captain over each band, and a general over the whole. After this body was formed, notice was given to several of the dissenters to leave the county, and they were threatened severely, in case of disobedience. The effect of this was, that many of the dissenters left; amongst these were David Whitmer, John Whitmer, Hiram Page, and Oliver Cowdery, all witnesses to the Book of Mormon; also Lyman Johnson, one of the Twelve Apostles. The day after John Whitmer left his house in Far West, it was taken possession of by Sidney Rigdon. About this time, Rigdon preached his famous "salt sermon."
William Harris, Mormonism Portrayed P 32

Book of Mormon

11. and he went unto those that sent him, and they all entered into a covenant, yea, swearing by their everlasting Maker, that they would tell no man that Kishkumen had murdered Pahoran.

Helaman Chapter 1 verse 11

JOSEPH SMITH'S PLAN IN FAR WEST

Joseph planned to restore the United Order, which would have solved the financial problems of the Church because the United Order required every member to transfer real estate, farms, business, homes, and money to him. As he looked around at past failures, he determined his past problems were due to "enemies" of the Church both within and without who were close neighbours. Joseph planned to purge key counties of "dissenters." To Joseph Smith in 1838 a dissenter was anyone who would not transfer his or her property to him. With this worldview, Joseph Smith was in need of a dependable security force with the intention of carrying out the will of the "presidency."

Problems at Church headquarters in Kirtland relating to the Kirtland Safety Society Bank, caused Joseph Smith, Jr., and Sidney Rigdon to relocate to Far West in early 1838. A brief leadership struggle ensued, which led to the excommunication of John Whitmer and the entire Whitmer family as well as Oliver Cowdery, W.W. Phelps and others. These men continued to live in Far West for a time and became known as the "dissenters". Sidney Rigdon, in his Salt Sermon, warned the dissenters to leave the county and his words were soon followed up by perceived threats from the newly formed Mormon confraternity known as the Danites.

The Danites

CHURCH LEADERS INVOLVED[2]

"Church leaders mobilized the Caldwell County militia and prepared to protect themselves. Some members of the Danites, originally organized to assist with Latter-day Saint community development, engaged in paramilitary activity, including burning the headquarters of mobbers at Gallatin and Millport who had threatened their destruction."

SPRING 1838 ORGANIZATION[3]

One of the three witnesses to the Book of Mormon, David Whitmer, had some inside information about the history and development of the early Danites

"In the spring of 1838, the heads of the Church and many of the members had gone deep into error and blindness.... In June, 1838, at Far West, Missouri, *a secret organization was formed*, Doctor Avard being put in as the leader of the band; a certain oath was to be administered to all the brethren to bind them to support the heads of the Church *in everything they should teach.*

All who refused to take this oath were considered *dissenters from the Church, and certain things were to be done concerning these dissenters, by Dr. Avard's secret band....* my persecutions, for trying to show them their errors, became or such a nature that I had to leave the Latter Day Saints..."

OFFICIAL CHURCH HISTORY[4]

"Avard initiated members into his band, firmly binding them, by all that was sacred, in the protecting of each other in all things that were lawful; and was careful to picture out a great glory that was then hovering over the Church, and would soon burst upon the Saints as a cloud by day, and a pillar of fire by night, and would soon unveil the slumbering mysteries of heaven, which would gladden the hearts and arouse the stupid spirits of the Saints of the latter-day, and fill their hearts with that love which is unspeakable and full of glory, and arm them with power, that the gates of hell could not prevail against them; and would often affirm to his company that the principal men of the Church had put him forward as a spokesman, and a leader of this band, which he named Danites."
SOME DANITES TURNED STATES EVIDENCE

SENATE DOCUMENT No.189

As soon as these members agreed to testify Joseph Smith excommunicated them. From this time forward these key leaders are always depicted as apostates.

DANITE LEADER TESTIMONY [5]

"Sampson Avard, a witness, produced, sworn, and examined, in behalf of the state, deposeth and saith:--That about four months since, a band called the Daughters of Zion, (since called the Danite band,) was formed of the members of the Mormon church, the original object of which was to drive from the county of Caldwell all those who dissented from the Mormon church; in which they succeeded admirably, and to the satisfaction of all concerned. I consider Joseph Smith, jr., as the prime mover and organizer of this band. The officers of the band, according to their grades, were brought before him, at a school house, together with Hiram Smith and Sidney Rigdon; the three composing the first presidency of the whole church. It was stated by Joseph Smith, jr., that it was necessary this band should be bound together by a covenant, that those who revealed the secrets of the society should be PUT TO DEATH. The covenant taken by all the Danite band was as follows, to wit:--They declared, holding up their right hand, 'In the name of Jesus Christ, the son of God, I do solemnly obligate myself ever to conceal and never to reveal the *secret purposes* of this society, called the Daughters of Zion. Should I ever do the same, I hold my *life* as the forfeiture." *La Roy Sunderland Mormonism Exposed chapter two. 1842*

The Adam-God Doctrine

On April 9, 1852, Brigham Young publicly preached the Adam-God doctrine. Brigham Young succeeded Joseph Smith as Prophet of the Church.
In this sermon he declared

Brigham Young[6]

"Now hear it, O inhabitants of the earth, Jew and Gentile, Saint and sinner! When our father Adam came to the Garden of Eden, he came with a celestial body, and brought Eve, one of his wives with him. He helped to make and organize this world. He is Michael, the Archangel, the Ancient of Days! About whom holy men have written and spoken--- He is our Father and our God, and the only God with whom we have to do. Every man upon the earth, professing Christians or non-professing, must hear it, and will know it sooner or later.... The earth was organized by three distinct characters, namely, Elohim, Yahovah, and Michael, these three forming a quorum, as in all heavenly bodies, and in organizing element, perfectly represented in the Deity, as Father, Son, and Holy Ghost"

Brigham Young[7]

"You believe Adam was made of the dust of this earth. This I do not believe, though it is supposed that it is so written in the Bible; but it is not to my understanding. You can write that information to the States, if you please-- that I have publicly declared that I do not believe that portion of the Bible as the Christian world do"

Eighth Article of Faith states

8. We believe the Bible to be the word of God as far as it is translated correctly; we also believe the Book of Mormon to be the word of God.

Brigham Young[8]

"When the Virgin Mary conceived the child Jesus, the Father had begotten him in his own likeness. He was not begotten by the Holy Ghost. And who is the Father? He is the first of the human family…. I could tell you much more about this; but were I to tell you the whole truth; blasphemy would be nothing to it, in the estimation of the superstitious and over-righteous of mankind. However, I have told you the truth as far as I have gone… Jesus, our elder brother, was begotten in the flesh by the same character that was in the Garden of Eden, and who is our Father in Heaven. Now, let all who hear these doctrines, pause before they make light of them, or treat them with indifference, for they will prove their salvation or damnation".

Brigham Young[9]

Now hear it, O inhabitants of the earth, Jew and Gentile, Saint and sinner! When our father Adam came into the Garden of Eden, he came into with a celestial body, brought Eve, one of his wives with him. He helped to make and organize this world. He is Michael, the Archangel, the Ancient of Days! about whom holy men have written and spoken, HE is our Father and our God, and only God with whom we have to do.

Mormon Church Historian B.H. Roberts said [10]

"As a matter of fact, the Mormon Church does not teach that doctrine. A few men in the Church have held such views: and several of them quite prominent in the councils of the Church.... Brigham Young and others have taught that doctrine..."

This doctrine is no longer taught in the Church even though some members still believe it. Anyone caught teaching this doctrine is liable to be excommunicated. This however shows the inconsistencies in the Mormon Church, they claim Brigham Young was a prophet, and at the same time excommunicate people for believing in his teachings or "revelations".

Ninth Article of Faith

9. We believe all that God has revealed, all that He does now reveal, and we believe that He will yet reveal many great and important things pertaining to the Kingdom of God.

Blacks holding the Priesthood

On June 9, 1978, the leaders in the Mormon Church announced a very important change in their doctrine concerning blacks. They stated that blacks would now be given "all of the privileges and blessings which the gospel affords "Deseret News, June 9, 1978).

Prior to that blacks of African lineage were not allowed to hold the Priesthood nor go through the temple, no matter how faithful in the Church they were.

Bruce R. Mc Conkie an LDS Apostle wrote the following in his book Mormon Doctrine published in 1958[11]

Negroes in this life are denied the priesthood; under no circumstances can they hold this delegation of authority from the Almighty. The gospel message of salvation is not carried affirmatively to them.... Negroes are not equal with other races where the receipt of certain spiritual blessings are concerned....

President Joseph Fielding Smith explained the LDS view concerning blacks[12]

Not only was Cain called upon to suffer, but because of his wickedness he became the father of an inferior race. A curse was placed upon him and that curse has been continued through his lineage and must do so while time endures. Millions of souls have come into this world cursed with a black skin and have been denied the privilege of Priesthood and the fullness of the blessings of the Gospel. These are the descendants of Cain. Moreover, they have been made to feel their inferiority and have been separated from the rest of mankind from the beginning.…

But what a contrast! The sons of Seth, Enoch, and Noah honoured by the blessings and rights of Priesthood! …. And the sons of Cain denied the Priesthood; not privileged to receive the covenants of glory in the kingdom of God! We will also hope that blessings may eventually be given our Negro brethren, for they are our brethren--- children of God--- notwithstanding their black covering emblematical of eternal darkness "

Brigham Young[13]

"How long is that race to endure the dreadful curse that is upon them? That curse will remain upon them, and THEY NEVER CAN HOLD THE PRIESTHOOD or share in it until all the other descendants of Adam have received the promises and enjoyed the blessings of the Priesthood and the keys thereof. Until the last ones of the residue of Adam's children are brought up to that favourable position, the children of Cain cannot receive the first ordinances of the Priesthood. They were the first that were cursed, and they will be the last from whom the curse will be removed. When the residue of the family of Adam come up and receive their blessings, then the curse will be removed from the seed of Cain, and they will receive blessings in like proportion.", Emphasis added.

Early Mormon leaders received a "revelation "commanding them to marry the Indians to make them a white and delightsome people.

Joseph Smith[14]

"Verily I say unto you that the wisdom of man in his fallen state, knoweth not the purposes and the privileges of my holy priesthood, but ye shall know when ye receive a fulness by reason of the anointing: For it is my will that in time, ye should take unto you wives of the Lamanites and Nephites, that their posterity may become white, delightsome and Just, for even now their females are more virtuous than the gentiles".

Brigham Young[15]

"Shall I tell you the law of God in regard to the African race? If the white man who belongs to the chosen seed mixes his blood with the seed of Cain, the penalty, under the law of God, is death on the spot. This will always be so" (Journal of Discourses, vol.10. P. 110)

Joseph Smith[16]

Letter for the Messenger and Advocate

Dear Sir: -- This place [Kirtland] having recently been visited by a gentleman who advocated the principles or doctrines of those who are called Abolitionists, I fear that the sound might go out, that "an Abolitionist" had held forth several times to this community… All, except a very few, attended to their own vocations, and left the gentleman to hold forth his own arguments to nearly naked walls. I am aware that many, who profess to preach the Gospel, complain against their brethren of the same faith, who reside in the South, and are ready to withdraw the hand of fellowship, because they will not renounce the principle of slavery, and raise their voice against everything of this kind. This must be a tender point, and one which should call forth the candid reflections of all men, and more especially before they advance in an opposition calculated to lay waste the fair states of the South, and let loose upon the world a community of people, who might, peradventure, overrun our country, and violate the most sacred principles of human society, chastity and virtue… I do not believe that the people of the North have any more right to say that the South shall not hold slaves, than the South have to say the North shall.

How any community can ever be excited with the chatter of such persons, boys and others, who are too indolent to obtain their living by honest industry, and are incapable of pursuing any occupation of a professional nature, is unaccountable to me; and when I see persons in the free states, signing documents against slavery, it is no less, in my mind, than an army of influence, and a declaration of hostilities, against the people of the South. What course can sooner divide our union? ....

I do not doubt, but those who have been forward in raising their voices against the South, will cry out against me as being uncharitable, unfeeling, unkind, and wholly unacquainted with the Gospel of Christ... the first mention we have of slavery is found in the Holy Bible.... And so far from that prediction being averse to the mind of God, it remains as a lasting monument of the decree of Jehovah, to the shame and confusion of all who have cried out against the South, in consequence of their holding the sons of Ham in servitude.... I can say, the curse is not yet taken off from the sons of Canaan, neither will be until it is affected by as great a power as caused it to come; and the people who interfere the least with the purpose of God in this matter, will come under the least condemnation before him; and those who are determined to pursue a course, which shows an opposition, and a feverish restlessness against the decrees of the Lord, will learn, when perhaps it is too late for their own good, that God can do his own work, without the aid of those who are not dictated by His counsel. (History of the Church, by Joseph Smith, vol. 2, pp. 436-38).

Mark E. Petersen LDS Apostle[17]

If a "Negro is faithful all his days, he can and will enter the celestial kingdom. He will go there as a servant, but he will get celestial glory"

A young black girl was permitted to be adopted and sealed to the Prophet Joseph Smith as his servant in the temple.

Bruce McConkie LDS Apostle[18]
"Worthy males of all races can now receive the Melchizedek Priesthood.... It means that members of all races may now be married in the temple, although interracial marriages are discouraged by the Brethren...."

Mormon Doctrine

"Here, then, is laid bare the nerve of the whole matter: Is the south [southern U.S.] Justified in this ABSOLUTE DENIAL OF SOCIAL EQUALITY TO THE NEGRO, no matter what his virtues or abilities or accomplishments? WE AFFIRM, then, that THE SOUTH IS ENTIRELY RIGHT in thus keeping open at all times, at all hazards, and at all sacrifices AN IMPASSIBLE SOCIAL CHASM BETWEEN BLACK AND WHITE. This she must do IN BEHALF OF HER BLOOD, her essence, of THE STOCK OF HER CAUCASIAN RACE." (William Benjamin Smith, The Color Line, as quoted in LDS Historian B.H. Roberts' book entitled "First Year Book in the Seventy's Course in Theology," 1931, p. 231)

New Testament

"For the grace of God that brings salvation has appeared to __ALL__ men."

Titus 2 verse 11

Colossians 3 verse 11

11. *Where there is neither Greek nor Jew, circumcision non circumcision, Barbarian, Scythian, bond nor free: but Christ is all, and in all.*

Animal Sacrifices

In the Old Testament the Israelites offered sacrifices to God. The first male out of every flock that was without blemish. A sheep, goat, calf, bullock, or any valuable livestock of the people of God. These sacrifices were representative of the great and last sacrifice of the Only Begotten Son, who was to come. When Jesus offered himself up to be the last sacrifice, he was the last living creature to be sacrificed.

Joseph Smith[19]

...." It is generally supposed that sacrifice was entirely done away when the Great sacrifice.... Was offered up, and that there will be no necessity for the ordinance of sacrifice in [the] future: but those who assert this are certainly not acquainted with the duties, privileges and authority of the Priesthood, or with the Prophets.

These sacrifices, as well as every ordinance belonging to the Priesthood, will, when the Temple of the Lord shall be built… Be fully restored and attended to in all their powers, ramifications, and blessings".

From the journal of Wandle Mace[20]

Joseph told them to go to Kirtland, and cleanse and purify a certain room in the Temple that they must kill a lamb and offer a sacrifice unto the Lord which should prepare them to ordain Willard Richards a member of the Quorum of the Twelve Apostles.

Joseph Fielding Smith Jr.[21]

RESTORATION OF BLOOD SACRIFICES

"We are living in the dispensation of the fulness of times into which all things are to be gathered, and *all things* are to be restored since the beginning. Even this earth is to be restored to the condition which prevailed before Adam's transgression. Now in the nature of things, the law of sacrifice will have to be restored, or *all things* which were decreed by the Lord would not be restored. It will be necessary, therefore, for the sons of Levi, who offered the blood sacrifices anciently in Israel, to offer such a sacrifice again to round out and complete this ordinance in this dispensation. Sacrifice by the shedding of blood was instituted in the days of Adam and of necessity will have to be restored. The sacrifice of animals will be done to complete the restoration when the temple spoken of is built; at the beginning of the millennium, or in the restoration, blood sacrifices will be performed long enough to complete the fulness of the restoration in this dispensation. Afterwards sacrifice will be of some other character".

Book of Mormon

19. Jesus said "And ye shall offer up unto me no more the shedding of blood; yea, your sacrifices and your burnt offerings shall be done away, for I will accept none of your sacrifices and burnt offerings."
                                        3rd Nephi chapter 9 verse 19

Old Testament

22. and Samuel said, Hath the Lord as great delight in burnt offerings and sacrifices, as in obeying the voice of the Lord? Behold, to obey is better than sacrifice, and to hearken than the fat of rams.

1ˢᵗ Samuel 15 verse 22

Cursing of one's Enemies

Joseph Smith gave a revelation, which sanctioned the cursing of ones enemies:

Doctrine and Covenants

"And inasmuch as mine enemies come against you... ye shall curse them; and whomsoever ye curse, I will curse, and ye shall avenge me of mine enemies"

Section 103 verses 24-25

This cursing of enemies was actually carried out in the Kirtland Temple.

Apostle George A. Smith[22]   March 18ᵗʰ 1855

"Now I will illustrate this still further. The Lord did actually reveal one principle to us there, and that one principle was apparently so simple, and so foolish in their eyes, that a great many apostatised over it, because it was so contrary to their notions and views. It was this, after the people had fasted all day, they sent out and got wine and bread... and they ate and drank, and prophesied, and bore testimony, and continued so to do until some of the High Council of Missouri stepped into the stand, and, as righteous Noah did when he awoke from his wine, commenced to curse their enemies. You never felt such a shock go through any house or company in the world as went through that. There was almost a rebellion because men would get up and curse their enemies"...

William Harris said concerning the cursing[23]

"I will now go back for a short period. In 1836, an endowment meeting, or solemn assembly, was called, to be held in the Temple at Kirtland. It was given out that those who were in attendance at the meeting should receive an endowment, or blessing, similar to that experienced by the Disciples of Christ on the day of Pentecost. When the day arrived, great numbers convened from the different churches in the country. They spent the day in fasting and prayer, and in washing and perfuming their bodies; they also washed their feet and anointed they called their holy oil, and pronounced blessings. In the evening, they met for the endowment.

The fast was then broken, by eating light wheat bread, and drinking as much wine as they saw proper. Smith knew well how to infuse the spirit which they expected to receive; so he encouraged the brethren to drink freely, telling them that the wine was consecrated, and would not make them drunk. As may be supposed, they drank to the purpose. After this they began to prophesy, pronouncing blessings upon their friends, and curses upon their enemies. If I should be so unhappy as to go to the regions of the damned, I never expect to hear language more awful, or more becoming the infernal pit, than was uttered that night. The curses were pronounced principally upon the clergy of the present day, and upon the Jackson county mobs in Missouri. After spending the night in alternate blessings and cursings, the meeting adjourned".

The Inhabitants of the Moon

In an 1892 LDS publication the heading "The Inhabitants of the Moon"

Oliver B. Huntington[24]

"Nearly all the great discoveries of men in the last half century have, in one way or another, either directly or indirectly, contributed to prove Joseph Smith to be a Prophet.

"As far back as 1837, I know that he said the moon was inhabited by men and women the same as this earth, and that they lived to a greater age than we do -- that they live generally to near the age of 1000 years. He described the men as averaging near six feet in height, and dressing quite uniformly in something near the Quaker style.

"In my Patriarchal blessing, given by the father of Joseph the Prophet, in Kirtland, 1837, I was told that I should preach the gospel before I was 21 years of age; that I should preach the gospel to the inhabitants upon the islands of the sea, and to the inhabitants of the moon, even the planet you can now behold with your eyes."

Brigham Young[25]

"Who can tell us of the inhabitants of this little planet that shines of an evening, called the moon? When you inquire about the inhabitants of that sphere you find that the most learned are as ignorant in regard to them as the ignorant of their fellows. So it is in regard to the inhabitants of the sun. Do you think it is inhabited? I rather think it is. Do you think there is any life there? No question of it; it was not made in vain."

In the early days of the Church many people left their homes and their countries to gather to Zion. Some of them made the ultimate sacrifice for what they believed to be of God. The Mormon Church teaches that Zion will be the New Jerusalem, which would be built in Missouri by the Mormon Church.

Old Testament, *Micah Chapter 4 verse 2*

2. *"For the law shall go forth of Zion, and the word of the Lord from Jerusalem".*

Some of those early Pioneers buried their loved ones along the way as they made their journey to America. In the 1800s travel was very difficult. For what did they do it?

The Mormon handcart pioneers were participants in the migration of members of the Church of Jesus Christ of Latter Day Saints to Salt

Lake City, Utah. They used handcarts to transport their belongings. The Mormon handcart movement began in 1856 and lasted until 1860. Motivated to join their fellow Church members but lacking funds for full ox or horse teams, nearly 3,000 Mormon pioneers came from England, Wales, Scotland and Scandinavia and then made the journey from Iowa or Nebraska to Utah in ten handcart companies.

The trek was disastrous for two of the companies, which started their journey dangerously late and were caught by heavy snow and severe temperatures in central Wyoming. Despite a dramatic rescue effort, more than 210 of the 980 pioneers in these two companies died along the way. John Chislett, a survivor, wrote, "Many a father pulled his cart, with his little children on it, until the day preceding his death."

New Testament, Book of Revelation Chapter 22 verses 18-19

18. for I testify unto every man that heareth the words of the prophesy of this book, if any man shall add unto these things, God shall add unto him the plagues that are in this book:

19. And if any man shall take away from the words of the book of this prophesy, God shall take away his part out of the book of life, and out of the holy City, and from the things, which are written in this book.

When I was a member of the Church this scripture was quoted to me many times by non-members and well meaning friends. I would quote the scripture.

New Testament, 2nd Corinthians 13 verse 1

1. In the mouth of two or three witnesses shall every word be established...

Orson Pratt[26]

The Book of Mormon claims to be a divinely inspired record... If false, it is one of the most cunning, wicked, bold, deep-laid impositions ever palmed upon the world, calculated to deceive and ruin millions... if true, no one can possibly be saved and reject it: if false, no one can possibly be saved and receive it....

"*If false, it is one of the most cunning, wicked, bold, deep-laid impositions ever palmed upon the world, calculated to deceive and ruin millions*".

This it has indeed done and continues to do.
This Church makes false promises, and desires a very big say in the lives in of its members.

Notes

1. William Harris, *Mormonism Portrayed*
2. Milton V. Backman, Jr., and Ronald K. Esplin, *History of the Church, Encyclopaedia of Mormonism.*
3. *An Address to All Believers in Christ*, David Whitmer, Richmond, Mo., 1887, pp. 27-28
4. *History of the Church*, Vol.3, Ch.13, p.179
5. La Roy Sunderland, *Mormonism Exposed* (1842) Chapter two
6. *Journal of Discourses*, vol. 1, pp. 50-51
7. *Journal of Discourses*, vol. 2, p6
8. *Journal of Discourses*, vol.1, p 51
9. *Journal of Discourses*, vol.1, p 51
10. *Deseret News, July 23, 1921* (As quoted in Jerald &Sandra Tanner's *The Changing World of Mormonism* p.20
11. *Mormon Doctrine*, 1958, p.447
12. Author of (*The Way to Perfection, Salt Lake City*, 1935, pp. 101-2)
13. *Journal of Discourses*, Vol. 7, pp. 290-291, 1859
14. *Revelation received West of Jackson county, Missouri, July 1831*
15. *Journal of Discourses*, vol.10. P. 110
16. *History of the Church*, by Joseph Smith, vol. 2, pp. 436-38
17. (*Race Problems-- As They Affect The Church*, a speech delivered at Brigham Young University, August 27, 1954)
18. *Mormon Doctrine*, pp. 526-528, 1979 (printing of 1966 edition)
19. *History of the Church*, vol. 4, p. 211
20. *Journal of Wandle Mace*, p. 32
21. Joseph Fielding Smith Jr., *Doctrines of Salvation*, Vol.3, p.94
22. *Journal of Discourses*, vol. 2, p. 216
23. William Harris, *Mormonism Portrayed*, pp. 31-32
24. *The Young Woman's Journal*, 1892, vol. 3, pp. 263-64
25. *Journal of Discourses*, vol. 13, p. 271
26. *Orson Pratt's Works, Divine Authenticity of the Book of Mormon*, Liverpool, 1851, pp.1-2

Chapter Fourteen

The following is by author and friend Marion Stricker[1]

LIFE AFTER MORMONISM and THE DOUBLE-BIND

This book is the culmination of a twenty-year odyssey, a personal quest for a solution to an unknown problem that had become emotionally and intellectually intolerable for me. My main symptom was that I could never quite think, or do things "right" --- I felt and thought that something must be terribly wrong with my mind, because significant others could always set things "right" for me, therefore I must be "stupid." It was implied that my problem wasn't shared by others; I was told that it was I who needed to change. I believed this assessment. But if I needed to change, how could I --- if I didn't't know what my problem was? Does it have a name? I was willing to abide by whatever I found to be true. What I found through a trial and error search, following threads and connections, was a pattern of behaviour I finally identified and named.

The Pattern of the Double-Bind

What I also discovered was that I was not alone in my dilemma; as I continued on, the Pattern began to assume Universal implications. At first, I found that my loved ones, and others in Mormonism, were also trapped inside it, unknowingly, the same as I; this created an urge to find its origins. It was in this extended search that I found that the Pattern went way beyond my own personal experiences in Mormonism.

The Pattern is not obvious, the reason being that its insidious nature operates silently with powerful cultural taboos and customs contained within it: one must not see, hear, speak, or question anything contrary to its unexamined "truth." Once I had discovered the Pattern in my own life, it was particularly painful to realize that I had "voluntarily" cooperated, as an "accomplice," in perpetuating a lie--- a lie masked as truth.

The Church of Jesus Christ of Latter-day Saints, better known as the Mormon Church-- and also referred to as Mormonism--- contains, as its psychological basis, this Pattern. I was raised exclusively within its environment, was married in the LDS Temple (1950), raised six children, and lived a life dedicated to the death covenants exacted in the Temple. Mormonism is not the only corporation of its kind to be based on this Pattern, but it is where I first discovered it.

In extending the ramifications of this Pattern to its logical end it is found that it causes the very problems it claims to be able to cure...by the use of the cause! It is a circular system used to control others, which reverses the possible evolution towards intellectual integrity. A form of de-volution, and in its extreme form leads to mental havoc and possible madness. Yet at the same time, it claims to be the means of obtaining peace of mind through "intelligence." In other words, The Pattern is a form of illogical "logic."

Needless to say, I found out what was "wrong" with me; my ability to think rationally, to question, was condemning me; Reason is the enemy of the Mormon Church.

The cure for this madness is its opposite...it is to be able to reason without fear. This is made possible by the exposure and understanding of the cause, hence the aim of this book... to expose the nature of the Pattern and to show how it is possible to live a life relatively free from its web of deceit.

The Nature of the Pattern and the Double Bind

What the Pattern Is and What the Pattern Does

The Pattern is a method used that subjugates and dehumanises. It does this by creating a new fabricated world, the direct opposite of this real world.

A REVIEW OF THE FACTS KNOWN IN THE REAL WORLD

The Basic Necessities for a Constructive Life worth Living are:
First, our BODY ... which houses and cooperates with...

Our SENSES ... by which we perceive the real world, and which in turn sends concrete messages to...

Our BRAIN ... which can then function in order to question and reason, which leads to *Self* -control over our own lives ... to make individual choices which are our means of survival as rational, individually aware *human* beings.

This is an OPEN SYSTEM, where there is always room for growth, expansion, and correction ... trial and error being included in the process of gaining more awareness and knowledge, which makes possible more life and happiness in its most constructive aspects.

* * *

ON THE CONTRARY

The Pattern destroys the awareness of all the above necessary faculties for the realization of our own individual identity; the most essential parts of us as *human* beings are missing. Therefore, all that is human and intrinsic to life, liberty, and the pursuit of happiness, is invalidated. The Pattern destroys *Identity*, along with *integrity of mind*, and the ability to *truly love*. IT DOES THIS BY TURNING THE REAL WORLD UPSIDE-DOWN THROUGH FRAUD AND THEFT

It operates by reversing the order of our natural functions, and by replacement, as follows:

1. The MIND of a controller, whom I call the "Binder," reverses the basic order, and replaces the individual's *brain* with the Mind of the Binder; as a result, sense perceptions to the brain are invalidated.

2. "FEELINGS" that are attached to the pre-conceived ideas in the Binder's Mind replace individual *authentic perceptions* and their accompanying *emotions*.

3. The BODY of the individual is now last in order, and becomes the property of the Binder, and is his to control, replacing *Self*-control.

This I call a CLOSED SYSTEM, which admits nothing that is not already preconceived by the Binder. To do this, the Binder must continually suppress the integrity of the body, separating the brain and emotions from the real world of *sense perceptions* ... our *means* of perceiving the real world.

Psychological Cannibalism - Suicide

The prelude to suicide is accumulated, unearned "Guilt" and the abandonment by those in whom all of one's trust has been deposited, plus the sense that one has failed in all things. Numbness sets in. One loses all feelings of sense perceptions, and feels nothing but a "Black Hole" of despair, and the desire to die, the pain unendurable.

Mormonism fosters an unconscious death wish through The Pattern which is designed to destroy individual identity ... to lose oneself totally for the "up building of the Kingdom of God on earth." The sincere devotee obeys the Law of Sacrifice of offering, literally, one's life and all of one's talents and possessions, if necessary, for the Church. All of the words and promises by the leaders of the Church have been believed and worked for diligently. Since the Gospel "plan" is based on fraud, i.e., the Double-Bind, failure is a built-in result. The stronger the individual is, the more basic intelligence the member has, the more the pain and devastation one feels at the final failure. This person is labelled "mentally ill," a "misfit," and becomes the "exception" that can't be tolerated and is literally abandoned. Instead of help given, the member is accused of having committed some terrible sin, which reinforces the desire to die; the member is punished again ... for being punished.

Abandonment will be masked by "Not I (*we*), But, you, are "evil." This member is abandoned in his or her most crucial time of need because he/she becomes a threat to the "Key" to "Salvation" ... the Double-Bind and what it does. The member reveals a fact that gets too close to the poisonous source; the Church is put on the spot with its own corruption of values that it must deny; it must have the *image* of "sanity," "joy," "happiness," "love," and, of course, "intelligence." Therefore, the member must be labelled the "enemy" of these "highest values." Mormonism *outwardly* fights what it *inwardly* is.

The victim is blamed and accused of needing "psychiatric" help; it is the member who is "mad," not the Church. Or, Church "psychologists" may recommend a drug of some kind (like Prozac) to "stabilize" a member by superficially erasing all of the anxiety that shows and indicates that something is radically wrong. The member is then able to continue his or her labours in the Church uninterrupted. They need only to "read the Book of Mormon and the Doctrine and Covenants" and to "work harder to increase their faith." It is this "lack" of effort that has caused their "illness" they are told. In reality, it is just the opposite. The cause is prescribed as the cure, which continues to destroy the ability to reason. However, the underlying reasons for the depression are still there; the drugs merely put the problems back into the "little box" of denial that Mormonism had encouraged before the current outbreak; thus, the problems that caused the crisis are "forgotten." On the other hand, if the member is leaving, or has left the Church (the real cause of the problem) and has sought help, certain calming drugs can elevate the desire to live and to give the energy necessary to probe the real cause of the depression. The problem once known and the Self Identity of the person re-established, the drug is no longer necessary. The chemical imbalance *caused by the anxiety inflicted by the Double-Bind Pattern* is restored to its balanced operating level. The brain is not separate from the body. What one thinks and feels affects the well being of the rest of the body. Our sense perceptions and their normal chemical messages to the brain are our means of survival.

The major difference is whether a Band-aid is used to cover a still festering abscess, or whether a fundamental cure is the goal. Without knowing the primary cause, there can be no real cure ... and an addiction to the drug results. At any time the desire to die could break through. Suicide is one of the "side effects" of the drug Prozac.

The Church is the Whited Sepulchre, which houses the living Dead. If this sounds grim, it is because the whitewashed deadly falsehoods are being taken away, and what is left are facts that have been denied for too long. The problem needs to be identified, named and exposed. And, contrary to Mormon expectations, the factual truths can actually set us free. Ernest Renan expressed it this way: "The Truths which Science

(Reason) reveals always surpass the dreams which it destroys." (*Italics, mine.*)

We cannot fight or defend ourselves from the invisible. This is what Mormonism fears ... that we will objectify and identify the fraud. The very things the Church considers its enemies, are the very things that contain hidden truths which they want to keep hidden. Boyd K. Packer has identified and is obsessed with three main "enemies" of the Church, Gays and Lesbians, Women, and Intellectuals ... (in other words, Sex, the issue of choice in Procreating, and Reason). The other subject it fears, and which is carefully avoided, and rarely spoken of or defined ... considered too "sacred" to speak about ... is *Love*. Love is one of the "Mysteries of Godliness." In Mormonism, the "Mysteries" are not to be delved into. This life is for *blind* "Obedience and Sacrifice" only.

> "Binders always punish with what they fear most ... abandonment and independence. They are the ones who most need others ... to feed them; it becomes a "life or death" matter for the Binder. For the Bound, if they have the courage to leave, it becomes possible for them to reclaim all the humanness that was stolen from them ... to live freely in the Real World which is the true home of all possibilities for understanding and love."

> LIFE AFTER MORMONISM and THE DOUBLE-BIND (p. 113)

An ex-member of the Church shares her "dream" or "nightmare"[2]

"Back in 1996, when I was no longer a believer in Mormonism, but still very active in the Church for family reasons I had a dream. Perhaps it was a daydream while I was in the shower. I don't remember now. At the time Mormonism was constantly on my mind for obvious reasons.

Anyhow, the dream was somewhat gruesome and graphic. It consisted of numerous adults being connected via individual umbilical cords to a giant placenta. Perhaps placentas were also on my mind at the time having just witnessed the birth of my first child. I remember getting a wide-eyed view of not only the delivery of my son's placenta but it sitting in a tray in the delivery room after the fact.

But back to the dream... The people that were all connected to this giant placenta appeared happy enough. They didn't have to search for food much and they appeared to be receiving their nourishment from it. Most of those connected were at a fair distance from the placenta itself and not too curious about its behaviour. On closer inspection, however, I found that they weren't free to go beyond the tether of the cords that bound them. When I took a really close look at this giant placenta I found it to be most hideous. Not only was it not providing much nourishment, it was concealing its true behaviour. Instead of providing food it was doing the feeding. It was sapping the life out of those it bound. They didn't have the will or an easy way to sever the connection. It was very creepy. Sort of like Invasion of the body Snatchers. Screams would not have been heard in this twisted world".

****

Basically what happens in the Church is that it produces Clones, everybody thinking and believing what the Church wants them to believe. Everyone abiding by their dress code, their health code and their religious creed. The mind is swallowed up and freedom of expression is stifled if not altogether crushed into anonymity.

I believe the church is alive and kicking, for power, financial and world. Some say their aim is to get the control of the Government completely.

Brigham Young[3]
July 4th 1854

"Will the Constitution be destroyed? No: it will be held inviolate by this people; and, as Joseph Smith said", "The time will come when the destiny of the nation will hang upon a single thread. At that critical juncture, this people will step forth and save it from the threatened destruction." It will be so".

The Church has billions of dollars collected from the tithing of its faithful members; some of these members are millionaires. The Church owns vast amounts of properties and invests in more and more. The Churches humanitarian effort is feeble compared to what they invest in property. They do spend millions on their temples and on their Missionary programmes.

Sidney Rigdon stole the Spalding Manuscript; he was a clever man who used his knowledge to add the religious tone to the Book of Mormon, claiming it to be a New Testament of Jesus Christ. Joseph Smith was a willing accomplice to it. Both of whom did not want to earn their living by the sweat of their brow.

Sidney Rigdon's grandson says their family understood it to be a fraud.

Notes

1. Marion Stricker, *LIFE AFTER MORMONISM and THE DOUBLE-BIND (p. 113)*
2. Letter posted on <u>www.exmormon.org</u>
3. *Journal of Discourses Vol. 7, p.15*

CHAPTER FIFTEEN

Who was Joseph Smith? (1805 to 1844)

Born on 23rd December 1805. Birth place Sharon Vermont. Died June 27th 1844 (aged 38) Death place Carthage, Illinois.

Founder:
Latter Day Saint Movement

Early life of Joseph Smith Jnr.

Joseph Smith, Jr. was born on December 23rd. 1805 in Sharon, Vermont to Joseph Smith Snr. and Lucy Mack Smith. After his birth, the family moved to western New York where they continued farming just outside the border of the town of Palmyra. This region was an area of intense revivalism and religious diversity during the Second Great Awakening. Although Smith had limited involvement with organized religion during his youth, he studied the Bible, held religious opinions, and was influenced by the common folk religion of the area.

A court record dated March 1826, when Joseph Smith was twenty-one, covers his trial in Bainbridge, New York, on a charge of being "a disorderly person and impostor. Mormon scholars continued to deny the authenticity of the court record until Rev. Wesley Pomade his discovery in 1971.

REVEREND WESLEY P. WALTERS[1]

Being first duly sworn upon his oath deposes and states:

On Saturday, May 22, 1971, while in Norwich, New York, I ...was shown by the County Historian, Mrs. Mae Smith, where Chenango County kept their dead storage, which was in a back, poorly-lit room in the basement of the County Jail....

On July 28, 1971, I was able to return to Norwich and in the late afternoon I went back to the County Jail accompanied by Mr. Fred Poffarl ...Mr. Poffarl discovered two cardboard boxes in the darkest area of the room, containing more bundles of bills, all mixed up as to date, and some badly watersoaked and mildewed.... It was in Mr. Poffarl's box that the 1826 bills were soon found.... When I opened the 1826 bundle and got part way through the pile of Bainbridge bills, all of which were very damp and mildewed, I came upon, first, the J. P. bill of Albert Neeley and then upon the Constable's bill of Philip M. DeZeng. On Mr. Neely's bill was the item of the trial of "Joseph Smith The Glass Looker" ....On the bill of Mr. DeZeng were the charges for arresting and keeping Joseph Smith, notifying two justices, subpoenaing 12 witnesses, as well as a mittimus charge for 10 miles travel "to take him," with no specification as to where he was taken on the Mittimus....

In my opinion, the bills are authentic, of the same paper quality and ink quality as the other 1826 and 1830 bills and appeared to me to have remained tied up and untouched since the day they were bound up and placed away in storage by the Board of Supervisors of Chenango County, New York...

STATE OF NEW YORK v. JOSEPH SMITH [2]

Warrant issued upon written complaint upon oath of Peter G. Bridgeman, who informed that one Joseph Smith of Bainbridge was a disorderly person and an impostor.

Prisoner brought before Court March 20, 1826. Prisoner examined: says that he came from the town of Palmyra, and had been at the house of Josiah Stowel in Bainbridge most of the time since; had small part of time been employed by said Stowel on his farm, and going to school. That he had a certain stone which he occasionally looked at to determine where hidden treasures in the bowels of the earth were; that he professed to tell in this manner where gold mines were a distance under ground, and had looked for Mr. Stowel several times, and had informed him where he could find these treasures, and Mr. Stowel had been engaged in digging for them.

That at Palmyra he pretended to tell by looking at this stone where coined money was buried in Pennsylvania, and while at Palmyra had frequently ascertained in that way where lost property was of various kinds; that he had occasionally been in the habit of looking through this stone to find lost property for three years, but of late had pretty much given it up on account of its injuring his health, especially his eyes making them sore; that he did not solicit business of this kind, and had always rather declined having anything to do with business.

Josiah Stowel sworn: says that prisoner had been at his house something like five months; had been employed by him to work on farm part of time; that he pretended to have skill of telling where hidden treasures in the earth were by means of looking through a certain stone; that prisoner had looked for him sometimes; once to tell him about money buried in Bend Mountain in Pennsylvania, once for gold on Monument Hill, and once for a salt spring; and that he positively knew that the prisoner could tell, and did possess the art of seeing those valuable treasures through the medium of said stone; that he found the (word illegible) at Bend and Monument Hill as prisoner represented it; that prisoner had looked through the said stone for Deacon Attleton for a mine, did not exactly find it, but got a p--(word unfinished) of ore which resembled gold, he thinks; that prisoner had told by means of this stone where a Mr. Bacon had buried money; that he and prisoner had been in search of it; that prisoner had said it was in a certain root of a stump five feet from surface of the earth, and with it would be found a tail feather; that Stowel and prisoner thereupon commenced digging, found a tail feather, but money was gone; that he supposed the money moved down. That prisoner did offer his services; that he never deceived him; that prisoner looked through stone and described Josiah Stowel's house and outhouses, while at Palmyra at Simpson Stowel's, correctly; that he had told about a painted tree, with a man's head painted upon it, by means of said stone. That he had been in company with prisoner digging for gold, and had the most implicit faith in prisoner's skill.

Arad Stowel sworn: says that he went to see whether prisoner could convince him that he possessed the skill he professed to have, upon which prisoner laid a book upon a white cloth, and proposed looking through another stone which was white and transparent, hold the stone to the candle, turn his head to book, and read. The deception appeared so palpable that witness went off disgusted.

Mc Master sworn: says he went with Arad Stowel, and likewise came away disgusted. Prisoner pretended to him that he could discover objects at a distance by holding this white stone to the sun or candle; that prisoner rather declined looking into a hat at his dark stone, as he said that it hurt his eyes.

Jonathon Thompson says that prisoner was requested to look for chest of money; did look, and pretended to know where it was; and prisoner,

Thompson, and Yeomans went in search of it; that Smith looked hat {sic} while there, and when very dark, and told how the chest was situated. After digging several feet, struck upon something sounding like a board or plank. Prisoner would not look again, pretending that he was alarmed on account of the circumstances relating to the trunk being buried, [which] came all fresh to his mind. That the last time he looked he discovered distinctly the two Indians who buried the trunk, that a quarrel ensued between them, and that one of the said Indians was killed by the other, and thrown into the hole beside the trunk, to guard it, as he supposed.

Thompson says that he believes in the prisoner's professed skil; [sic] that the board that he struck his spade on was probably the chest, but on account of an enchantment the trunk kept settling away from under them when digging; that not, withstanding they continued constantly removing the dirt, yet the trunk kept about the same distance from them. Says prisoner said that it appeared to him that salt might be found at Bainbridge, and that he is certain that prisoner can divine things by means of said stone. That as evidence of the fact prisoner looked into his hat to tell him about some money witness lost sixteen years ago, and that he described the man that witness supposed had taken it, and the disposition of the money.

And therefore the Court find(s) the Defendant guilty. Costs Warrant, 19cc. Complaint upon oath, 251/2 c. Seven witnesses, 871/2 c. Recognisance's, 25c. Mittimus, 19 c.
Recognisances of witnesses, 75. Subpoena, 18c. --$2.68

Mormon leaders declared that this record was a forgery.

Apostle John A. Widtsoe[3]

"This alleged court record...seems to be a literary attempt of an enemy to ridicule Joseph Smith....There is no existing proof that such a trial was ever held" (*Joseph Smith—Seeker After Truth*, Salt Lake City, 1951, p. 78)

Mr. Walters made his discovery in 1971. The document which Walters found is Justice Albert Neely's bill showing the costs involved in several trials in 1826.

In addition to Justice Neely's bill for the trial of "Joseph Smith The Glass Looker," Mr. Walters discovered the bill of Constable Philip M. DeZeng, which tells of "Serving Warrant on Joseph Smith." Mr. Walters has given an account of the discovery of these bills in an affidavit.

Before Mr. Walters made his discovery of the bills, Mormon scholars were willing to admit that if the 1826 trial were authentic, it would disprove Mormonism.[4]

(As quoted in *The Changing World of Mormonism* Jerald & Sandra Tanner. P. 71-72

Joseph Smith suppressed the 1826 trial in his History of the Church. The trial was mentioned in a letter published in the Evangelical Magazine and Gospel Advocate.

Evangelical Magazine & Gospel Advocate [5]

Utica, N. Y., April 9, 1831

MORMONITES.

A.W. Benton

Messrs. Editors --

In the sixth number of your paper I saw a notice of a sect of people called Mormonites; and thinking that a fuller history of their founder, Joseph Smith, Jr., might be interesting to community, and particularly to your correspondent in Ohio, where, perhaps, the truth concerning him may be hard to come at, I will take the trouble to make a few remarks on the character of that infamous imposter.

For several years preceding the appearance of his book, he was about the country in the character of a glass-looker: pretending, by means of a certain stone, or glass, which he put in a hat, to be able to discover lost goods, hidden treasures, mines of gold and silver, &c. Although he constantly failed in his pretensions, still he had his dupes who put implicit confidence in all his words. In this town, a wealthy farmer, named Josiah Stowell, together with others, spent large sums of money in digging for hidden money, which this Smith pretended he could see, and told them where to dig; but they never found their treasure.

At length the public, becoming wearied with the base imposition which he was palming upon the credulity of the ignorant, for the purpose of sponging his living from their earnings, had him arrested as a disorderly person, tried and condemned before a court of Justice. But, considering his youth, (he being then a minor,) and thinking he might reform his conduct, he was designedly allowed to escape. This was four or five years ago. From this time he absented himself from this place, returning only privately, and holding clandestine intercourse with his credulous dupes, for two or three years.

It was during this time, and probably by the help of others more skilled in the ways of iniquity than himself, that he formed the blasphemous design of forging a new revelation, which, backed by the terrors of an endless hell, and the testimony of base unprincipled men, he hoped would frighten the ignorant, and open a field of speculation for the vicious, so that he might secure to himself the scandalous honor of being the founder of a new sect, which might rival, perhaps, the Wilkinsonians, or the French Prophets of the 17th century.

During the past Summer he was frequently in this vicinity, and others of baser sort, as Cowdry, Whitmer, etc., holding meetings, and proselyting a few weak and silly women, and still more silly men, whose minds are shrouded in a mist of ignorance which no ray can penetrate, and whose credulity the utmost absurdity cannot equal.

In order to check the progress of delusion, and open the eyes and understandings of those who blindly followed him, and unmask the turpitude and villainy of those who knowingly abetted him in his infamous designs; he was again arraigned before a bar of Justice, during last Summer, to answer to a charge of misdemeanor. This trial led to an investigation of his character and conduct, which clearly evinced to the unprejudiced, whence the spirit came which dictated his inspirations. During the trial it was shown that the Book of Mormon was brought to light by the same magic power by which he pretended to tell fortunes, discover hidden treasures, &c. Oliver Cowdery, one of the three witnesses to the book, testified under oath, that said Smith found with the plates, from which he translated his book, two transparent stones, resembling glass, set in silver bows. That by looking through these, he was able to read in English, the reformed Egyptian characters, which were engraved on the plates.

So much for the gift and power of God, by which Smith says he translated his book. Two transparent stones, undoubtedly of the same properties, and the gift of the same spirit as the one in which he looked to find his neighbor's goods. It is reported, and probably true, that he commenced his juggling by stealing and hiding property belonging to his neighbors, and when inquiry was made, he would look in his stone, (his gift and power) and tell where it was.

Josiah Stowell, a Mormonite, being sworn, testified that he positively knew that said Smith never had lied to, or deceived him, and did not believe he ever tried to deceive any body else. The following questions were then asked him, to which he made the replies annexed.

Did Smith ever tell you there was money hid in a certain glass which he mentioned?
    Yes.

Did he tell you, you could find it by digging?
    Yes.

Did you dig?
    Yes.

Did you find any money?
> No.

Did he not lie to you then, and deceive you?
> No! the money was there, but we did not get quite to it!

How do you know it was there?
> Smith said it was!

Addison Austin was next called upon, who testified, that at the very same time that Stowell was digging for money, he, Austin, was in company with said Smith alone, and asked him to tell him honestly whether he could see this money or not. Smith hesitated some time, but finally replied, "to be candid, between you and me, I cannot, any more than you or any body else; but any way to get a living."

Here, then, we have his own confession, that he was a vile, dishonest impostor. As regards the testimony of Josiah Stowell, it needs no comment. He swears positively that Smith did not lie to him. So much for a Mormon witness. Paramount to this, in truth and consistency, was the testimony of Joseph Knight, another Mormonite. Newell Knight, son of the former, and also a Mormonite, testified, under oath, that he positively had a devil cast out of himself by the instrumentality of Joseph Smith, Jr., and that he saw the devil after it was out, but could not tell how it looked.

Those who have joined them in this place, are, without exception, children who are frightened into the measure, or ignorant adults, whose love for the marvellous is equalled by nothing but their entire devotedness to the will of their leader; with a few who are as destitute of virtue and moral honesty, as they are of truth and consistency. As for his book, it is only the counterpart of his money-digging plan. Fearing the penalty of the law, and wishing still to amuse his followers, he fled for safety to the sanctuary of pretended religion.

A. W. Benton

S. Bainbridge, Chen, Co., March, 1831
(Evangelical Magazine and Gospel Advocate, April 9, 1831, p.120)

This date on the court record shows that Joseph Smith was involved in magic practises at the very time he was supposed to preparing himself to receive the plates for the Book of Mormon.

CHENANGO UNION

Vol. 30.	Norwich, N. Y., Thursday, May 2, 1877	No. 33.

William D. Purple
(1803-1886)
"Joseph Smith, The Originator of Mormonism"

Historical Reminiscences of the town of Afton.

BY W. D. PURPLE [6]

More than fifty years since, at the commencement of his professional career, the writer spent a year in the present village of Afton, in this County. It was then called South Bainbridge, and was in striking contrast with the present village at the same place. It was a mere hamlet, with one store and one tavern. The scenes and incidents of that early day are vividly engraven upon his memory, by reason of his having written them when they occurred, and by reason of his public and private rehearsals of them in later years. He will now present them as historical reminiscences of old Chenango, and as a precursor of the advent of that wonder of the age, Mormonism.

In the year 1825 we often saw in that quiet hamlet, Joseph Smith, Jr., the author of the Golden Bible, or the Books of Mormon. He was an inmate of the family of Deacon Isaiah [sic] Stowell, who resided some two miles below the village, on the Susquehanna. Mr. Stowell was a man of much force of character, of indomitable will, and well fitted as a pioneer in the unbroken wilderness that this country possessed at the close of the last century. He was one of the Vermont sufferers, who for defective titles, consequent on the forming a new State from a part of Massachusetts, in 1791, received wild lands in Bainbridge. He had been educated in the spirit of orthodox puritanism, and was officially connected with the first Presbyterian church of the town, organized by Rev. Mr. Chapin. He was a very industrious, exemplary man, and by severe labor and frugality had acquired surroundings that excited the envy of many of his loss [sic] fortunate neighbors. He had at this time grown up sons and daughters to share his prosperity and the honors of his name.

About this time he took upon himself a monomaniacal impression to seek for hidden treasures that he believed were buried in the earth. He hired help and repaired to Northern Pennsylvania, in the vicinity of Lanesboro, to prosecute his search for untold wealth, which he believed to be buried there. Whether it was the

"Ninety bare of gold
"And dollars many fold"

That Capt. Robert Kidd, the pirate of a preceding century, had despoiled the commerce of the world, we are not able to say, but that he took his help and provisions from home, and camped out on the black hills of that region for weeks at a time, was freely admitted by himself and family.

What success, if any, attended these excursions, is unknown, but his hallucination adhered to him like the fabled shirt of Nessus, and had entire control over his mental character. The admonition of his neighbors, the members of his church, and the importunities of his family, had no impression on his wayward spirit.

There had lived a few years previous to this date, in the vicinity of Great Bend, a poor man named Joseph Smith, who, with his family, had removed to the western part of the State, and lived in squalid poverty near Palmyra, in Ontario County. Mr. Stowell, while at Lanesboro, heard of the fame of one of his sons, named Joseph, who, by the aid of a magic stone had become a famous seer of lost or hidden treasures. These stories were fully received into his credulous mind, and kindled into a blaze his cherished hallucination.

Visions of untold wealth appeared through this instrumentality, to his longing eyes. He harnessed his team, and filled his wagon with provisions for "man and beast," and started for the residence of the Smith family. In due time he arrived at the humble log-cabin, midway between Canandaigua and Palmyra, and found the sought for treasure in the person of Joseph Smith, Jr., a lad of some eighteen years of age.

He, with the magic stone, was at once transferred from his humble abode to the more pretentious mansion of Deacon Stowell. Here, in the estimation of the Deacon, he confirmed his conceded powers as a seer, by means of the stone which he placed in his hat, and by excluding the light from all other terrestrial things, could see whatever he wished, even in the depths of the earth. This omniscient attribute he firmly claimed. Deacon Stowell and others, as firmly believed it. Mr., Stowell, with his ward and two hired men, who were, or professed to be, believers, spent much time in mining near the State line on the Susquehanna and many other places, I myself have seen the evidences of their nocturnal depredations on the face of Mother Earth, on the Deacon's farm, with what success "this deponent saith not."

In February 1826, the sons of Mr. Stowell, who lived with their father, were greatly incensed against Smith, as they plainly saw their father squandering his property in the fruitless search for hidden treasures, and saw that the youthful seer had unlimited control over the illusions of their sire. They made up their minds that "patience had ceased to a virtue," and resolved to rid themselves and their family from this incubus, who, as they believed, was eating up their substance, and depriving them of their anticipated patrimony. They caused the arrest of Smith as a vagrant, without visible means of livelihood. The trial came on in the above mentioned month, before Albert Neeley, Esq., the father of Bishop Neeley, of the State of Maine. I was an intimate friend of the Justice, and was invited to take notes of the trial, which I did. There was a large collection of persons in attendance, and the proceedings attracted much attention.

William D. Purple

William Stafford Statement on Joseph Smith, Jr.

Manchester, Ontario Co. N. Y. Dec. 8th, 1833

I, William Stafford, having been called upon to give a true statement of my knowledge, concerning the character and conduct of the family of Smiths, known to the world as the founders of the Mormon sect, do say, that I first became acquainted with Joseph, Sen., and his family in the year 1820. They lived, at that time, in Palmyra, about one mile and a half from my residence. A great part of their time was devoted to digging for money: especially in the night time, when they said the money could be most easily obtained. I have heard them tell marvellous tales, respecting the discoveries they had made in their peculiar occupation of money digging. They would say, for instance, that in such a place, in such a hill, on a certain man's farm, there were deposited keys, barrels and hogsheads of coined silver and gold -- bars of gold, golden images, brass kettles filled with gold and silver -- gold candlesticks, swords, &c. &c. They would say, also, that nearly all the hills in this part of New York, were thrown up by human hands, and in them were large caves, which Joseph, Jr., could see, by placing a stone of singular appearance in his hat, in such a manner as to exclude all light; at which time they pretended he could see all things within and under the earth, -- that he could see within the above mentioned caves, large gold bars and silver plates -- that he could also discover the spirits in whose charge these treasures were, clothed in ancient dress. At certain times, these treasures could be obtained very easily; at others, the obtaining of them was difficult. The facility of approaching them, depended in a great measure on the state of the moon. New moon and Good Friday, I believe, were regarded as the most favorable times for obtaining these treasures. These tales I regarded as visionary. However, being prompted by curiosity, I at length accepted of their invitations, to join them in their nocturnal excursions. I will now relate a few incidents attending these excursions.

Joseph Smith, Sen., came to me one night, and told me, that Joseph Jr. had been looking in his glass, and had seen, not many rods from his house, two or three kegs of gold and silver, some feet under the surface of the earth: and that none others but the elder Joseph and myself could get them. I accordingly consented to go, and early in the evening repaired to the place of deposit. Joseph, Sen. first made a circle, twelve or fourteen feet in diameter. This circle, said he, contains the treasure. He then stuck in the ground a row of witch hazel sticks, around the said circle, for the purpose of keeping off the evil spirits. Within this circle he made another, of about eight or ten feet in diameter. He walked around three times on the periphery of this last circle, muttering to himself something which I could not understand. He next stuck a steel rod in the centre of the circles, and then enjoined profound silence upon us, lest we should arouse the evil spirit who had the charge of these treasures. After we had dug a trench about five feet in depth around the rod, the old man by signs and motions, asked leave of absence, and went to the house to inquire of young Joseph the cause of our disappointment. He soon returned and said, that Joseph had remained all this time in the house, looking in his stone and watching the motions of the evil spirit--that he saw the spirit come up to the ring and as soon as it beheld the cone which we had formed around the rod, it caused the money to sink. We then went into the house, and the old man observed, that we had made a mistake in the commencement of the operation; if it had not been for that, said he, we should have got the money.

At another time, they devised a scheme, by which they might satiate their hunger, with the mutton of one of my sheep. They had seen in my flock of sheep, a large, fat, black weather. Old Joseph and one of the boys came to me one day, and said that Joseph Jr. had discovered some very remarkable and valuable treasures, which could be procured only in one way. That way, was as follows: -- That a black sheep should be taken on to the ground where the treasures were concealed -- that after cutting its throat, it should be led around a circle while bleeding. This being done, the wrath of the evil spirit would be appeased: the treasures could then be obtained, and my share of them was to be four fold. To gratify my curiosity, I let them have a large fat sheep. They afterwards informed me, that the sheep was killed pursuant to commandment; but as there was some mistake in the process, it did not have the desired effect. This, I believe, is the only time they ever made money-digging a profitable business. They, however, had around them constantly a worthless gang, whose employment it was to dig money nights, and who, day times, had more to do with mutton than money.

When they found that the people of this vicinity would no longer put any faith in their schemes for digging money, they then pretended to find a gold bible, of which, they said, the book of Mormon was only an introduction. This latter book was at length fitted for the press. No means were taken by any individual to suppress its publication: No one apprehended any danger from a book, originating with individuals who had neither influence, honesty nor honor. The two Josephs and Hiram, promised to show me the plates, after the book of Mormon was translated. But, afterwards, they pretended to have received an express commandment, forbidding them to show the plates. Respecting the manner of receiving and translating the book of Mormon, their statements were always discordant. The elder Joseph would say that he had seen the plates and that he knew them to be gold; at other times he would say that they looked like gold; and other times he would say he had not seen the plates at all. I have thus briefly stated a few of the facts, in relation to the conduct and character of this family of Smiths; probably sufficient has been stated without my going into detail.

WILLIAM STAFFORD.

State of New York, Wayne County, ss:

I certify, that on this 9th day of December, 1833, personally appeared before me, William Stafford, to me known, and made oath to the truth of the above statement, and signed the same.

TH. P. BALDWIN,
Judge of Wane County Court.

William Stafford, a neighbour of Joseph Smith's swore that Joseph Smith told him there was money buried on his property, but that it could not be secured until a black sheep was taken to the spot, "led around a circle" bleeding with its throat cut.

This ritual was necessary to appease the evil spirit guarding the treasure. "To gratify my curiosity," Stafford admitted, "I let them have a large fat sheep. They afterwards informed me that the sheep was killed pursuant to commandment; but as there were some mistakes in the process, it did not have the desired effect. This, I believe is the only time they ever made money digging a profitable business."

MORMONISM IS A SYSTEM OF MONEY MAKING[7]

Such are some of the facts, which are proved beyond the possibility of confutation, by the affidavits of respectable witnesses, persons who were well acquainted with Joseph Smith, jun., and his associates, both before and since the pretended discovery of his golden plates. And, perhaps, we cannot better close the investigation of this subject, than by quoting a specimen of those testimonies. It is numerously signed, as will be seen; and by persons well acquainted with the "author and proprietor" of the book of Mormon: --

PALMYRA, Dec. 4, 1833.

"We, the undersigned, have been acquainted with the Smith family, for a number of years, while they resided near this place, and we have no hesitation in saying, that we consider them destitute of that moral character, which ought to entitle them to the confidence of any community. They were particularly famous for visionary projects, spent much of their time in digging for money, which they pretend was hid in the earth; and to this day, large excavations may be seen in the earth, not far from their, residence, where they used to spend their time in digging for hidden treasures. Joseph Smith, sen., and his son Joseph, were, in particular, considered *entirely destitute of moral character, and addicted to vicious habits.*

Martin Harris was a man who had acquired a handsome property, and in matters of business his word was considered good; but on moral and religious subjects, he was perfectly visionary -- sometimes advocating one sentiment, and sometimes another. And in reference to all with whom we were acquainted, who have embraced Mormonism, from this neighbourhood, we are compelled to say, were very visionary, and most of them destitute of any moral character, and without influence in this community, and this may account why they were permitted to go on with their impositions undisturbed.

It was not supposed that any of them were possessed of sufficient character or influence, to make any one believe their book or their sentiments, and we know not of a single individual in this vicinity that puts the least confidence in their pretended revelations.

W. Parke,

L. Durfee S. Ackley,

E. S. Townsend,

Amos Hollister,

Jesse Townsend,

C. E. Thayer,

D. C. Ely,

T. P. Baldwin,

John Sothington,

G. Beckwith,

Durfy Chase,

W. Anderson,

H. Payne,

A. H. Beckwith,

R. S. Williams,

L. Hurd,

G. S. Ely,

M. Butterfield,

E. D. Robinson,

Pelatian West,

D. S. Jackways,

E. Ensworth,

Linus North,

R. W. Smith,

T. Rogers, 2d,

Clark Robinson,

Josiah Francis,

Josiah Rice,

H. P. Alger,

G. A. Hathaway,

R. D. Clark,

G. W. Anderson,

H. K. Jerome,

H. P. Thayer,

L. Williams,

Lewis Foster,

G. W. Crosby,

Leve Thayer,

P. Grandin,

Philo Durfee,

P. Sexton,

Joel Thayer,

G. N. Williams,

H. Sinnell,

Israel F. Chilson..

The following is taken from an affidavit by Mr. Isaac Hale, father of Emma Smith nee Hale, father-in-law of Joseph Smith Jnr.[8]

I first became acquainted with Joseph Smith, Jun. In November 1825. He was at that time in the employ of a set of men who were called "money-diggers;" and his occupation was that of seeing, or pretending to see by means of a stone placed in his hat, and his hat closed over his face. In this way he pretended to discover minerals and hidden treasures.... Smith, and his father, with several other "money-diggers" boarded at my house... Young Smith gave the "money-diggers" great encouragement, at first, but when they had arrived in digging, to near the place where he had stated an immense treasure would be found-- he said the enchantment was so powerful that he could not see.

After these occurrences, young Smith made several visits at my house... and while I was absent from home, carried off my daughter, into the state of New York, where they were married without my approbation or consent... In a short time they returned...

Smith stated to me, that he had given up what he called "glass-looking," and that he expected to work hard for a living.... He also made arrangements with my son Alva Hale, to go up to Palmyra, and move his (Smith's) furniture &c. to this place...

Soon after this, I was informed they had brought a wonderful book of plates down with them... The manner, in which he pretended to read and interpret, was the same as when he looked for the money-diggers, with the stone in his hat, and his hat over his face, while the book of plates were at the same time hid in the woods!
(Affidavit of Isaac Hale, as printed in the Susquehanna Register, May 1, 1834)

David Whitmer frankly admitted that Joseph Smith placed the "seer stone" into a hat to translate the Book of Mormon[9]

"I will now give you a description of the manner in which the Book of Mormon was translated. Joseph would put the seer stone into a hat, and

236

put his face in the hat, drawing it closely around his face to exclude the light; and in the darkness the spiritual light would shine. A piece of something resembling parchment would appear, and on that appeared the writing"

Emma Smith related the following to her son[10]

"In writing for your father I frequently wrote day after day, sitting by the table close by him, he sitting with his face buried in his hat, with the stone in it, and dictating hour after hour with nothing between us "

Lucy Smith, Joseph Smith's mother wrote

Emma and Joseph brought home the plates on September 22, 1827. Joseph showed her the magic spectacles, which she described as "two smooth three-cornered diamonds set in glass and the glasses set in silver bows."

Divining Rods

The money diggers used diving rods to find buried treasure. They were also used as
"A medium of revelation."

Book of Commandments[11]
This was said to Cowdery. "Now this is not all, for you have another gift, which is the gift of working with the rod: behold it has told you things: behold there is no other power save God that can cause this rod of nature, to work in your hands..."

By the time that Joseph Smith approached the reinterpretation and rewording of this document for the 1835 edition of the Doctrine and Covenants, he had had time and experience necessary to place his 1829 assessment of the meaning of Cowdery's gift of working with the rod in a somewhat more accurate perspective.

Both he and Cowdery had developed away from an emphasis on the religious or mystical meanings in such mechanical objects as the water-witching rod. Joseph's 1835 wording of this document.... Left behind the apparent 1829 reliance on external media, which by 1835 had assumed in Joseph's mind overtones of superstition and speculative experimentation

Doctrine and Covenants

"Now this is not all thy gift, for you have another gift, which is the gift of Aaron; behold it has told you many things;

"Behold there is no other power, save the power of God, that can cause this gift of Aaron to be with you"

Richard P. Howard, RLDS. Reorganized Church of the Latter-Day Saints states in a book published by his Church.

"Several writers have established that both in Vermont and in western New York in the early 1800s, one of the many forms which enthusiastic religion took was the adaptation of the witch hazel stick.... For example, one Nathaniel Wood in Rutland County, Vermont, used the "diving rod" effectively in 1801. Wood, Winchell, William Cowdery, Jr., and his son, Oliver Cowdery, all had some knowledge of and association with the various uses, both secular and sacred, of the forked witch hazel rod. Winchell and others used such a rod in seeking buried treasure... When Joseph Smith met Oliver Cowdery in April 1829, he found a man peculiarly adept in the use of the forked rod... and against the background of his own experiments with and uses of oracular media, Joseph Smith's April, 1829, affirmations about Cowdery's unnatural powers related working the rod are quite understandable."

Joseph Smith continued to hunt for treasure even after he published the Book of Mormon.

Old Testament, Deuteronomy Chapter 18 verses 10-11

10. There shall not be found among you any that maketh his son or daughter to pass through the fire, or that useth divination, or an observer of times, or an enchanter, or a witch.

11. *or a charmer, or a consulter with familiar spirits, or a wizard, or a necromancer.*

Div·i·na·tion

The practice of attempting to foretell future events or discover hidden knowledge by occult or supernatural means.

Daniel Henrix, who helped set type for the Book of Mormon, once wrote that Joseph had "jovial, easy, don't-care way about him that made him a lot of warm friends. He was a good talker, and would have made a fine stump speaker if he had had the training. He was known among the young men I associated with as a romancer of the first water. I never knew so ignorant a man as Joe was to have such a fertile imagination. He could never tell a common occurrence in his daily life without embellishing the story with his imagination; yet I remember that he was grieved one day when old Parson Reed told Joe that he was going to hell for his lying habits."

Lucy Smith had cherished the details of several of her husband's (Joseph Smith Snr's.) dreams. The similarities in this dream are so close to the Lehi's Vision in the Book of Mormon.

Dream of Joseph Smith, Sr.[12]

I thought I was thus travelling in an open and desolate field, which appeared very barren..., a tree, such as I had never seen before... I found it delicious beyond description. As I was eating, I said in my heart, "I cannot eat this alone; I must bring my wife and children."...
I beheld a beautiful stream of water, which ran from the east to the west...
I could see a rope running along the bank of it...
I beheld a spacious building... filled with people, who were very finely dressed.
When these people observed us in the low valley, under the tree, they pointed the finger of scorn at us.

Lehi's Vision. (Book of Mormon (1830), pp. 18-20)

... Me thought I saw a dark and dreary wilderness....
I beheld a tree, whose fruit was desirable to make one happy... most
sweet above all that I ever had before tasted.
.... I began to be desirous that my family should partake of it also...
And I beheld a rod of iron; and it extended along the bank of the river,
and led to the tree...
... a great and spacious building... filled with people, both old and young,
both male and female; and their manner of dress was exceeding fine, and
they were in the attitude of mocking and pointing their finger towards
those which had come at, and were partaking of the fruit.

Benjamin F. Johnson[13]
Recalled how Joseph Smith sometimes lost his temper and resorted to
physical violence:

"And yet, although so social and even convivial [sic] at times, he would
allow no arrogance or undue liberties. Criticisms, even by his associates,
were rarely acceptable. Contradictions would arouse in him the lion at
once. By no one of his fellows would he be superseded. In the early days
at Kirtland, and elsewhere, one or another of his associates were more
than once, for their impatience, helped from the congregation by his
foot... He soundly thrashed his brother William... While with him
in such fraternal, social and sometimes convivial moods, we could not
then so fully realize the greatness and majesty of his calling. But since
his martyrdom, it has continued to magnify in our view as the glories of
this last dispensation have more fully unfolded to our comprehension".

Entry from Joseph Smith's diary records: January 1 and 2, 1843, Joseph
Smith related that he had "whipped "seven men at once and on another
occasion had "whipped "a Baptist minister
"till he begged".

Four years after Joseph Smith published the Book of Mormon; he
organized an army and marched to Missouri to 'redeem Zion.' This
project was a complete failure.

At Nauvoo, Illinois, the Mormons organized the Nauvoo Legion. Bruce Flanders explains[14]

"The crowning provision of the charter gave the city its own little army, the famous Nauvoo Legion... The Legion was therefore independent of and not subject to the military laws of Illinois"

Mormon writer Hyrum L. Andrus[15]
Recorded of the Prophet's appearance as Lieutenant General at the head of the Nauvoo Legion.

Lyman L. Woods recalled, "I have seen him on a white horse wearing the uniform of a general... He was leading a parade of the Legion and looked like a god" (Joseph Smith, The Man And The Seer, p.5).

In the History of the Church[16]
Dated May 7, 1842

"The Nauvoo Legion. Was reviewed by Lieutenant-General Joseph Smith, who commanded through the day... At the close of the parade, Lieutenant-General Joseph Smith remarked, "that his soul was never better satisfied than on this occasion"

In 1843 a reporter who visited Joseph Smith wrote[17]

We spent about an hour conversing on various subjects, the prophet himself, with amazing volubility, occupying the most of the time, and his whole theme was himself. Let us give what turn we would to the conversation, he would adroitly bring it back to himself... He said: "The world persecutes me, it has always persecuted me... When I have proved that I am right, and get all the world subdued under me, I think I shall deserve something".

Joseph Smith set up a secret "Council of Fifty" and had himself ordained to be a King.

In 1853 William Marks, who had been a member of the Council of Fifty[18]

"I was also witness of the introduction (secretly,) of a kingly form of government, in which Joseph suffered himself to be ordained a king, to reign over the house of Israel forever; which I could not conceive to be in accordance with the laws of the Church, but I did not oppose this move, thinking it none of my business"
(Zion's Harbinger and Baneemy's Organ, St. Louis, July, 1853, p.53)

Kenneth W. Godfrey, who was director of the LDS Institute at Stanford University, admitted that Joseph Smith was "ordained ' King over the immediate House of Israel' by the Council of Fifty" (Brigham Young University Studies, Winter 1968, pp. 212-13).

Among other things, Dr. Godfrey's footnote refers to the
"Diary of George A. Smith, May 8, 1844," which is in the "Library of the Church Historian."
In a dissertation written at Brigham Young University, Dr. Godfrey observed:

Davidson states that Joseph Smith had himself anointed King and Priest. In a revelation dated 1886 given to President John Taylor, mention is made of Joseph Smith being crowned a king in Nauvoo. Not only was he ordained a king but the leading members of the Church were assigned governmental responsibilities. Brigham Young was to be president, John Taylor vice president, members of the Church were assigned to represent different states in the house and senate of the United States, and a full cabinet was appointed.
(Causes of Mormon Non-Mormon Conflict in Hancock County, Illinois, 1839-1846," Ph.D. dissertation, BYU, 1967, pp. 63-65) As quoted in *The Changing World of Mormonism. Jerald & Sandra Tanner.*

In 1844 the Council of Fifty decided to put forward Joseph Smith to run for the presidency of the United States. At a special meeting of the Elders on April 9, 1844, Brigham Young declared:
"It is now time to have a President of the United States. Elders will be sent to preach the Gospel and electioneer" (History of the Church, vol. 6, p.322).

The Nauvoo Expositor was a newspaper in Nauvoo, Illinois that published only one issue, which was dated June 7th 1844. Several disaffected associates of Joseph Smith Jnr. some of whom claimed that Smith had attempted to seduce their wives in the name of plural marriage founded the Expositor.

The bulk of the *Expositor's* single issue was devoted to criticism of Smith, who was also the mayor of Nauvoo and founder of the Latter Day Saint Movement. After two days of consultation, Smith and the Nauvoo city council voted on June 10, 1844 to declare the paper a public nuisance, and ordered the paper's printing press destroyed. The town marshal carried out the order that evening. These actions generated considerable disturbance, and culminated in Smiths' assassination by a vigilante group while he was in legal custody and awaiting a trial in nearby Carthage jail.

11th Article of Faith

11. We claim the privilege of worshipping Almighty God according to the dictates of our own conscience, and allow all men the same privilege, let them worship how, where, or what they may.

Mormons believe that Joseph Smith went to his death like a lamb to the slaughter, without putting up a struggle.

In the History of the Church the following account is given.

Immediately there was little rustling at the outer door of the jail, and a cry of surrender, and also a discharge of three or four firearms followed instantly.... Joseph sprang to his coat for his six-shooter, Hyrum for his single barrel...

When Hyrum fell, Joseph exclaimed, " Oh dear, brother Hyrum!" and opening the door a few inches he discharged his six shooter in the stairway (as stated before), two or three barrels of missed fire.

Joseph, seeing there was no safety in the room, and no doubt thinking that it would save the lives of his brethren in the room if he could get out, turned calmly from the door, dropped his pistol on the floor, and sprang into the window... and he fell outward into the hands of his murderers... (History of the Church, vol. 6, pp. 617-18)
As quoted in *The Changing World of Mormonism* Sandra & Jerald Tanner

Address of the Prophet-- His Testimony Against the Dissenters at Nauvoo

(Sunday, May 26, 1844)

God is in the still small voice. In all these affidavits, indictments, it is all of the devil-- all corruption. Come on! Ye prosecutors! Ye false swearers! All hell boil over! Ye burning mountains roll down your lava! For I will come out on top at last. I have more to boast of than ever any man had. I am the only man that has ever been able to keep a whole Church together since the days of Adam. A large majority of the whole have stood by me. Neither Paul, John, Peter, nor Jesus ever did it. I boast that no man ever did such a work as I. The followers of Jesus ran away from Him; but the Latter-Day Saints never ran away from me yet. You know my daily walk and conversation. I am in the bosom of a virtuous and good people. How I do love to hear the wolves howl! When they can get rid of me, the devil will also go.

Notes

1. Affidavit by Wesley P. Walters, dated Oct. 28, 1971
2. *Frazer's Magazine, February, 1873, pp. 229-30*
3. *Joseph Smith—Seeker After Truth*, Salt Lake City, 1951, p. 78
4. *(As quoted in The Changing World of* Mormonism Jerald & Sandra Tanner. P. 71-72)
5. *Evangelical Magazine and Gospel Advocate, April 9, 1831, p.120*
6. William D. Purple (1803-1886) *"Joseph Smith, The Originator of Mormonism"*
7. *AN EXPOSURE OF MORMONISM, BEING A STATEMENT OF FACTS RELATING TO THE SELF-STYLED "LATTER DAY SAINTS," And the Origin of the Book of Mormon. P.4-5.* BY RICHARD LIVESEY, MINISTER OF THE METHODIST EPISCOPAL CHURCH. 1838
8. *Affidavit of Isaac Hale, as printed in the Susquehanna Register, May 1, 1834*
9. *An Address To All Believers In Christ*, David Whitmer, p.12
10. *The Saints' Herald, May 19, 1888, p. 310*
11. (Restoration Scriptures, Independence, Mo., 1969, pp. 211-14) As Quoted in *The Changing World of Mormonism.* Jerald & Sandra Tanner. p 86-87
12. *Lucy Smith: Biographical Sketches, pp. 58-9.*
13. *Letter by Benjamin F. Johnson, 1903, as printed in the Testimony of Joseph Smith's Best Friend, pp. 4-5*
14. *Nauvoo: Kingdom On The Mississippi, p.100*
15. *Joseph Smith, The Man And The Seer, p.5*
16. *History of the Church, May 7, 1842 (Vol. 5, p.3)*
17. *The New York Spectator, September 23, 1843*
18. *Zion's Harbinger and Baneemy's Organ, St. Louis, July, 1853, p.53*

CHAPTER SIXTEEN

The following letters were written by Ezra Booth, a Methodist Clergyman, and addressed to a presiding Elder. Ezra was an early convert to Mormonism, and renounced it as soon as he was fully convinced of its nature and design. They were originally published in the Ohio Star.

Ezra Booth letters

LETTER I.
NELSON, Portage Co. Sept. 1831.
Rev. Ira Eddy ---
Dear Sir: I received yours of the 2d inst. and heartily thank you for the favour. It revives afresh in my recollection the scenes of past years, upon the remembrance of which, I dwell with a mixture of pleasurable and painful sensations. I arrived at my home on the 1st of the present month, having finished my tour to the west; since which time the scenes and events in the history of my life, for the last few months, have passed in review before my mind.
You are not, it is probable, ignorant of the designs of my most singular and romantic undertaking: sufficient to say, it was for the purpose of exploring the promised land -- laying the foundation of the city of Zion, and placing the corner stone of the temple of God. A journey of one thousand miles to the west, has taught me far more abundantly, than I should have probably learned from any other
176b
source. It has taught me quite beyond my knowledge, the imbecility of human nature, and especially my own weakness. It has unfolded in its proper character, a delusion to which I had fallen a victim, and taught me the humiliating truth, that I was exerting the powers of both my mind and body, and sacrificing my time and property, to build up a system of delusion, almost

unparalleled in the annals of the world.

If God be a God of consistency and wisdom I now know Mormonism to be a delusion; and this knowledge is built upon the testimony of my senses. In proclaiming it, I am aware I proclaim my own misfortune -- but in doing it, I remove a burden from my mind, and discharge a duty as humbling to myself, as it may be profitable to others. You had heard the story of my wanderings, and "was induced to believe that I had been visited with a species of mental derangement," and therefore, you "had given me up, as one among those friends of early association, who in the lapse of time, would be as though they had not existed." You had concluded that the magic charm of delusion and falsehood, had so wrapped its sable mantle around me, as to exclude the light of truth and secure me a devoted slave. But thanks be to God! The spell is dissipated, and the "captive exile hasteneth that he may be loosed, and not die in the pit." When I embraced Mormonism, I conscientiously believed it to be of God. The impressions of my mind were deep and powerful, and my feelings were excited to a degree to which I had been a stranger. Like a ghost, it haunted me by night and by day, until I was mysteriously hurried, as it were, by a kind of necessity, into the vortex of delusion. -- At times I was much elated; but generally, things in prospect were the greatest stimulants to action. On our arrival in the western part of the State of Missouri

177

the place of our destination, we discovered that prophecy and vision had failed, or rather had proved false. -- The fact was so notorious, and the evidence so clear, that no one could mistake it -- so much so, that Mr. Rigdon himself said, "Joseph's vision was a bad thing." This was glossed over, apparently, to the satisfaction of most persons present; but not fully to my own. It excited a suspicion that some things were not right, and prepared my mind for the investigation of a variety of circumstances, which occurred during my residence there, and indeed, to review the whole subject, from its commencement to that time. My opportunities for a thorough investigation were far greater than they could have been, had I remained at home; and therefore, I do not regret that I made the journey, though I sincerely regret the cause of it. Since my return, I have had several interviews with Messrs. Smith, Rigdon and Cowdery, and the various shifts and turns, to which they resorted in order to obviate objectors and difficulties, produced in my mind additional evidence, that there was nothing else than a deeply laid plan of craft and deception. The relation in which Smith stands to the Church, is that of a Prophet, Seer, Revealer, and Translator; and when he speaks by the Spirit, or says he knows a thing by the communication of the Spirit, it is received as coming directly from the mouth of the Lord. When he says he knows a thing to be so, thus it must stand without controversy. A question is agitated between two Elders of the Church -- whether or not a bucket of water will become heavier by putting a living fish in it. Much is said by each of the disputants; when at length, Smith decides in the negative, by saying -- "I know by the spirit, that it will be no heavier." Any person, who chooses, may easily ascertain by actual experiment, whether the Prophet was influenced in this decision by a true or false spirit.

178

It is not my design, at this time, to enter into particulars relative to the evidence upon which my renunciation of Mormonism is founded. This evidence is derived from various sources, and is clear and full, and the conviction, which it produces, at least on my mind, is irresistible. You are not aware of the nature of this deception, and the spirit that uniformly attends it; nor can you ever know it, unless you yield to its influence, and by experience learn what it is to fall under its power: "from which my earnest prayer is, that you may ever, ever escape." There probably never was a plan better suited to lead the sinner and the conscientious, when in an unguarded hour they listen to its fatal insinuations. The plan is so ingeniously contrived, having for its aim one principal point, viz: the establishment of a society in Missouri, over which the contrivers of this delusive system, are to possess unlimited and despotic sway. To accomplish this, the Elders of the Church, by commandment given in Missouri, and of which I was both an eye and an ear witness, are to go forth to preach Mormonism to every creature; and now, said Mr. Rigdon --"The Lord has set us our stint; no matter how soon we perform it -- for when this is done, he will make his second appearance." I do sincerely, and I trust in deep humility, return unfeigned gratitude to the God of infinite mercy, who, in condescension to my weakness, by a peculiar train of providences, brought me to the light, enabled me to see the hidden things of darkness, and delivered me from the snare of the fowler, and from the contagious pestilence which threatened my entire destruction. The scenes of the past few months are so different from all others in my life, that they are in truth to me "as a dream when one awaketh." Had my fall affected only myself, my reflections would be far less painful than they now are. But to know -- that whatever influence

179

I may have possessed, has been exerted to draw others into a delusion, from which they may not soon be extricated, is to me a source of sorrow and deep regret. They are at this moment the object of my greatest anxiety and commiseration. I crave their forgiveness, and assure them, that they will ever have an interest in my addresses to the throne of grace. It shall be my endeavour to undo, as far as possible, what I have done in this case, and also to prevent the spread of a delusion, pernicious in its influence, and destructive in its consequences to the body and the soul -- to the present and eternal interests of all men. I am, through restoring mercy and grace, as in former years, though unworthily, yet affectionately yours in Christ, EZRA BOOTH.

LETTER II.

Were there none but myself interested in the exposition of Mormonism, I can assure you my time would be otherwise employed than in writing upon a subject which has heretofore been to me one of deep interest, and at times has occasioned a painful anxiety of mind. I could wish, if possible, to bury it in oblivion; and to remember it no more forever. But as this is a thing which cannot be accomplished in a moment, for the sake of others, who may be exposed to the delusion, from which, through the mercy of God, I have been recovered, and others who are at present involved in it: and also in compliance with your request, I will, as far as I have

ability, unfold a system of darkness, fraught with glaring absurdity, and deceptive as falsehood itself. This system, to some, carries the face of plausibility, and appears under an imposing form. It claims the Bible for its patron and proffers the restoration of the apostolic Church, with all the gifts and graces with which the primitive saints
180
were endowed. It is called the fullness of the gospel of both Jew and Gentile: and is the test by which every man's faith is to be tried. Judgments are denounced against the sinners of this generation; or in other words, all who reject the Book of Mormon, are threatened with eternal damnation. Great promises are made to such as embrace it, signs and wonders are to attend them, such as healing the sick, the blind made to see, the lame to walk, &c,; and they are to receive an everlasting inheritance in "the land of Missouri," where the Saviour will make his second appearance; at which place the foundation of the temple of God, and the City of Zion, have been laid, and are soon to be built. It is also to be a city of Refuge, and a safe asylum when the storms of vengeance shall pour upon the earth, and those who reject the Book of Mormon, shall be swept off as with the besom of destruction. Then shall the riches of the Gentiles be consecrated to the Mormonites; they shall have lands and cattle in abundance, and shall possess the gold and silver, and all the treasures of their enemies. The Mormonite preachers go forth proclaiming repentance and baptism for the remission of sins, and the laying on of hands for the reception of the Holy Ghost. The form of baptism is similar to other orders; only it is prefaced with -- "having authority given me of Jesus Christ;" also, the laying on of hands -- "In the name of Jesus Christ, receive ye the Holy Ghost." Many of them have been ordained to the High Priesthood, or the order of Melchisedec; and profess to be endowed with the same power as the ancient apostles were. But they have been hitherto unsuccessful in finding the lame, the halt, and the blind, who had faith sufficient to become the subjects of their miracles: and it is now concluded that this work must be postponed until they get to Missouri; for the Lord will not show those signs

181

to this wicked and adulterous generation. In the commandment
given to the Churches in the State of New York, to remove to the
State of Ohio, they were assured that these miracles should be
wrought in the State of Ohio; but now they must be deferred until
they are settled in Missouri. As the Mormonite Church depends
principally upon the commandments, and as most of them are
concealed from the world, it will be necessary to make some
statement respecting them. These commandments come from
Smith, at such times and on such occasions as he feels disposed
to speak, and Rigdon or Cowdery to write them. Their exact
number I have never taken pains to ascertain. I have the "27th
commandment to Emma my daughter in Zion;" and should
presume there are betwixt fifty and a hundred. -- They received
the addition of five or six while in Missouri; and these are
considered a miracle in themselves, sufficient to convince any
rational mind. But none but the strong in faith are permitted to
witness their origin. I had an opportunity of seeing this wonderful
exhibition of the wisdom and power of God, at three different
times; and I must say, that it bore striking marks of human
weakness and wickedness. They are received in the Church as
divinely inspired, and the name of the Lord is substituted for that
of Smith. They are called "The Commandments of the Lord," They
are considered "The mysteries of the Kingdom;" and to divulge
them to the world, is the same as casting pearls before swine.
When they and the Scriptures are at variance, the Scriptures are
wrongly translated; and Smith, though totally ignorant of the
original, being a translator or an alterator, can easily harmonize
them. Every thing in the Church is done by commandment: and yet
it is said to be done by the voice of the Church. For instance,
Smith gets a commandment that he shall be the "head of the
Church," or that he "shall rule the Conference," or that the Church
182
shall build him an elegant house, and give him 1000 dollars. For this
the members of the Church must vote, or they will be cast off for
revelling against the commandments of the Lord. In addition to the
Book of Mormon, and the commandments, there are revelations

, which are not written. -- In this department, though Smith is the principal, yet there are others who profess to receive revelations; but after all, Smith is to decide whether they come from the Lord or the devil. Some have been so unfortunate as to have their revelations palmed off upon the latter. These revelations entirely supersede the Bible, and in fact, the Bible is declared too defective to be trusted, in its present form; and it is designed that it shall undergo a thorough alteration, or as they say, translation. This work is now in operation. The Gospel of St. Matthew has already received the purifying touch, and is prepared for the use of the Church. It was intended to have kept this work a profound secret, and strict commandments were given for that purpose; and even the salvation of the Church was said to depend upon it. The secret is divulged, but the penalty is not as yet inflicted. -- Their revelations are said to be an addition to the Bible. -- But instead of being an addition, they destroy its use; for everything, which need be known, whether present, past or future, they can learn from Smith, for he has declared to the Church, that he "knows all things that will take place from this time to the end of the world." If then, placing the Bible under circumstances, which render it entirely useless, is infidelity, Mormonism is infidelity. Joseph Smith, Jun., Sidney Rigdon, Oliver Cowdery and Martin Harris, may be considered as the principals in this work; and let Martin Harris tell the story, and he is the most conspicuous of the four. -- He informed me, that he went to the place where Joseph resided, and Joseph had given it up, on account of the opposition of his wife and

183

others; but he told Joseph. "I have not come down here for nothing, and we will go on with it." Martin Harris is what may be called a great talker, and extravagant boaster; so much so, that he renders himself disagreeable to many of his society. The money he has expended, and the great things he has done, form a considerable topic of his conversation; he understands all prophecies, and knows every thing by the spirit, and he can silence almost any opposer by talking faster, and louder than he can: or by telling him, "I know every thing and you know nothing:

I am a wise man and you are a fool;" and in this respect he
stands a fair sample of many others in the Church. Yours
affectionately, E. BOOTH.
LETTER III.
Mormonism has in part changed its character, and assumed a
different dress, from that under which it made its first appearance
on the Western Reserve. Many extraordinary circumstances which
then existed have vanished out of sight; and the Mormonites
desire, not only to forget them, but wish them blotted out of the
memory of others. Those wonders, which they wish to have
forgotten, stand as the principal foundation of the faith of several
hundred of the members of their Church. With the wonders of
Mormonism, or some of them, I design to occupy your attention in
this letter; and I wish you to observe here, and hereafter
remember, that the evidence by which all my statements are
supported, is derived from my own experience and observation, or
from testimony of persons who still adhere to Mormonism; and I
hold myself responsible to any tribunal, whether on earth or in
heaven, for the truth of what I write, or at least for an intention
to write the truth, and nothing but the truth. "Being carried away
by the spirit" and "I know it to be
184
so by the spirit," are well known phrases, and in common use in
the Mormonite Church. We will first notice the gift of tongues,
exercised by some when carried away in the spirit. These persons
were apparently lost to all surrounding circumstances, and wrapt
up in the contemplation of things, and in communion with persons
not present. -- They articulated sounds, which but few persons
professed to understand; and those few declared them to be the
Indian language. A merchant, who had formerly been a member of
the Methodist society, observed, he had formerly traded with the
Indians, and he knew it to be their dialect. Being myself present on
one of these occasions, a person proffered his services as my
interpreter, and translated these sounds to me, which were
unintelligible, into English language. One individual could read any
chapter of the Old or New Testament, in several different
languages. This was known to be the case by a person who

professed to understand those languages. In the midst of this
delirium they would, at times, fancy themselves addressing a
congregation of their red brethren; mounted on a stump, or the
fence, or from some elevated situation, would harangue their
assembly until they had convinced or converted them. They would
then lead them into the water, and baptize them, and pronounce
their sins forgiven. In this exercise, some of them actually went
into the water; and in the water, performed the ceremony used in
baptizing. These actors assumed the visage of the savage, and so
nearly imitated him, not only in language, but in gestures and
actions, that it seemed the soul and body were completely
metamorphosed into the Indian. No doubt was then entertained
but that was an extraordinary work of the Lord, designed to
prepare those young men for the Indian mission; and many who are
still leaders of the Church, could say, "we know by the spirit that
it is the work of the Lord." And now
185
they can say, "they know it is the work of the devil." Most of
those who were the principal actors have since apostatised, and
the work is unanimously discarded by the Church. The limits which
my want of time to write, as well as your want of patience to read
compel me to prescribe for myself, will allow me only to touch on
some of the most prominent parts of this newly invented and
heterogeneous system. A new method of obtaining authority to
preach the Gospel was introduced into the Church. One declared
he had received a commission, directly from Heaven, written upon
parchment. Another, that it was written upon the palm of his hand,
and upon the lid of his Bible, &c. three witnesses, and they were
formerly considered persons of veracity, testified they saw the
parchment, or something like it, when put into the hands of the
candidate. These commissions, when transcribed upon a piece of
paper, were read to the Church, and the persons who had received
them, were ordained to the Elder's office, and sent out into the
world to preach. But this also sunk into discredit, and experienced
the fate of the former. Visions also, were in high credit, and
sounded abroad as an infallible testimony in favour of Mormonism.
The visionary, at times, imagined he saw the city of New

Jerusalem, unlocked its gate, and entered within the walls; passed through its various apartments, and then returned, locked the gate, and put the key into his pocket. When this tour was finished, he would entertain admiring friends, with a detailed description of the Heavenly City. The condition of the ten tribes of Israel since their captivity, unto the present time, has excited considerable anxiety, and given rise to much speculation among the learned. But after all the researches, which have been made, the place of their residence has never been satisfactorily ascertained.

186

But these visionaries have discovered their place of residence to be contiguous to the North Pole; separated from the rest of the world by impassable mountains of ice and snow. In this sequestered residence, they enjoy the society of Elijah the Prophet, and John the Revelator, and perhaps the three immortalized Nephites -- By and by, the mountains of ice and snow are to give way, and open a passage for the return of these tribes, to the land of Palestine. About this time the ministration of angels was supposed to be frequent in the Church. The heavenly visitants made their appearance to certain individuals: they seldom made any communication, but presented themselves as spectacles to be gazed upon, with silent admiration. Smith is the only one at present, to my knowledge, who pretends to hold converse with the inhabitants of the celestial world. It seems, from his statements, that he can have access to them when and where he pleases. He does not pretend that he sees them with his natural, but with his spiritual, eyes; and he says he can see them as well with his eyes shut, as with them open. So also in the translating. The subject stands before his eyes in print, but it matters not whether his eyes are open or shut; he can see as well one way as the other. You have probably read the testimony of the three witnesses appended to the Book of Mormon. These witnesses testify that an angel appeared to them, and presented them the golden plates, and the voice of God declared it to be a divine record. To this they frequently testify, in the presence of large congregations. When in Missouri, I had an opportunity to examine a commandment given to these witnesses, previous to their seeing the plates. They were

informed that they should see and hear these things by faith, and then they should testify to the world, as though
187
they had seen and heard, as I see a man, and hear his voice: but after all, it amounts simply to this -- that by faith or imagination, they saw the plates and the angel, and by faith or imagination they heard the voice of the Lord. Smith describes an angel as having the appearance of a "tall, slim, well-built, handsome man, with a bright pillar upon his head." The devil once, he says, appeared to him in the same form, excepting upon his head he had a "black pillar," and by this mark he was able to distinguish him from the former. It passes for a current fact in the Mormon Church, that there are immense treasures in the earth, especially in those places in the state of New-York from whence many of the Mormons emigrated last spring: and when they become sufficiently purified, these treasures are to be poured into the lap of their Church; to use their own language, they are to be the richest people in the world. These treasures were discovered several years since, by means of the dark glass, the same with which Smith says he translated the most of the Book of Mormon. Several of those persons, together with Smith, who were unsuccessfully engaged in digging and searching for these treasures, now reside in this county, and from themselves I received this information. EZRA BOOTH
LETTER IV.
From the time that Mormonism first made its appearance upon the stage, until the grand tour of the Missouri, an expectation universally pervaded the Church, that the time was not far distant, when the deaf, the dumb, the maimed, the blind, &c. would become the subjects of the miraculous power of God, so that every defect in their systems would be entirely removed. This expectation originated from, and was grounded upon
188
a variety of premises, included in a number of commandments, or verbal revelations from Smith, or, as he is styled "the head of the Church." As the 4th of June last was appointed for the sessions of the conference, it was ascertained, that that was the time

specified, when the great and mighty work was to be commenced, and such was the confidence of some, that knowledge superseded their faith, and they did not hesitate to declare themselves perfectly assured that the work of miracles would commence at the ensuing conference. With such strong assurances, and with the most elevated expectations, the conference assembled at the time appointed. To give, if possible, energy to expectation, Smith, the day before the conference, professing to be filled with the spirit of prophecy, declared, "Not three days should pass away, before some should see their Savior, face to face." Soon after the session commenced, Smith arose to harangue the conference. He reminded those present of the prophecy, which he said "was given by the spirit yesterday." He wished them not to be overcome with surprise, when that event ushered in. He continued, until by long speaking, himself and some others became much excited. He then laid his hands on the head of Elder Wight, who had participated largely in the warm feeling of his leader, and ordained him to the High Priesthood. He was set apart for the service of the Indians, and was ordained to the gift of tongues, healing the sick, casting out devils, and discerning spirits; and in like manner he ordained several others; and then called upon Wight to take the floor. Wight arose, and presented a pale countenance, a fierce look, with arms extended, and his hands cramped back, the whole system agitated, and a very unpleasant object to look upon. He exhibited himself as an instance of the great power of God, and called upon those around him "if you want to see a sign, look at me." He then

189

stepped upon a bench, and declared with a loud voice, he saw the Savior: and thereby, for the time being, rescued Smith's prophecy from merited contempt. -- It, however, procured Wight the authority to ordain the rest. So said the spirit, and so said Smith. The spirit in Smith selected those to be ordained, and the spirit in Wight ordained them. But the spirit in Wight proved an erring dictator; so much so, that some of the candidates felt the weight of hands thrice, before the work was rightly done. Another Elder, who had been ordained to the same office as Wight, at the bidding of Smith, stepped upon the floor. Then ensued a scene, of which you can form no adequate conception; and which, I would forbear relating, did not the truth require it. The Elder moved upon the floor, his legs inclining to a bend; one shoulder elevated above the other, upon which the head seemed disposed to recline, his arms partly extended; his hands partly clenched; his mouth partly open, and contracted in the shape of an italic O; his eyes assumed a wild ferocious cast, and his whole appearance presented a frightful object to the view of the beholder. -- "Speak, Brother Harvey" said Smith. But Harvey intimated by signs, that his power of articulation was in a state of suspense, and that he was unable to speak. Some conjectured that Harvey was possessed of the devil, but Smith said, "The Lord binds in order to set at liberty." After different opinions had been given, and there had been much confusion, Smith learnt by the spirit, that Harvey was under a diabolical influence, and that Satan had bound him; and he commanded the unclean spirit to come out of him. It now became clearly manifest, that "the man of sin was revealed," for the express purpose that the elders should become acquainted with the devices of Satan; and after that they would possess knowledge sufficient to manage him. This, Smith declared to be a miracle, and his success in

190

this case, encouraged him to work other and different miracles. Taking the hand of one of the Elders in his own, a hand which by accident had been rendered defective, he said, "Brother Murdock, I command you in the name of Jesus Christ to straighten your hand;" in the mean while endeavouring to accomplish the work by using his own hand to open the hand of the other. The effort proved unsuccessful; but he again articulated the same commandment, in a more authoritative and louder tone of voice; and while uttering with his tongue, his hands were at work; but after all the exertion of his power, both natural and supernatural, the deficient hand returned to its former position, where it still remains. But ill success in this case, did not discourage him from undertaking another. One of the Elders who was decrepit in one of his legs, was set upon the floor, and commanded, in the name of

Jesus Christ to walk. He walked a step or two, his faith failed, and he was again compelled to have recourse to his former assistant, and he has had occasion to use it ever since. A dead body which had been retained above ground two or three days, under the expectation that the dead would be raised, was insensible to the voice of those who commanded it to awake into life, and is destined to sleep in the grave till the last trump shall sound, and the power of God easily accomplishes the work, which frustrated the attempts, and bid defiance to the puny efforts of the Mormonite. ** That an attempt was made to raise the child is denied, of course, as every other attempt has been, after the entire failure was obvious to all. The parents of the deceased child, however, state, that they were prevented from procuring medical aid for the child, by the representations of the elders, that there was no danger -- that it would certainly be restored. The father had no other idea but that the child was to be raised; neither did his faith fail him till preparations were made for its interment. He then awoke from his dream of delusion, and dissolved his connection with the impostors.

191

Under these discouraging circumstances, the horizon of Mormonism gathered darkness, and a storm seemed to hang impending over the Church. The gloom of disappointed expectation overspread the countenances of many, while they laboured to investigate the cause of this failure. To add. If possible, to their mortification, a larger assembly collected on the Sabbath, in order to hear preaching. In the midst of the meeting the congregation was dismissed by Rigdon, and the people sent to their homes. He was directed to do this, he said, by the spirit. But it was generally believed, that he was directed solely by fear; and that he had mistaken the spirit of cowardice, for the spirit of the Lord. Several of the Elders said they "felt the spirit to preach" to the congregation: and Rigdon felt the spirit to send the people home: such was the unity which then prevailed among them. You will doubtless say, can it be possible that the minds of men, and men who possess the appearance of honesty, can be so strangely infatuated, as still to adhere to a system, after it had occasioned

so much agitation, and so much disappointment. One reason which can be assigned for this, is, the adherents are generally inclined to consider the system so perfect, as to admit of no suspicion; and the confusion and disappointment, are attributed to some other cause. Another, and principal reason is, delusion always effects the mind with a species of delirium, and this delirium arises in a degree proportionate to the magnitude of the delusion. These men, upon other subjects, will converse like other men; but when their favourite system is brought into view, its inconsistencies and contradictions are resolved into inexplicable mystery; and this will not only apply to the delusions now under consideration, but in my view, to every delusion, from the highest to the lowest; and it matters
not whether it carries the stamp of popularity or its opposite.
Yours affectionately, EZRA BOOTH
192

LETTER V.
In my last letter I gave you a faint representation of the events which transpired and the circumstances which attended the meeting of the Mormonite Conference. Though many stumbled, yet none irrecoverably fell. Another grand object was presented, and the attention was somewhat diverted from these scenes of disappointment, through which we had recently passed. The tour to the Missouri, revived the sinking expectations, and gave new energy to faith and hope. In that distant region, anticipation was to be realized in full, and the objects of faith and hope, were to become the objects of knowledge and fruition. A commandment was received, and Elders were directed to take their journey for the "promised land." They were commanded to go two by two, with the exception of Rigdon, Smith, Harris, and Partridge; and it was designed that these should find an easier method of transporting themselves, than to travel that distance on foot. They were careful to make suitable provision for themselves, both in money and other articles, that while on their journey, they might carry the appearance of gentlemen filling some important station in life; while many, who were destined to travel on foot, with packs on

their backs, were so fixed with the ardor of enthusiasm, that they
supposed they could travel to Missouri with but little or no money.
These carried the appearance, and were justly entitled to the
character of beggars, for when the little money they took with
them was expended; they subsisted by begging, until they arrived
at their journey's end. Being myself one of the number selected to
perform the journey by land, and not being much accustomed to
travel

193

on foot, I hesitated for a while; but believing it to be the will of
God, I resolved on an unreserved surrender of myself to the work,
and on the 15th of June, in company with one appointed to travel
with me, took up my line of march for Missouri. I do not design to
trouble you with a relation of the particulars, but will observe, that
after I left the north part of the State of Ohio, I made a speedy
and prosperous journey to Missouri. I preached twice in Ohio,
thrice in Indiana, once in Illinois, and once in Missouri. We were
commanded to preach by the spirit, and my impressions were, that
farther to the westward, I should enjoy more of the spirit's
influence; and though I travelled one thousand miles to the west,
my anticipations in this respect, were never realized. I seldom
proclaimed Mormonism with that liberty which I enjoyed in my
public exercises, while a member of the Methodist Episcopal
Church. I supposed that at some future time, the spirit would
endow me to preach with an unusual degree of liberty. That period
has never arrived, and I am persuaded it never will, and I now
sincerely desire the spirit of truth to direct my pen, while I
endeavour to expose the errors and absurdities of the system I then
advocated. When we arrived at the place to which our mission
destined us, we perceived to our mortification, that
disappointment, instead of being confined to the State of Ohio,
had journeyed thither before us. We would gladly have avoided
here an interview with this, our old companion; but this was
impossible, she met us, and stared us in the face which way
soever we turned, nor was it possible to look her out of
countenance, or put the blush upon her pallid features, or expel
her from our society. Some were for making the best of her they

could; but for myself, I resolved that she should be expelled, or at any rate, that her visits should be less frequent, or I would abandon the habituation entirely.

194

When we commenced our journey for Missouri, we expected an "effectual door" would be opened, to proclaim the new system of faith, in that region; and that those who were ordained to the gift of tongues, would have an opportunity to display their supernatural talent, in communicating to the Indians, in their own dialect. Some who were ordained to this office, absolutely knew that through this medium, they should gain access to the natives; and I will venture to say, I know, that their success will be similar to that of their predecessor, Oliver Cowdery, who stated that he was endowed with the same fore knowledge. But the event has proved his presumption false. For more than two weeks, while I remained there, the disposition of the Elders appeared to be averse to preaching, either to the white or the red people, and indeed adverse circumstances prevented it. We expected to assemble together in conference according to the commandment, and the Lord would signally display his power, for the confirmation of our faith; but we commenced our journey home before most of the Elders arrived. It is true, a conference was held, but it was considered so unimportant, that myself and another man were permitted to be absent, for the purpose of procuring the means of conveyance down the river. We expected to find a large Church, which Smith said, was revealed to him in a vision, Oliver had raised up there. This large Church was found to consist of four females. We expected to witness the exercise if those miraculous gifts, to which some were ordained while in the State of Ohio. But the same difficulty, the same want of faith among the people, which counteracted them here, prevailed there; consequently no miracles could be wrought. We expected to see the foundation of the City and temple laid; and this we were permitted to see, and it was in fact a curiosity,

195

but not worth going to Missouri to see. The honour of consecrating the land, &c. was conferred on Rigdon. -- The commandment reads thus: "let my servant Sidney consecrate and dedicate the land, and the spot for the Temple" -- again, "Behold I give unto my servant Sidney a commandment, that he shall write a description of the land of Zion, and a statement of the will of God, as it shall be made known to him by the spirit, and a subscription to be presented to the Churches, to obtain money to purchase lands, for the inheritance of the children of God; for behold the Lord willeth that his Disciples, and the children of men, should open their hearts, to purchase the whole region of country, lest they receive none inheritance, save it be by the shedding of blood." The childish exultation of the Mormonite leaders, while they echoed and re-echoed, the Lord has given us this whole region of country; "this whole region of country is ours;" when it was manifest, agreeable to the commandment, that the gift was only obtained, by purchasing it at a dear rate with money, and that, in order to save themselves the trouble of "the shedding of blood," would, under other circumstances, have been truly diverting. But when viewing it as an instance of a deep laid scheme, and the cunning artifice of crafty impostors, designed to allure the credulous and the unsuspecting, into a state of unqualified vassalage, it presents a melancholy picture of the depravity of the human heart, while destitute of those virtues, inculcated in the Gospel by the blessed Redeemer.

It was conjectured by the inhabitants of Jackson county, that the Mormonites, as a body are wealthy, and many of them entertain fears, that next December, when the list of land is exposed for sale, they will out-bid others, and establish themselves as the most powerful body in the county. -- But they may dismiss their fears in this respect; for the

196

Mormonites as a body, are comparatively poor, and destined so to remain, until they pursue a different course as it relates to economy and industry, from what they have hitherto pursued. There were ten families, which came by water, landed there the day on which I arrived; and all the land which the Bishop said they had means to purchase, was less than thirty acres to the family; and thirty acres in that country, is little enough for wood and

timber land; as fifteen acres upon an average here, are worth
thirty there. Neither need they fear that the Mormonites, were
they so disposed, will obtain the possession of their lands "by
shedding of blood," until the spirit selects more courageous leaders
than Smith or Rigdon. Yours affectionately, EZRA BOOTH
LETTER VI.
It is well know [n] that the ostensible design of the Mormonites in
settling in the western part of Missouri is to convert the Indians
to the faith of Mormonism. In this, the leaders appear to have in
view, as a mode, the Jesuits of the 16th century, who established
themselves in South America, by gaining an entire ascendancy
over the hearts and consciences of the natives, and thereby
became their masters. As Independence is the place of general
rendezvous and head quarters of the Mormonites, it may not be
amiss to notice it. It is a new town, containing a court house built
of brick, two or three merchant's stores, and 15 or 20 dwelling
houses, built mostly of logs hewed on both sides; and is situated
on a handsome rise of ground, about three miles south of [the]
Missouri river, and about 12 miles east of the dividing line between
the United States and the Indian Reserve, and is the county seat
of Jackson county. In this place it is designed to establish the
Lord's printing press, of which Wm. W. Phelps and O. Cowdery are
to have the management;
197
and also, the Lord's storehouse, committed in charge to S.
Gilbert. By the means of these two grand engines, they expect to
make the wicked feel the weight of their tremendous power. West
of the line lies the territory, selected by the government of the
United States, for the future residence of the Indians; to which
place, a number of tribes have recently moved. The question is
frequently asked, do the Indians seem disposed to receive
Mormonism; or have any of them yet embraced it? To which
question I have heard some of the leaders reply, "O yes," when
the truth is, not an individual had embraced it when I left that
place. Nor is there any prospect they will embrace it. It is true,
that some of the Indians appear to listen with a degree of
attention, while the Mormonite teacher pretends to disclose to

them the secrets of their origins, the history of their ancestors, and that the great Spirit designs, in this generation, to restore them to the possession of their lands, now occupied by the whites; and the Indians shall go forth among the white people, "as a lion among the beasts of the forests, and as a young lion among the flocks of sheep, who, if he goeth through, both treadest down and teareth to pieces, and no man can deliver. Thy hand shall be lifted up against thy adversaries, (the whites) and all their enemies (the whites) shall be cut off." Here you have a fair specimen of the method adopted in the Book of Mormon, and preached by the Mormonite teachers, for the purpose of enlisting the feelings, and in gratiating themselves with the Indians; and should success attend their endeavours, and the minds of the Indians become inflamed with the enthusiastic spirit which Mormonism inspires, they may be inclined to try the experiment, whether "by shedding of blood," they can expel the white inhabitants, or reduce them to a state of servitude; and by this means, regain the possession of the lands occupied by their forefathers.

198

The laying of the foundation of Zion was attended with considerable parade, and an ostentatious display of talents, both by Rigdon and Cowdery. The place being designated as the site where the city was to commence, on the day appointed we repaired to the spot, not only as spectators, but each one to act the part assigned him in the great work of laying the foundation of the "glorious city of New Jerusalem." Rigdon consecrated the ground, by an address, in the first place, to the God whom the Mormons profess to worship; and then making some remarks respecting the extraordinary purpose for which we were assembled, prepared the way for administering the oath of allegiance to those who were to receive their "everlasting inheritance" in that city. He laid them under the most solemn obligations to constantly obey all the commandments of Smith. He enjoined it upon them to express a great degree of gratitude for the free donation, and then, as the Lord's Vicegerent, he gratuitously bestowed upon them that for which they had paid an exorbitant price in money. These preliminaries being ended, a shrub oak, about ten inches in diameter at the butt, the best that could be obtained near at hand, was prostrated, trimmed, and cut off at a suitable length; and twelve men, answering to the twelve apostles, by means of handspikes, conveyed it to the place. Cowdery craved the privilege of laying the corner stone. He selected a small rough stone, the best he could find, carried it in one hand to the spot, removed the surface of the earth to prepare a place for its reception, and then displayed his oratorical power, in delivering an address, suited to the important occasion. The stone being placed, one end of the shrub oak stick was laid upon it; and there was laid down the first stone and stick, which are to form an essential part of the splendid city of Zion. The next day the ground for the temple was consecrated,

199

and Smith claimed the honour of laying the corner stone himself. Should the inhabitants of Independence feel a desire to visit this place, destined at some future time to become celebrated, they will have only to walk one half of a mile out of the town, to a rise of ground, a short distance south of the road. They will be able to ascertain the spot by the means of a sapling, distinguished from the others by the bark being broken off on the north and on the east side. On the south side of the sapling will be found the letter T., which stands for temple; and on the east side Zom! For Zomas; which Smith says is the original word for Zion. Near the foot of the sapling they will find a small stone covered over with bushes, which were cut for that purpose. This is the corner stone for the temple. They can there have the privilege of beholding the mighty work, accomplished by about thirty men, who left their homes, travelled one thousand miles, most of them on foot, and expended more than $1000 in cash. Having completed the work, or rather finding but little business for us to accomplish in Missouri, most of us became anxious to return home. And none appeared to be more so than Rigdon and Smith, whose plans for future subsistence were considerably frustrated. They expected to find a country abounding with the necessaries and comforts of life. But the prospect appeared somewhat gloomy, and will probably remain so for some years to come. That they were disappointed is evident from the change, which appeared in their calculations. Before they went to Missouri, their language was "we shall winter in Ohio but one winter more;" and when in Missouri, "it will be many years before we come here, for the Lord has a great work for us to do in Ohio," and the great work is, to make a thorough alteration of the Bible, and invent new revelations, and these are to be sent to Missouri, in order to be printed.

200

This coming to save the expense of postage is parallel with their other calculations. But no matter for that, it will save them the difficulties and hardships incident to the settling of a new country; and also the dangers to which they would be exposed, in case the Indians should commence hostilities upon the whites; and moreover, they have an easy method to supply themselves with cash at any time when occasion requires. The authority of a commandment will easily untie the purse strings of those whose consciences are under their control; and they find it much easier, and better suited to their dispositions, to write commandments, than to gain a livelihood by the sweat of the brow: and indeed, Smith has commanded himself not to labour, and by his mandate, has enjoined it upon the Church to support him. The Bishop, when we were in Missouri, intimated that he and others were too much inclined to indolence. -- He replied, "I am commanded not to labour." Yours affectionately, EZRA BOOTH

LETTER VII.

The following, with but a little variation, is the copy of a letter to the Bishop of the Mormonite Church, who by commandment, has received his station, and now resides in Missouri. His business is to superintend the secular concerns of the Church. He holds a deed to the lands, and the members receive writing from him, signifying that they are to possess the land as their own, so long as they are obeisant to Smith's commandments. The Bishop is, in reality, the Vicegerent of Smith, and those in coalition with him; and holds his office during their will and pleasure. I think him to be an honest man as yet, but there is a point beyond which he cannot go, unless he prostrates his honour in the dust, and

prostitutes his conscience to the vilest of purposes. He has frequently staggered
201
and been ready to fall. The conference last year, gave him a tremendous shock, from which with difficulty he recovered. The law of the Church enjoins, that no debt with the world shall be contracted. But a thousand acres of land in the town of Thompson could be purchased for one half its value, and he was commanded to secure it; and in order to do it, he was under the necessity to contract a debt to the world. He hesitated, but the command was repeated, "you must secure the land." He was one of the number who was ordained to the gift of discerning spirits; and in a commandment, a pattern was given by which the good spirit might be distinguished from the bad, which rendered the gift of supernatural discernment useless; for the division was to be made from external appearances, and not from any thing discovered internally. He saw the impropriety, and it shook his faith. I am suspicious the time is not far distant, when by commandment, this office will be bestowed upon a more trusty and confidential person; perhaps Smith's brother or father, or some one who has been disciplined in the State of New York. Then it will become his business to make over the whole property, by deed of conveyance, to the person appointed by the commandment to supersede him. The Mormonites will tell you, that business of this nature is done by the voice of the Church. It is like this: a sovereign issues his decrees, and then says to his subjects, hold up your right hands, in favour of my decree being carried into effect. Should any refuse, they are sure to be hung for rebellion.
September 20, 1831.
Mr. Partridge: Sir -- From a sense of duty, I take up my pen, to communicate to you the present impressions of my mind, which originated from facts, which occurred during my stay there, and while returning home. I arrived safely at my home,
202
on the 1st instant, after having passed through a variety of scenes, some of which, I design to disclose to you in this letter. You will probably be surprised, when you learn, that I am no longer

a member of the Mormonite Church. -- The circumstances which led to this are numerous, and of such a character, that I should have been compelled to sacrifice every principle of honesty, or cease to support a system, which I conceive to be grossly inconsistent, and in opposition to the best interests of human society. The first thing that materially affected my mind, so as to weaken my confidence, was the falsehood of Joseph's vision. You know perfectly well, that Joseph had, or said he had, a vision, or revelation, in which it was made known to him by the spirit, that Oliver had raised up a large Church in Missouri. This was so confidently believed, previous to our leaving Ohio, that while calculating the number of the Church, several hundred were added, supposed to be in Missouri. The great Church was found to consist of three or four families. The night we took lodgings in the school house, and the morning, which succeeded it, presented circumstances, which I had not anticipated. When you intimated to Joseph that the land which he and Oliver had selected, was inferior in point of quality to other lands adjoining, had you seen the same spirit manifested in me, which you saw in him, would you not have concluded me to be under the influence of violent passions, bordering on madness, rather than the meek and gentle spirit which the Gospel inculcates? When you complained that he had abused you, you observed to him, "I wish you not to tell us any more, that you know these by the spirit when you do not; you told us, that Oliver had raised up a large Church here, and there is no such thing;" he replied, "I see it, and it will be so." This appeared to me, to be a shift, better suited to an impostor, than to a true Prophet of the Lord.

203

And from that time I resolved to weigh every circumstance; and I can assure you that no one that has a bearing on the subject, escaped my notice. But the spirit considered your insolence to Joseph too intolerable to be passed over unnoticed. Hence the commandment: "If he repent not of his sins, which is unbelief and blindness of heart, let him take heed lest he fall. Behold his mission is given unto him, and it shall not be given again." -- You are to be careful, to submit to all the abuse which Joseph sees fit

to pour upon you; and to swallow, passively, all the spurious visions, and false prophecies, that he in his clemency thinks proper to bestow upon you, lest you fall from your Bishoprick, never to regain it. These men under whose influence you act, were entire strangers to you until you embraced this new system of faith. Now, permit me to inquire, have you not frequently observed in Joseph, a want of that sobriety, prudence and stability, which are some of the most prominent traits in the Christian character? Have you not often discovered in him, a spirit of lightness and levity, a temper easily irritated, and an habitual proneness to jesting and joking? Have you not often proven to your satisfaction that he says he knows things to be so by the spirit, when they are not so? You most certainly have. Have you not reason to believe, or at least to suspect, that the revelations, which come from him, are something short of infallible, and instead of being the production of divine wisdom, emanate from his own weak mind? Some suppose his weakness, nay, his wickedness, can form no reasonable objection to his revelations; and "were he to get another man's wife, and seek to kill her husband, it could be no reason why we should not believe revelations through him, for David did the same." So Sidney asserted, and many others concurred with him in sentiment. The commandment we received to purchase, or make a water
204
craft, directed us to proceed down the river in it as far as St. Louis, and from thence, with the exception of Joseph and his two scribes, we were to proceed on our journey home two by two. The means of conveyance being procured, we embarked for St. Louis, but unpropitious events rolled on, superseded the commandment, frustrated our plans, and we had separated before we had accomplished one half of the voyage. The cause, which produced this disastrous result, was a spirit of animosity and discord, which made its appearance on board, the morning after we left Independence. The conduct of the Elders became very displeasing to Oliver, who, in the greatness of his power, uttered this malediction: "as the Lord God liveth, if you do not behave better, some accident will befall you." The manner in which this was

handed out, evinced it to be the ebullition of a spirit, similar to that which influenced Joseph in the schoolhouse. No accident, however, befell them, until Joseph, in the afternoon of the third day, assumed the direction of affairs on board that canoe, which, with other matters of difference, together with Oliver's curse, increased the irritation of the crew, who, in time of danger, refused to exert their physical powers, in consequence of which they ran foul of a sawyer, and were in danger of upsetting. This was sufficient to flutter the timid spirit of the Prophet and his scribe, who had accompanied him on board of that canoe, and like the sea-tossed mariner, when threatened with a watery grave, they unanimously desired to set their feet once more upon something more firm than a liquid surface; therefore, by the persuasion of Joseph, we landed before sunset, to pass the night upon the bank of the river. Preparations were made to spend the night as comfortably as existing circumstances would admit, and then an attempt was made to effect reconciliation between the contending parties. The business
205
of settlement elicited much conversation, and excited considerable feeling on both sides. Oliver's denunciation was brought into view; his conduct and equipage were compared to "a fop of a sportsman;" he and Joseph were represented as highly imperious, and quite dictatorial; and Joseph and Sidney were reprimanded for their excessive cowardice. Joseph seemed inclined to arm himself, according to his usual custom, in case of opposition, with the judgments of God, for the purpose of pouring them, like a thunder bolt, upon the rebellious elders; but one or two retorted, "None of your threats;" which completely disarmed him, and he reserved his judgments for a more suitable occasion. Finding myself but little interested in the settlement, believing the principles of discord too deeply rooted to be easily eradicated, I laid myself down upon the ground, and in silence contemplated awhile the events of the evening, as they passed before me. These are the men to whom the Lord has intrusted the mysteries, and the keys of his kingdom; whom he has authorized to bind or loose on earth, and their decision shall be ratified in Heaven. These are the men sent forth,

to promulgate a new revelation, and to usher in a new dispensation -- at whose presence the "Heavens are to shake, the hills tremble, the mountains quake, and the earth open and swallow up their enemies." -- These are the leaders of the Church, and the only Church on earth the Lord beholds with approbation. Surely, I never witnessed so much confusion and discord, among the Elders of any other Church; nevertheless they are all doomed to be a perpetual curse; except they receive the doctrines and precepts which Mormonism [allocates], and place themselves under the tuition of men, more ignorant and unholy than themselves. In the midst of meditations like these, I sunk into the arms of sleep, but was awakened at a late hour, to witness and consent to a reconciliation
206
between the parties. The next morning Joseph manifested an aversion to risk his person any more upon the rough and angry current of the Missouri, and, in fact, upon any other river; and he again had recourse to his usual method of freeing himself from the embarrassments of a former commandment, by obtaining another in opposition to it. A new commandment was issued, in which a great curse was pronounced against the waters: navigating them was to be attended with extreme danger; and all the saints, in general, were prohibited in journeying upon them, to the promised land. From this circumstance, the Missouri river was named the river of Destruction. It was decreed that we should proceed on our journey by land, and preach by the way as we passed along. Joseph, Sidney, and Oliver were to press their way forward with all possible speed, and to preach only in Cincinnati; and there they were to lift up their voices, and proclaim against the whole of that wicked city. The method by which Joseph and Co. designed to proceed home, it was discovered, would be very expensive. "The Lord don't care how much money it takes to get us home," said Sidney. Not satisfied with the money they received from the bishop, they used their best endeavours to exact money from others, who had but little, compared with what they had; telling them, in substance "You can beg your passage on foot, but as we are to travel in the stage we must have money."

You will find, sir, that the expense of these three men was one hundred dollars more than three of our company expended, while on our journey home; and, for the sake of truth and honesty, let these men never again open their mouths, to insult the common sense of mankind, by contending for equality, and the community of goods in society, until there is a thorough alteration in their method of proceeding. It seems, however, they had drained their pockets, when they arrived at Cincinnati,
207
for there they were under the necessity of pawning their trunk, in order to continue their journey home. Here they violated the commandment, by not preaching; and when an inquiry was made respecting the cause of that neglect, at one time they said they could get no house to preach in; at another time they stated that they could have had the court-house, had they stayed a day or two longer, but the Lord made it known to them that they should go on; and other similar excuses, involving like contradictions. Thus they turn and twist the commandments to suit their whims, and they violate them when they please with perfect impunity. They can any time obtain a commandment suited to their desires, and as their desires fluctuate and become reversed, they get a new one to supercede the other, and hence the contradictions which abound in this species of revelation. The next day after, we were cast upon the shore, and had commenced our journey by land, myself and three others went on board of a canoe, and recommenced our voyage down the river. From this time a constant gale of prosperity wafted us forward, and not an event transpired, but what tended to our advancement, until we arrived at our much-desired homes. At St. Louis, we took passage in a steamboat, and came to Wellsville; and from thence in the stage home. We travelled afloat eight hundred miles further than the three who took their passage in the stage, and arrived at our homes but a few days later. -- It is true, we violated the commandment by not preaching by the way, and so did they by not preaching at Cincinnati. But it seems that none of us considered the commandment worthy of much notice. In this voyage upon the waters, we demonstrated that the great dangers

existed only in imagination, and the commandment to be the offspring of a pusillanimous spirit. -- The spirit also revealed to Joseph, that "on the steamboats,

208

plots were already laid for our destruction." This too we proved to be false. While descending the Missouri river, Peter and Frederick, two of my company, divulged a secret respecting Oliver, which placed his conduct on a parallel with Ziba's; for which Ziba was deprived of his Elder and Apostleship: "Let that which was bestowed upon Ziba be taken from him, and let him stand as a member in the Church, and let him labor with his own hands with the brethren." And thus by commandment, poor Ziba, one of the twelve Apostles, is thrust down; while Oliver the scribe, also an Apostle, who had been guilty of similar conduct, is set on high, to prepare work for the press; and no commandment touches him, only to exalt him higher. -- These two persons stated, that had they known previous to their journey to Missouri, what they then knew, they never should have accompanied Oliver thither, Sidney, since his return has written a description of Zion. But it differs essentially from that which you wrote; so much so, that either yours or his must be false. Knowing him to be constitutionally inclined to exaggerate, and suspecting that this habit would be as likely to preponderate in his written as in his oral communications, you cautioned him against it. "What I write will be written by the most infallible inspiration of the holy spirit," said he with an air of contempt. You must be careful, sir, or it will again sound in your ears, "if he repent not" for giving a false description of the land of Zion, let him take heed lest he fall from his office. This, Sidney said, was one reason why you were not permitted to return to the State of Ohio. The want of time and paper warn me to bring this letter to a close. And now permit me to entreat you, to candidly view the whole matter, from the commencement unto the present time. Look at it with your eyes, and no longer suffer these strangers to blind your eyes, and daub you over with

209

their untempared mortar. Think how often you have been stumbled by these discordant revelations, false visions, and lying prophecies.

Put into practice the resolutions you expressed to me the morning after the collision in the schoolhouse, that you would go home, and attend to your own business. Transfer the lands you hold in your hands, to the persons whose money paid for it. Place yourself from under the influence of the men who have deceived you; burst asunder the bands of delusion; fly for your life, fly from the habitations haunted by impostors; and having done this, you most surely will be glad and rejoice, and prove to your own satisfaction, as I have done, the falsity of Joseph's prophetic declaration, "if you turn against us you will enjoy no more satisfaction in the world." E. B.

Some things are intimated in the foregoing letter, which more properly belongs to Cowdery's mission to the Indians; and when I come to notice that mission, those things will probably be more fully exhibited. It is also indirectly stated, that Rigdon has acquired the habit of exaggeration. The truth of this statement, I presume, will be doubted but by few, who have been long acquainted with him. Most of his communications carry the appearance of high and false coloring; and I am persuaded, that truth by this embellishing touch, often degenerates into fiction, I have heard him several different times, give a representation of the interview between him lf, and to use his own phraseology, "the far-famed Alexander Campbell." This man's wonted shrewdness and presence of mind forsook him when in the presence of this gigantic Mormonite; so much so, that "he was quite confused and silly." I will give to you a specimen of the language, with which Rigdon said he assailed him: "You have lied, Alexander. Alexander you have lied. If you do not receive the Book of Mormon, you will be damned." With such like arguments

210

he browbeat his antagonist, until he had silenced and set him down, like the pusillanimous cur, at the feet of his chastising master. "You are a liar, you are a child of the Devil, you are an enemy to all righteousness, and the spirit of the Devil is in you," and the like is dealt out profusely against an obstinate opponent, and especially, one whom they are pleased to nickname apostate. I regret the necessity I am under of making such statements, and could wish there had been no occasion for them. But truth compels me to it, and the good of society demands it. -- Yours, &c. EZRA BOOTH

LETTER VIII.

The origin of the aborigines of this country, and the history before the introduction of the eastern literature into the western hemisphere, has afforded a subject for much speculation, and deep research among the learned; and has occasioned considerable curiosity, among various classes of people. But the subject still remains an impenetrable obscurity; and will so remain, unless He who has the power to speak. "Let there be light," and the light shall break forth out of obscurity. But as this is a subject better calculated to gratify the speculative inquirer, then to purify the heart, by rectifying wrong principles in the mind, or to increase that kind of knowledge intimately connected with, and essential to practical improvements either in civil or religious society, we may reasonably doubt, whether the great Jehovah will soon, if ever, condescend to clear away the darkness, by giving a revelation, merely to gratify the desires of persons, who delight to wander in the region of conjecture and speculation. But he has already done it, cries the Mormonite herald. The Book of Mormon, which I hold in my hand, is a divine revelation, and the very thing we need, to burst the cloud and remove the darkness, which
211
has long surrounded the mysteries and degraded aborigines. We now know that the natives, who inhabit the forests of America, are a "branch of the House of Israel;" and by means of this blessed book, they are soon, even in this generation, to be restored to the knowledge, and the true worship of the God of Israel. -- Among them is to be built, the "glorious city of the New Jerusalem." In the midst of which is to stand, the splendid and magnificent temple, dedicated to the Most High God, and "Oliver being called and commanded of the Lord God, to go forth among the Lamanites, to proclaim glad tidings of great joy unto them, by presenting unto them, the fullness of the gospel of the only begotten son of God," &c. The grand enterprise of introducing this new dispensation, or the fullness of the Gospel, among the Indian

tribes, who have recently received the appellation of Lamanites, was committed in charge to Oliver Cowdery, a young man of high fame among the Mormonites. His credentials, and the credentials of the three others associated with him in the mission, will be found in the following revelations, which I transcribe for your perusal, and also for some future remarks, which I design to offer.
A REVELATION UNTO OLIVER, GIVEN SEPTEMBER 1830.
Behold I say unto you, Oliver, that it shall be given unto thee, that thou shalt be heard by the Church, in all things whatsoever thou shalt teach them by the comforter, concerning the revelations and commandments which I have given. But, verily, verily I say unto you, no one shall be appointed to receive commandments and revelations in this Church, excepting my servant Joseph, for he receiveth them even as Moses, and thou shalt be obedient unto the things which I shall give unto him, even as Aaron, to declare faithfully the commandments and the revelations, with power and authority
212
unto the Church. And if thou art led at any time by the comforter to speak or teach, or at all times by the way of commandment unto the Church, thou mayest do it; but thou shalt not write by way of commandment but by wisdom: and thou shalt not command him who is at thy head, and at the head of the Church; for I have given him the keys of the mysteries of the revelations which are sealed, until I shall appoint unto him another in his stead -- and now, behold I say unto you, that you shall go unto the Lamanites and preach my gospel unto them; and thou shalt have revelations but write them not by way of commandment. -- And now I say unto you, that it is not revealed, and no man knoweth where the city shall be built, but it shall be given hereafter. Behold I say unto you, that it shall be among the Lamanites. Thou shalt not leave this place until after the conference, and my servant Joseph shall be appointed to rule the conference, by the voice of it; and what he saith unto thee that thou shalt tell. And again, thou shalt take thy brother Hiram between him and thee alone, and tell him that the things which he hath written from that stone are not of me, and that Satan hath deceived him, for behold these things have

not been appointed unto him, neither shall any thing be appointed
unto any in this Church, contrary to the Church covenant, for all
things must be done in order and by commandment, by the prayer
of faith, and thou shalt settle all these things before thou shalt
take thy journey among the Lamanites; and it shall be given from
the time, that thou shalt go, until the time that thou shalt return,
what thou shalt do; and thou must open thy mouth at all times
declaring my gospel with the sound of rejoicing. -- Amen.
Manchester, Oct. 17, 1830.
I, Oliver, being commanded of the Lord God to go forth unto the
Lamanites to proclaim glad tidings of great joy
213
unto them by presenting unto them the fullness of the gospel, of
the only begotten son of God; and also to rear up a pillar as a
witness where the temple of God shall be built, in the glorious New
Jerusalem; and having certain brothers with me, who are called of
God to assist me, whose names are Parley, Peter, and Ziba, do
therefore most solemnly covenant with God, that I will walk humbly
before him, and do this business, and this glorious work according
as he shall direct me by the Holy Ghost; ever praying for mine and
their prosperity, and deliverance from bonds, and from
imprisonment, and whatsoever may befall us, with all patience and
faith. -- Amen. OLIVER COWDERY
We, the undersigned, being called and commanded of the Lord
God, to accompany our brother Oliver Cowdery to go to the
Lamanites and to assist in the above mentioned glorious work and
business. We do therefore, most solemnly covenant before God,
that we will assist him faithfully in this thing, by giving heed unto
all his words and advice, which is, or shall be given him by the
spirit of truth, ever praying with all prayer and supplication, for our
and his prosperity, and our deliverance from bonds, and
imprisonments, and whatsoever may come upon us, with all
patience and faith. -- Amen.
Signed in presence of
JOSEPH SMITH, Jun.
DAVID WHITMER.P. P. PRATT,
ZIBA PETERSON,

PETER WHITMER.

In the preceding revelation, the principal thing, which claims your attention, is the mission to the Indians; for with that mission many circumstances are connected, which clearly evince, that it originated from human imbecility, and diabolical depravity. -- There are also some other things the meaning of which you will not be likely to apprehend, without some explanation. In this, as well as several of the commandments, it is clearly and explicitly stated, that

214

the right of delivering written commandments, and revelations, belong exclusively to Smith, and no other person can interfere, without being guilty of sacrilege. In this office he is to stand, until another is appointed in his place, and no other can be appointed in his stead, unless he falls through transgression; and in such a case, he himself is authorized to appoint his successor. But how is he to be detected, should he become guilty of transgression. The commandment makes provision for this. His guilt will become manifest by his inability to utter more revelations, and should he presume "to get another man's wife," and commit adultery; and "by the shedding of blood, seek to kill her husband," if he retain the use of his tongue, so as to be able to utter his jargon, he can continue as long as he pleases in the bed of adultery, and wrap himself with garments stained with blood, shed by his own hands, and still retain the spotless innocence of the holiest among mortals; and must be continued in the office of revelator, and head of the Church. Some others, and especially Cowdery, have earnestly desired to relieve Smith of some part of his burden. Cowdery's desires for this work were so keen and excessive, as, to use his own language, "it was unto me a burning fire shut up in my bones, and I was weary with forbearing, and I could forbear no longer;" and he did in fact, issue some productions, which he said bore the divine impress; but Smith fixed upon them the stamp of devilish. But it seems, in order to compromise the matter, that Cowdery was permitted to "speak or to teach, at all times, by way of commandment unto the Church; but not to write them by way of commandment:" thus Cowdery is authorized to give verbal

commandments to the Church by the inspiration of the spirit, which, if he afterwards writes, ceases to be inspiration; therefore, a commandment delivered orally, may be divinely inspired; but the same
215
communicated, written verbatim, so far loses its former character, that it degenerates into a prediction of an infernal stamp. Here is the mystery, for aught I know, peculiar to Mormonism; and none but Mormonites, I presume, will attempt to unravel it. But it finds its parallel in the following: Smith assures his followers, that what he speaks by the spirit, and is written, is infallible in operation. But if it is not written, he may sometimes be mistaken. -- He tells them that the right to deliver written revelations, belongs exclusively to himself, and no other person shall interfere in the business; and if he transgresses he will graciously condescend to appoint another in his stead, and the only proof produced for the support of such assertions, is barely his word, upon which they implicitly rely, and because entirely resigned to place their person and property under his control, and even risk the salvation of their souls upon his say-so. Such glaring duplicity on the one hand, and unaccountable credulity on the other, seldom have a parallel in the annals of men. Never was there a despot more jealous of his prerogative than Smith; and never was a fortress guarded with more vigilance and ardor against every invading foe, than he guards these. Smith apprehended a rival in the department of written inspiration, from another quarter, and hence Cowdery was commissioned to commence an attack and suppress the enemy, before he had acquired sufficient stability and strength so as to become formidable. "Thou shalt take thy brother Hiram, between him and thee alone, and tell him that the things he hath written from that stone, &c." Hiram Page, one of the eight witnesses, and also one of the "money diggers," found a smooth stone, upon which there appeared to be a writing, which when transcribed upon paper, disappeared from the stone, and another impression appeared in it place. This when copied, vanished,
216
and so it continued, alternately appearing and disappearing; in the

meanwhile, he continued to write, until he had written over considerable paper. It bore striking marks of a Mormonite revelation, and was received as an authentic document by most of the Mormonites, till Smith, by his superior sagacity, discovered it to be a satanic fraud. A female professing to be a prophetess, made her appearance in Kirtland, and so ingratiated herself into the esteem and favour of some of the Elders, that they received her, as a person commissioned to act a conspicuous part in mormonizing the world. Rigdon, and some others, gave her the right hand of fellowship, and literally saluted her with what they called the kiss of charity. But Smith, viewing her as an encroachment upon his sacred premises, declared her an impostor, and she returned to the place from whence she came. Her visit, however, made a deep impression on the minds of many, and the barbed arrow, which she left in the hearts of some, is not yet eradicated. Yours affectionately, EZRA BOOTH

LETTER IX.

In this letter the mission to the Indians will be brought into view, and with it are connected circumstances and facts, sufficient, one would suppose, to convince every honest and unprejudiced Mormonite, of the fallacy and deception of Mormonism. But a Mormonite of the highest grade is invulnerable by facts the most notorious, and evidence as glaring as the noon-day sun; for they affirm, they know by the spirit that Mormonism is what it pretends to be, and should Smith acknowledge it to be a fabrication, they would not believe him. This forms the highest climax in Mormonism, and but few have attained it. After Cowdery and his three associates had left the State of New York,

217

while bending their course to the west, he was directed by the spirit to Kirtland, for the special purpose of enlisting Rigdon in the Mormonite cause. I have since learned that the spirit, which directed in this enterprise, was no other than Pratt, who had previously become acquainted with Rigdon and had been proselyted by him into what is called the Campbellite faith. This new system appears to have been particularly suited to Rigdon's taste, and calculated to make an impression on his mind. But before he could fully embrace it, he must "receive a testimony from God." In order to do this he labored as he was directed by his Preceptor, almost incessantly and earnestly in praying, till at length his mind was wrapped up in a vision; and to use his own language, "to my astonishment I saw the different orders of professing Christians passing before my eyes, with their hearts exposed to view, and they were as corrupt as corruption itself. That society to which I belonged also passed before my eyes, and to my astonishment it was as corrupt as the others. Last of all that little man who bro't me the Book of Mormon, passed before my eyes with his heart open, and it was as pure as an angel; and this was a testimony from God; that the Book of Mormon was a Divine Revelation." Rigdon is one who has ascended to the summit of Mormonism; and this vision stands as the foundation of his knowledge. He frequently affirms, that these things are not a matter of faith with him, but of absolute knowledge. He has been favoured with many remarkable and extraordinary visions, in some of which he saw Kirtland, with the surrounding country consecrated as the promised land, and the Churches in the state of New York expected to receive their everlasting inheritance in the state of Ohio, and this expectation was grounded on Rigdon's vision while in the state of New York. These visions are considered by the Church as entitled to no credit and laid aside as mere rubbish.

218

As it relates to the purity of the heart of "that little man," if a pure and pleasant fountain can send forth corrupt and bitter streams, then may the heart of that man be pure, who enters into a matrimonial contract with a young lady, and obtains the consent of her parents; but as soon as his back is turned upon her, he violates his engagements, and prostitutes his honor by becoming the gallant of another, and resolved in his heart, and expresses resolutions to marry her. But as the practice of a man will ever stand as a general criterion by which the principles of the heart are to be tested, we say that the heart of such a man is the reverse of purity, From Kirtland, Cowdery & Co. were directed by the spirit to Sandusky, where they contemplated opening their

mission and proselyting the Indians residing at that place. But
neither Cowdery, nor the spirit which directed him was able to
open the way to, or make any impression upon their minds. Being
frustrated in this, his first attempt to convert the natives, he
turned his attention and course to the Missouri, and when near the
eastern line of that state, he halted for several days, for the
purpose of obtaining, by inquiry, information respecting the Indians
still further west. It appears that he was fearful that his infallible
guide, (the spirit,) was incapable to direct him, while proceeding
further to the west; consequently, he applied to men more capable
of giving instruction than the spirit, by which he was influenced.
When he arrived at the western line of Missouri, he passed into the
Indian territory, where he remained but a short time, before he
was notified by the U. S. Agent, that he must either re-cross the
line, or be compelled to take up his residence in the garrison, forty
miles up the Arkansas river. As there was no other alternative, the
former seemed to him the most expedient; and he never possessed
courage sufficient to pass the line, or visit the residence of
219
the Indians since. Thus you behold a man, "called and commanded
of the Lord God, to go forth unto the Lamanites," and establish his
Church among them; but no sooner is he set down in the field of
his mission, and surrounded by his anticipated converts, than he
is driven by a comparative nothing, from the fields, and obliged to
relinquish his contemplated harvest. -- This is the person
commissioned by the Lord to proceed to the western wilds, and as
he himself stated, "to the place where the foot of a white man
never trod," to rear up a pillar for a witness, where the temple of
God shall be built, in the glorious New Jerusalem. But alas! He was
arrested by man in his course, and by the breath of man the
mighty undertaking was blown into the air, and Cowdery was
thrown back among the Gentiles, to wait for the spirit to devise
some new plans in the place of those, which had been frustrated.
But as the city and temple must be built, as every avenue leading
to the Indians was closed against the Mormonites, it was thought
that they should be built among the Gentiles, which is in direct
opposition to the original plan -- as foreign from the design of the

spirit, expressed in several commandments, as it would have been had the Directors, who were appointed to build the court-house in Ravenna, built it in Trumbull county, foreign from the design of those who intrusted them with the business. Though their plans had hitherto failed, they were unwilling to abandon the Indian enterprise; and in a commandment it was stated, that Cowdery and others should receive a written recommendation, signed by the Elders, for the purpose of presenting it to the Indian agent, in order to obtain permission to visit the Indians in their settlements. -- The recommendation was written according to the commandment, and frequent opportunities occurred in which it might have been presented to the agent, but it never was

220

presented, and of course was useless; he was censured by some for not presenting it, but I suppose the spirit directed him not to do it. Another method has been invented, in order to remove obstacles, which hitherto had proved insurmountable. "The Lord's store-house," is to be furnished with goods suited to the Indian trade, and persons are to obtain license from the government to dispose of them to the Indians in their own territory; at the same time they are to disseminate the principles of Mormonism among them. From this smuggling method of preaching to the Indians, they anticipate a favourable result. In addition to this, and to co-operate with it, it has been made known by revelation, that it will be pleasing to the Lord, should they form a matrimonial alliance with the natives; and by this means the Elders, who comply with the thing so pleasing to the Lord, and for which the Lord has promised to bless those who do it abundantly, gain a residence in the Indian territory, independent of the agent. It has been made known to one, who has left his wife in the State of New York, that he is entirely free from his wife, and he is at pleasure to take him a wife from among the Lamanites. It was easily perceived that this permission was perfectly suited to his desires. I have frequently heard him state that the Lord had made it known to him, that he is as free from his wife as from any other woman; and the only crime I have ever heard alleged against her is, she is violently opposed to Mormonism. But before this contemplated marriage can

be carried into effect, he must return to the State of New York and settle his business, for fear, should he return after that affair had taken place, the civil authority would apprehend him as a criminal. It is with pleasure I close this exposition, having in part accomplished what I intended when I commenced it. The employment has been an unpleasant one to me, and from
221
the first, I should gladly have avoided it, could I have done it, and maintained a conscience void of offence, towards God and man. -- But should an individual by this exposition be extricated or prevented from falling into the delusion, which has been the subject of consideration; I shall be amply compensated, for the painful task which I have performed.

Yours affectionately,
EZRA BOOTH

In the last letter to the Ohio Star Ezra Booth states.

"Another method has been invented, in order to remove obstacles which hitherto have proved insurmountable. "The Lord's store-house," is to be furnished with goods suited to the Indian trade, and persons are to obtain license from the government to dispose of them to the Indians in their own territory; at the same time, they are to disseminate the principles of Mormonism among them. From this smug[g]ling method of preaching to the Indians, they anticipate a favorable result.

In addition to this, and to co-operate with it, it has been made known by revelation, that it will be pleasing to the Lord, should they form a matrimonial alliance with the Natives; and by this means the Elders, who comply with the thing so pleasing to the Lord, and for which the Lord has promised to bless those who do it abundantly, gain a residence in the Indian territory, independent of the agent. It has been made known to one, who has left his wife in the state of N. Y. that he is entirely free from his wife, and he is at liberty to take him a wife from among the Lamanites".

This is in direct contradiction to what it says in the Book of Mormon.

Alma

6 And the skins of the Lamanites were dark, according to the mark which was set upon their fathers, which was a curse upon them because of their transgression and their rebellion against their brethren, who consisted of Nephi, Jacob, and Joseph, and Sam, who were just and holy men.

7 And their brethren sought to destroy them, therefore they were cursed; and the Lord God set a mark upon them, yea, upon Laman and Lemuel, and also the sons of Ishmael, and Ishmaelitish women.

8 And this was done that their seed might be distinguished from the seed of their brethren that thereby the Lord God might preserve his people that they might not mix and believe in incorrect traditions which would prove their destruction.

9 And it came to pass that whosoever did mingle his seed with that of the Lamanites did bring the same curse upon his seed.

Chapter 3, verses 6, 7, 8,& 9

CHAPTER SEVENTEEN

D.N.A

The evidence against the Book of Mormon

Where did the American Indians come from? Since D.N.A fingerprinting has come about this can be addressed. Thomas W.Murphy Anthropologist said:

"Any Mormon that takes an honest look at the genetic evidence is going to struggle with it. It raises fundamental questions about what we call scripture,about the Book of Mormon; it raises fundamental questions about Joseph Smith. Was he a prophet?"
Used with the kind permission of Thomas Murphy.

Thomas W. Murphy has a Ph.D. (2003) and M.A. (1996) in anthropology from the University of Washington and a B.A. (1993) in anthropology and religion from the University of Iowa.

Thomas Murphy has since left the Mormon Church.

America 589 B.C is the estimated time and place of the arrival of Lehi and his family from Jerusalem.

By the year 326 A.D. Mormon was the General of the Nephite Army.

Book of Mormon

"And I Mormon wrote an epistle to the Lamanites that we might gather together our people to the hill which was called Cumorah and there we could give them battle."

Mormon Chapter 6 verse 2

Recorded in Mormon chapter 6.

In this final battle the Lamanites are completely destroyed by the Nephites. When the Nephite causalities on the hill Cumorah are added up, they number 230,000. Not one piece of archeological evidence has been found to support this. Mormon's son Moroni was the only Nephite to escape death. Moroni hid the golden plates but before doing so he added his own written accounts to them.

Moroni writes that after the great and tremendous battle at Cumorah the Nephites who had escaped in the country southward were hunted by the Lamanites until they were all destroyed. And my father was also killed by them and I remain alone to write the sad tale of the destruction of my people. Therefore the Book of Mormon claims the Lamanites to be sole surviving race of people living in the Americas. This is why the title page in the Book of Mormon declares that it is specifically written to the Lamanites who are a remnant of the house of Israel. And why the introduction page in the Book of Mormon concludes that after thousands of years all were destroyed except the Lamanites and they are the principal Ancestors of the American Indians.

Moroni is the angel whom Joseph Smith said visited him more than fourteen hundred years later.

Human D.N.A research has allowed scientists to determine the relatedness of different populations around the world. Children inherit a mixture of their parents DNA that is a mixture of their grandparents DNA and so forth. With each subsequent generation that DNA becomes increasingly mixed and blended with DNA from other ancestors. However smaller isolated amounts of DNA exist in the cells of both mothers and fathers that do not mix when passed to their children. The father's Y Chromosome DNA remains intact, as it is passed to his son and his son's son and so on through multiple generations.

In the same way the mother's Mitochondrial DNA also remains intact as it is passed down to both her sons and daughters from one generation to the next. Scientists are then able to trace these intact DNA markers back through hundreds of generations to determine ancestry. When the Y chromosome and the Mitochondrial DNA are tested in hundreds and even thousands of individuals from two different populations of people, results can be compared to see how similar or dissimilar these intact DNA markers are between people groups.

Dr. David Glenn Smith a Molecular Anthropologist has spent more than 30 years studying Native American genes.

He said: "If you look at genes in Native Americans they come from their ancestors, they had to come from their ancestral populations and those ancestors lived somewhere. You can look for these genes in Jewish populations but you don't find them. If you look at genes that are now commonly found in Native American populations and those that are most commonly found in Jewish populations, they don't coincide at all."

Dr. David Glenn Smith
University of Kentucky, Lexington. B.A., in Anthropology, May, 1969
University of Colorado, Boulder M.A., in Anthropology, December, 1970
Ph.D. in Anthropology, May, 1973
Used with the kind permission of Dr.David Glenn Smith

Dr. Stephen L. Whittington Anthropologist said:

"Archaeologists and physical anthropologists have not found any evidence of Hebrew origins for the people of North, South and Central America"
Used with the kind permission of Dr. Stephen L. Whittington.

Dr. Stephen L. Whittington has been Director of the Museum of Anthropology and Adjunct Associate Professor in the Department of Anthropology since 2002. He is a bioarcheologist who has excavated and studied human skeletal material from Maya sites in Honduras and Guatemala. He is currently directing the Teozacoalco Archaeological Project in Oaxaca, Mexico.

Dr. Whittington specialises mainly in Central America, which was the main setting for the Book of Mormon.

Some Mormon Apologists have gone against tradition and suggested that the people referred to in the Book of Mormon may have stayed in Central America.

One Mormon Biologist says that Lehi and his descendents may have occupied a very small stage in the Americas.

Book of Mormon "scriptures" contradict this opinion

Helaman Chapter 3 verse 8

8. *And it came to pass that they did multiply and spread, and did go forth from the land southward to the land northward, and did spread insomuch that they began to cover the face of the whole earth, from the sea south to the sea north, from the sea west to the sea east.*

Book of Mormon

1. *And it came to pass that the angel said unto me: Look, and behold thy seed, and also the seed of thy brethren. And I looked and beheld the land of promise; and I beheld multitudes of people, yea, even as it were in number as many as the sand of the sea.*

1ˢᵗ Nephi chapter 12 verse 1

One response among Mormons wrestling with genetic data is that the founding populations of the Book of Mormon would have been small and would have made a small genetic contribution to the larger populations that were already on the American Continent.

However, the Book of Mormon records otherwise

5. *But, said he, notwithstanding our afflictions, we have obtained a land of promise, a land which is choice above all other lands; a land which the Lord God hath covenanted with me should be a land for the <u>inheritance of my seed</u>. Yea, the Lord hath covenanted this land unto me, and to my children forever, and also all those who should be led out of other countries by the hand of the Lord. (Emphasis added).*

8. *And behold, it is wisdom that this land should be kept as yet from other nations; for behold, many nations would overrun the land, that there would be no place for an inheritance. (Emphasis added).*

2nd Nephi chapter 1 verses 5 & 8

Thomas Murphy Anthropologist

"This response also rests on a rejection of statements from the Book of Mormon; it also requires a rejection of the teachings of Joseph Smith, Brigham Young and virtually every other Church President who has commented on the subject. It requires setting aside statements in the Doctrine and Covenants about the Lamanites being the Indigenous people near present day Missouri. This approach is like trying to defend the prophetic status of Joseph Smith by denying his prophesies.
If Hebrew immigrants populated the Americas there would also be a strong Hebrew influence found in the languages and archaeology of the New World".

Dr. John Mc Laughlin, Linguistic, Utah State University said:

"All the evidence we have and we have evidence from probably in the neighbourhood of 800 to 900 different languages that are or have been spoken on this continent within the last few centuries points against it. None of these languages that we have has ever shown any indication of having descended from Hebrew"
Used with the kind permission of Dr. John Mc Laughlin, Linguistic, Utah State University.

Thomas Murphy Anthropologist said:

"With the Book of Mormon we do not have a single, not one source from Ancient America outside of the Book of Mormon validating a single place, a single person, a single event in both the Book of Mormon and external evidence from Ancient America. We don't have any of that so the problems that DNA poses for the Book of Mormon in a sense exemplify the difficulties that we already have in archaeology. There's never been any evidence that would show us that there was an Israelite migration to

291

the New World, none in genetics or for that matter in any other source Historical, Archaeological, or Linguistic. <u>We are in a dilemma now</u>. The genetic evidence shows clearly that the Native American Indians are not Hebrew, they are not Israelites. Not only do the ancestors of Native Americans not come from Israel, but we know where in fact they came from and that's from the Northern part of East Asia"
Author's note.(Emphasis added)

Dr. Stephen L. Whittington Anthropologist

"The evidence acceptable to most archaeologists and physical anthropologists both from dental traits and Mitochondrial DNA is that the origin of the people in North, South and Central America before the coming of the Europeans in 1492 was North Asian"

Simon Southerton Ph.D. Molecular Biologist

" If Y Chromosomes all came from Asia and Mitochondrial g gnomes all came from Asia then the only explanation for where all the rest of the chromosomes came from, is Asia. That is a very scientifically valid explanation; it's the only explanation. In excess of 150 tribes have been tested and these are from all over America even into Greenland and from that survey in excess of 5,500 individuals have been tested. From those 5,500 99.4% of Native Americans have a Mitochondrial lineage that originated in Asia. 0.6% have a European or African Mitochondrial lineage. Very tiny minority of African and European lineages that they do find came after Columbus"
Used with the kind permission of Simon Southerton.

The journey from Jerusalem to America is 8,500 miles.

Book of Mormon
17. And they were built after a manner that they were exceedingly tight, even that they would hold water like unto a dish; and the bottom thereof was tight like unto a dish; and the sides thereof were tight like unto a dish; and the ends thereof were peaked; and the top thereof was tight like unto a dish; and the length thereof was the length of a tree; and the door thereof, when it was shut, was tight like unto a dish.

Ether Chapter 6 verse 7

7. And it came to pass that when they were buried in the deep there was no water that could hurt them, their vessels being tight like unto a dish, and also they were tight like unto the ark of Noah; therefore when they were encompassed about by many waters they did cry unto the Lord, and he did bring them forth again upon the top of the waters.

Ether Chapter 2 verse 20

20. And the Lord said unto the brother of Jared: Behold, thou shalt make a hole in the top, and also in the bottom; and when thou shalt suffer for air thou shalt unstop the hole and receive air. And if it be so that the water come in upon thee, behold, ye shall stop the hole, that ye may not perish in the flood.

Ether Chapter 6 verse 10

10. And thus they were driven forth; and no monster of the sea could break them, neither whale that could mar them; and they did have light continually, whether it was above the water or under the water.

Ether Chapter 6 verse 4

4. And it came to pass when they had prepared all manner of food, that thereby they might subsist on the water, and also food for their flocks and herds, and whatsoever beast or animal or fowl that they should carry with them—and it came to pass that when they had done all these things they got aboard of their vessels or barges, and set forth into the sea, commending themselves unto the Lord their God.

Ether Chapter 6 verse 11

11. And thus they were driven forth, three hundred and forty and four days upon the water.

A single gramme of feces can contain 10 million viruses, one million bacteria, 1,000 parasite cysts and 100 worm eggs. Feces not disposed of properly can be carried on people's shoes, hands and clothes and contaminate water, food and cutlery. It's an impossiblity to survive in the conditions which are recorded in the Book of Mormon.

The journey from Jerusalem to America is 8,500 miles.

The journey from Asia across the Bering Strait is 58 miles.

Thomas Murphy Anthropologist

" In living Native Americans DNA there will inevitably be a few individuals even in the most remote native communities that have had some intermarriage with Europeans or Africans and that will show up in their DNA, the small percentage that's there can be distinguished from the possibility of an Israelite migration to the New World by looking at the dates in which those types of lineages separated from other forms of DNA very similar to them, so in other words you can identify which ones came after 1492.

Dr. Stephen Whittington Anthropologist

"In general the tool kits that were being used in the New World fit what was coming out of Asia at the same time"

Thomas Murphy Anthropologist

"What is most significant about the genetic research and its applicability to the Book of Mormon is that it validates what we already knew from other scientific disciplines. From biological anthropology more generally we knew a long time ago that American Indians resembled Asians and particularly the people from the regions around Mongolia and Siberia, more than they did other peoples.

Archeologically we knew that there were similarities between the cultures of North East Asia and those of the early Americans that are in the types of artefacts they used and left behind. We also knew based on linguistic evidence that American Indians shared a common ancestry with at least some of North East Asians and the Siberians. So we had all of this evidence from scientific disciplines as diverse as linguistics and archaeology and human biology all showing us the Asian origin of American Indians. Now the genetic evidence confirms what we already knew from that other material "

This DNA evidence had been firmly established and widely published long before the 2002 Winter Olympics focussed the world's attention on Utah and to a certain extent on the Mormon Church. The foreign press was given a rare opportunity to interview the leader of the Church Gordon B. Hinckley.

A German reporter asked President Hinckley. "What will be your position when DNA analysis will show that in the History there never has been an emigration from Israel to North America? It could be that the scientists will find out".

President Hinckley replied. "It hasn't happened, that hasn't been determined yet. All I can say is that's speculative. No one really knows that, the answer to that, not at this point".

Recent Book of Mormon change: Instead of being the "principal ancestors" of American Indians, Lamanites are now......"among the ancestors of the American Indians."

Genetic principles explain a lack of Jewish Markers?

Mormon apologists have cited possible genetic effects to explain the lack of Jewish genetic markers in Native American populations. (Mormon apologetics is the systematic defense of Mormonism against its critics)

Frequently cited are the founder's effect and genetic drift. Although the terms sound scientific and possibly could explain the contradictory evidence, there is not a non-Mormon scientist who would accept those kinds of explanations as being valid. Let's first explain the principles and how they might apply to these studies.

Founder effects can result from one individual becoming the dominant ancestor of a population. In the founder effect, if that one individual harbours a significant mutation compared to the population he came from, the genetics would be skewed toward that one individual. Genetic drift results in isolated populations as selective breeding occurs, skewing the genetics in a particular direction different from other isolated populations.

How could founder effect and genetic drift account for the data from these genetics studies? In the Book of Mormon, all the male founders of the Nephites and Lamanites were descended from one man, Lehi. If Lehi harboured some kind of skewed genetics, it would be reflected in his sons and their offspring. This could explain some of the Y-chromosome data, which is passed on only through the male line. However, since there are many different Y-chromosome haplotypes found at many loci, it is virtually impossible that *all* of those loci would be mutated in any one individual.

It gets much worse for the Mormon apologist. Lehi's genetics could not explain the mtDNA genetics, since these genes are passed on only though the female line. The wives of Lehi's sons were also from one family line - Ishmael. Since there are four main Native American specific mtDNA haplotypes, one would have to hypothesize that all of these haplotypes were developed in the wives of Lehi's sons or their immediate daughters *and* that those haplotypes just happened to match those of East Asians. A third genetic technique examined the polymorphic Alu insertions found in the autosomal (non-X or Y) chromosomes. With results similar to the two other genetic techniques, the founder effect would require the additional simultaneous mutation of at least 5 polymorphic Alu insertions in Lehi's sons and son's wives -

Not only do Mormon apologists have to deal with human genetics, they also have to explain the genetics of certain intestinal bacteria in domesticated dogs. In order for Native Americans to have been founded by Israelites, the *Helicobacter pylori* in their gut would have had to mutate to match that of the Asian variety. In addition, the dogs they took over to the Americas would have had to mutate to Asian type genetics. *All of* these five extremely improbable, multiple mutation effects would have had to have happened within one or two generations in the same small populations. The idea is scientifically ludicrous.

The authenticity of Moroni, the golden plates and Joseph's Smith's testimony concerning them are all invalidated if in fact it is discovered that the Book of Mormon story is not real history. The status of prophet is also at stake for Joseph Smith because he claimed the history told in the Book of Mormon was God's word, the most correct book on earth and the keystone of the religion he was building.

Randall Shortridge Ph.D. Molecular Biologist

"If the Book of Mormon is not a literal history, then it should follow what happens in it isn't history. Yes the crowning event, Jesus appearing in the Americas. If the people didn't exist it couldn't have happened."
Used with kind permission of Randall Shortridge
Randall D. Shortridge, Ph.D. Associate Professor, SUNY-Buffalo 1996-present.

Thomas Murphy, Anthropologist

"When we compare the Book of Mormon with the Bible especially when we deal with themes like archaeology, there are some stark difference. There are specific battles, events, people and places named in the Bible that we know from external sources. But with the Book of Mormon we don't have a single person, place or event from Ancient America validated by external sources"

Randall Shortridge Ph.D.

"If this was taken into a court of law, it would be an open and shut case and that's because the DNA fingerprinting evidence is unquestionable. The American Indians came from Asia"

There was no angel Moroni, there was no First Vision, there were no plates, there were no people from Israel on the American Continent whatsoever.

Jesus did not appear to the Book of Mormon people for they did not exist. There was no emigration of a group of Jews to the New World.

THE DESIGNS OF MORMONISM
By William Harris 1841

The designs of Smith and his coadjutors, at the time of the first publication of the Book of Mormon, was, doubtlessly, nothing more than pecuniary aggrandisement. I do not believe, at that time, they expected at that time that so many could ever be duped to admit it true. When, however, the delusion began to spread, the publishers saw the door opened not only for wealth, but also for extensive power; and their history throughout, shows that they have not been remiss in their efforts to acquire both. The extent of their desires is now by no means limited, for their writings and actions show a design to pursue the same path, and attain the same end by the same means, as did Mahomet.

The idea of a second Mahomet arising in the nineteenth century, may excite a smile; but when we consider the steps now taken by the Mormons to concentrate their numbers, and their ultimate design to unite themselves with the Indians, it will not be at all surprising, if scenes unheard of since the days of Feudalism, should soon be re-enacted.

In the first place, Smith, by proclamations and by revelations, has called all his followers to settle immediately around him. The last revelation on this subject is published in the "Times and Seasons" dated June 1st, 1841, from which I extract the following, "Awake! O! Kings of the Earth! Come ye, O! Come ye, with your gold and your silver, to the help of my people, to the house of the Daughter of Zion. And again, verily I say unto you, let all my saints come from afar; and send ye swift messengers, yea, chosen messengers, and say unto them, come ye with all your gold, and your silver, and your precious stones, and with your antiquities'" &c. They are further informed, in the course of this revelation, that after sufficient time has been allowed to build a baptismal font at Nauvoo, their baptisms for the dead shall not be acceptable in other places. The object of Smith, in all this, is evidently to collect all his followers into one place, and thus to concentrate all his power and enable him the better to secure wealth.

CHAPTER EIGHTEEN

The Burning in the bosom

Book of Mormon Moroni Chapter 10 verses 3- 5.

3. Behold, I would exhort you that when ye shall read these things, if it be wisdom in God that ye should read them, that ye would remember how merciful the Lord hath been unto the children of men, from the creation of Adam even down until the time that ye shall receive these things, and ponder it in your hearts.

4. And when ye shall receive these things, I would exhort you that ye would ask God, the Eternal Father, in the name of Christ, if these things are not true; and if ye shall ask with a sincere heart, with real intent, having faith in Christ, he will manifest the truth of it unto you, by the power of the Holy Ghost.

5. And by the power of the Holy Ghost ye may know the truth of all things.

Can we rely alone on our feelings? No! In The New Testament, John has already said that our hearts can condemn us and that we should not rely on them alone to confirm that we are in the truth.

New Testament, 1 John 5:13

13. I write these things to you who believe in the name of the Son of God so that you may know that you have eternal life.

David Whitmer [1]

David Whitmer used his position as one of the Three Witnesses to condemn Joseph Smith's Church. "If you believe my testimony to the Book of Mormon," wrote Whitmer, " if you believe that God spake to

us three witnesses by his own voice, then I tell you that in June, 1838, God spake to me again by his own voice from the heavens and told me to 'separate myself from among the Latter Day Saints, for as they sought to do unto me, so it should be done unto them.'
An Address To All Believers In Christ 1887 p27

Some of the Book of Mormon witnesses were so credulous that they were influenced by a man named James Jesse Strang. Strang like Joseph Smith claimed he found some plates that he translated with the Urim and Thummim. He had witnesses who claimed they saw the plates and their testimony is recorded in almost the same way that the testimony of the eleven witnesses is recorded in the Book of Mormon. Brigham Young and other Mormon leaders denounced Strang as an impostor, but some Book of Mormon witnesses became very interested in his claims. On 20th January 1848 Strang wrote the following:

James Strang [2]

... Early in 1846 the tract reprint of the first number of the Voree Herald, containing the evidence of my calling and authority, strayed into upper Missouri. Immediately I received a letter from Hiram Page, one of the witnesses of the Book of Mormon, and a neighbour and friend to the Whitmers' who lived near him, and that they rejoiced with exceeding joy that God has raised up one to stand in the place of Joseph.... He goes on to say that all the witnesses of the Book of Mormon living in that region received the news with gladness, and finally that they held a council in which David and John Whitmer and this Hiram Page were the principle actors; and being at a loss what they ought to do about coming to Voree, sent up to me as a prophet of God to tell them what to do... last April (1847) I received another letter from the same Hiram Page, acknowledging the receipt of mine... and giving me the acts of another council of himself at the Whitmers',......they invite me to come to their residence in Missouri and receive from them, David and John Whitmer, Church records, and manuscript revelations, which they had kept in their possession from the time that they were active members of the Church. These documents they speak of as great importance to the Church, and offer them to me as the true shepherd who has a right to them.

Although the Book of Mormon witnesses were attracted to Strang for a short time, they soon became interested in a new movement, which William E. Mc Lellin (who had served as an Apostle under Joseph Smith) was trying to start. William E. Mc Lellin tells how David Whitmer, one of the three witnesses to the Book of Mormon, gave revelations supporting his organization and condemning the Mormon Church.

William E. Mc Lellin [3]

.... After a few moments of solemn secret prayer, the following was delivered solely through and by David Whitmer, as the Revelator, and written by me as scribe, viz:

"Verily, verily thus saith the Lord unto my servants David, and John, and William, and Jacob, and Hiram... Behold I have looked upon you from the beginning, and have seen that in your hearts dwelt truth, and righteousness [sic]...it must needs have been that ye were cast out from among those who had polluted themselves and the holy authority of their priesthood... For verily, verily saith the Lord, even Jesus, your Redeemer, they have polluted my name, and have done continually wickedness in my sight, Thou shalt write concerning the downfall of those who once composed my Church..."

But here David Whitmer said a vision was opened before him, and the spirit, which was upon him bid him to stop and talk to me concerning it. He said that in the bright light before him he saw a small chest or box of very curious and fine workmanship, which seemed to be locked, but he was told that it contained precious things... I was told that it contained "the treasure of wisdom, and knowledge from God." David and I turned aside, and called upon the Lord, and received direct instruction how we should further proceed... I ordained Hiram Page to the office of High Priest, ... we two ordained Jacob Whitmer to the same office. Then we all laid hands on John Whitmer and re-ordained him.... We stepped forward and all laid hands on upon David and re-ordained him...
The Ensign of Liberty, August 1849, pp. 101-4. As quoted in The Changing World of Mormonism.

Brigham Young[4]

"Some of the witnesses of the Book of Mormon, who handled the plates and conversed with the angels of God, were afterwards left to doubt and to disbelieve that they had ever seen an angel."
Journal of Discourses, vol. 7, p. 164

David Whitmer stood by his Testimony.

Thomas Ford [5]
Governor of Illinois, who was very aware of the Mormon movement in his state, had given his own opinion as to how Joseph Smith collected the testimony of the witnesses, having known several well-known men of Smith's acquaintance:
They (Smith's key men) told Ford, that the witnesses were "set to continual prayer, and other spiritual exercises. " Then at last " he assembled them in a room, and produced a box which he said contained the precious treasure. The lid was opened; the witnesses peeped into it, but making no discovery, for the box was empty, they said, "Brother Joseph, we do not see the plates." The prophet answered them, " O ye of little faith! How long will God bear with this wicked and perverse generation? Down on your knees, brethren every one of you, and pray God for the forgiveness of your sins, and for a holy and living faith which cometh down from heaven." The disciples dropped to their knees, and began to pray in the fervency of their spirit, supplicating God for more than two hours with fanatical earnestness; at the end of which time, looking again into the box, they were now persuaded that they saw the plates".

Newspaper reports at that time said that all three witnesses told different versions.

The written witness account was apparently written first by Joseph Smith and then he got them to sign it.

Notes

1. *An Address To All Believers In Christ. 1887 p 27*
2. *Gospel Herald,* January 20, 1848. As quoted in *The Changing World of Mormonism p 99-100*
3. *The Ensign of Liberty, August 1849, pp. 101-4 as quoted in The Changing World of Mormonism p.102*
4. *Journal of Discourses, vol.7 p.164*
5. Gov. Thomas Ford (1800-1850) *History of Illinois* (Chicago: S. C. Griggs & Co. 1854)

Chapter Nineteen

The Second Endowment

The rank and file members of the Mormon Church do not know about this ordinance.

Account by ex-Church member.

My Second Anointing Experience[1]

I am posting this account to confirm the ordinance does actually take place currently, as I have received the ordinance, and how it is currently performed.

I state the names of the Apostle and Seventy involved as well as the date and actual temple so that the credibility cannot be questioned. I have not mentioned my own name as I wish the emphasis to be on the topic of the ordinance itself. It is not to protect my anonymity from the Church, as the First Presidency will be able to identify me from this account within minutes, if not immediately.

Invitation
Preparation
The day itself – what happened
Feelings afterwards
Asked to nominate others
Aftermath

Invitation

In April 2002 Elder Harold G. Hillam of the First Quorum of Seventy, as President of the Europe West Area, called me into his office. He said he was extending to me and my wife (she was not present), on behalf of President Hinckley, an invitation to receive a "special blessing" in the Preston England Temple. He asked whether I had heard of the "second endowment" to which I replied no. I later told him that I had heard of it, but was so stunned by his invitation my mind went blank regarding the matter.

He told me very few people receive this blessing and it must be kept secret. He said if the general membership knew about it there would be problems. More would want to receive the ordinance than the apostles have time to accommodate and members would wonder why "so and so" had received it but they had not. I must not even tell my children. He said I should just tell them that their mother and I were going away for the day or weekend. He recommended I read all that Elder Bruce R. McConkie had written on the subject of "making your calling and election sure".

Elder Hillam promised me it would be a "life changing" experience. He said the ordinance was performed in Joseph Smith's time but had been discontinued during President David O. McKay's time. This resulted in only 2 of the then apostles, Harold B. Lee and Spencer W. Kimball, having had this ordinance on the death of President Joseph Fielding Smith. It was therefore re-introduced and is still practiced today. (I have seen no source that quotes this suspension of the ordinance, only Elder Hillam's word).

We were to be at the Preston England Temple on Sunday 19th May 2002 where Elder M. Russell Ballard, of the Quorum of the Twelve Apostles, would perform the ordinance. We should have our temple recommends and our temple robes etc. with us.

Preparation

I went home and told my wife. She accepted it quite calmly. I reflected on my own life and personal worthiness. I read all that Elder McConkie had written on the subject and looked forward to the day with excitement. Basically, Elder McConkie wrote that , during the first endowment you are given certain blessings to become a king and a priest (queen and priestess) to the most high God, and these blessings are conditional on you remaining worthy of them. With the second endowment, the conditions are removed as you have already proven your faithfulness and entitlement to the blessings. Therefore, you are sealed up to the highest degree of the celestial kingdom unconditionally. Any sins committed afterward may render you liable to the "buffetings in the flesh" but they will not prevent you from attaining your exaltation.

The only sin that is unpardonable is denying the Holy Ghost (or in some passages the shedding of innocent blood).

I had never expected this to happen to me. I assumed I would be judged in the next life, not have that judgment made in this life. It meant my wife and I would be guaranteed a celestial glory unless we committed the "unpardonable sin" which seemed to be unthinkable at the time. We had made it, the Lord, through his prophet, had informed us we were worthy of this high exaltation. I never thought it would be done in this way. I had assumed that, if anyone did deserve to have their calling and election made sure, the Lord would appear to them Himself. Like most members of the Church I assumed all the apostles had made sure their calling and election and many of the other General Authorities of the Church.

I felt a power helping me be a better person and more dedicated to the Church. I telephoned the temple to book accommodation for my wife and myself on Saturday 18th May so that we could make the most of the experience. I did not like lying to my family and friends as to our whereabouts that weekend. I did not feel comfortable as it was dishonest but I was instructed not to disclose what was happening. To tell people you will be at the temple on a Sunday, when supposedly all temples are closed, would raise further questions. I therefore told my children we were going to the temple for the weekend and would be attending a special meeting with Elder Ballard and the Area President on Sunday. This was not too unusual for my children to accept as I regularly attended Area Presidency meetings and had been assisting these same brethren the day before at a training session for stake presidents. Also, it was as truthful as I considered I could be while still keeping the second anointing secret.

On Saturday 18th May 2002, after Priesthood Leadership Training by Elder Ballard in Birmingham England, my wife and I drove to the Preston England Temple. We were surprised and delighted to discover that we had been given a "bridal suite" as our accommodation. It added to the special occasion. While walking in the temple grounds in the early evening we unexpectedly met a member of our ward who had attended a family wedding that day. She asked us what we were doing at the temple on a Saturday evening. I quickly mentioned something about Area Presidency meetings (she knew of my calling at the time, that I worked closely with the Area Presidency) and changed the subject. Again, I did not feel comfortable "lying for the Lord".

Anyway, my wife and I had a very pleasant evening preparing ourselves spiritually for our "life changing" experience.

At the Temple

Upon entering the temple we changed into our temple robes, met the other couples who were to receive the ordinance that day, and were led to an upper room that had been set apart for this purpose. I knew 3 of the other 4 couples. 2 of the husbands were former stake presidents and 1 was a mission president who had just completed his mission.

We were all seated in the room with Elder Ballard officiating, Elder Harold G. Hillam assisting, with Sister Carol Hillam, Elder Wayne S. Peterson and Sister Peterson as observers. A counsellor in the temple presidency was also present. The temple president was absent because his wife was seriously ill in hospital.

Elder Ballard explained what would be happening. We were to have our feet washed and be anointed by him. He was acting under the direction of the Prophet, President Gordon B. Hinckley. We would then be allocated a sealing room for each couple to be alone and perform the second part of the ordinance. We would then all meet again with Elder Ballard in the celestial room.

The following is my best recollection of what happened in performing this ordinance. It has been nearly 6 years since it happened so I may well have omitted some things. I have briefly reviewed published accounts of the second anointing to jog my memory.

I. THE ORDINANCE OF THE WASHING OF THE FEET

I was beckoned to sit on a particular chair. Elder Ballard knelt and washed my feet, then dried them. This ordinance cleansed me from the blood and sins of this generation.

II. THE ORDINANCE OF SECOND ANOINTINGS -- Part One
Anointed & Ordained a King/Priest, Queen/Priestess

I was anointed with oil, on the top of my head, and then hands were laid upon my head, and I was ordained a king and a priest unto the Most High God, to rule and reign in the House of Israel forever. My head, brow, eyes, ears nose, lips etc. were anointed with oil and specific blessings were given related to knowing, understanding and speaking the truth. This ordinance gave me the fullness of the priesthood and a blessing was given which included the following :-

Sealing power to bind & loose, curse & bless.
Blessings of Abraham, Isaac & Jacob.
The Holy Spirit of Promise bestowed.
Blessed to live as long as life is desirable.
Blessed to attain unto the Godhood.
Power to be a member of Godhead bestowed.
Sealed up to eternal life
Power to have the heavens opened.

We were charged not to reveal to other individuals that we had received this ordinance. My wife was also anointed and ordained a queen and priestess.

THE ORDINANCE OF SECOND ANOINTINGS -- Part Two

"The Washing of The Feet", Wife to Husband

The second part of the second anointing was explained to us. We (my wife and I) were to go to another sealing room where we would be alone as a couple. There would be a bowl of water and a towel. My wife was to wash my feet (as Mary did to Jesus) and dry them. She would then place her hands upon my head and pronounce a blessing upon me as the spirit dictated.

This was a very moving and personal experience for us as a couple and we both ended in tears of great joy.

Following this we met in the celestial room with Elder Ballard and the others. Elder Ballard summarized what had happened and asked if there were any questions as they could only be answered at this time, in this place as we were charged to tell nobody that we had received this ordinance.

I have stated earlier some of the things mentioned in the blessing given to me. I cannot recall everything and I did not record it at the time.

Feelings Afterwards

There is no doubt this had been a "life changing experience" as promised by Elder Hillam. I felt the "spirit" even stronger.

Nominating others for the Ordinance

A little time after this "life changing experience" Elder Hillam asked me to nominate 2 couples I knew to receive this ordinance. I took this charge very seriously and asked Elder Hillam what qualities I should consider. He answered, "find another you, mature people who have been tried and tested yet remained absolutely committed and dedicated to the Church". This was a flattering response. I knew the final decision would not be mine but, nevertheless, I considered it a very grave responsibility to make such nominations. I therefore went about it in the same manner I had done all my Church life. I prayed for guidance to know Heavenly Father's will in this respect, made a list of all the people I knew who could be considered, worked it out in my own mind and fasted and prayed.

Previously I had assumed, if anyone made sure their calling and election, it was received at a personal visit from Jesus Christ. He knows us and is the perfect judge. Now I was in a position of nominating others for something so sacred, more onerous than nominating bishops, patriarchs, stake presidency counsellors etc. I still assumed all nominations from all sources would be whittled down by an Area President and Apostle and the final decisions would be made by President Hinckley as he personally consulted with the Lord. (Years later I saw that these, like everything else in the Church, were purely the decisions of mortal men. What arrogance for a Church leader to assume he has the right to decide who will go to the "highest heaven".)

Aftermath

Seventeen months later, in October 2003, I was studying in preparation for serving a full-time mission with my wife. Since June 2001 I had been told by General Authorities of the Church that, when I was ready to submit my mission papers, they would recommend me as a mission president.

I decided there was one question regarding the Book of Mormon I had answered many times before but I doubted anyone with a good scientific background would accept such an answer. As I considered God would not prevent someone joining his one true Church simply because they had a better scientific education and understanding ("the glory of God is intelligence"), I studied to find an acceptable answer which I assumed would be to demonstrate the flaws in the scientific hypothesis.

I wanted this answer for myself to teach others and for my missionaries if I were called as a mission president. NOT FOR ONE MINUTE, at that time, did I think the Church was false. I KNEW, beyond any shadow of doubt, it was true. I just needed to know what was wrong with the currently held scientific views. After studying the specific scientific methodology, to my amazement, it stood up. These were not simply hypotheses and theories of scientists but demonstrable FACTS. I believed God to be the "Master Scientist" how else can He be the creator of all things. Therefore, true science cannot be in conflict with His revealed word.

This led me to consider in more depth other truth claims of the Church and discuss them with two general authorities and consult two Brigham Young University professors.

CONCLUSION – THE CHURCH WAS NOT TRUE, I HAD ALLOWED MYSELF TO BE DECEIVED.

Notes

1. www.exmormon.org

CHAPTER TWENTY

Spiritual Abuse and Its Effects

Post Traumatic Stress Disorder (PTSD) is a term for certain psychological consequences of exposure to, or confrontation with, stressful experiences that the person experiences as highly traumatic. The experience must involve actual or threatened death, serious physical injury, or a threat to physical and/or psychological integrity. It is occasionally called post-traumatic stress reaction to emphasize that it is a routine result of traumatic experience rather than a manifestation of a pre-existing psychological weakness on the part of the patient.

Experiences, which may induce the condition. I will put the experience that related to me.

* Being subjected to psychological or physical abuse as a member or adherent of ---

Or separation from --- a cult, religious sect, or New Religious Movement

Diagnostic Criteria[1]

The diagnostic criteria for PTSD, according to *Diagnostic and Statistical Manual of Mental Disorders-IV*, are stressors listed from A to F.

Notably, the stressor criterion A is divided into two parts.

The first (A1) requires that

"The person experienced, witnessed, or was confronted with an event or events that involved actual or threatened death or injury, or a threat to the physical integrity of self or others."

The second (A2) requires that

"The person's response involved intense fear, helplessness, or horror."
It is possible for individuals to experience traumatic stress without manifesting Post-Traumatic Stress Disorder.

Symptoms of PTSD can include the following: nightmares, flashbacks, emotional detachment or numbing feelings (emotional self-mortification or dissociation), insomnia, avoidance of reminders and extreme distress when exposed to reminders ("triggers"), irritability, hyper vigilance, memory loss, and excessive startle response, clinical depression and anxiety, loss of appetite.

For most people, the emotional effects of traumatic events will tend to subside after several months; if they last longer, then a psychiatric disorder may be diagnosed. Most people who experience traumatic events will not develop PTSD. PTSD is thought to be primarily an anxiety disorder and should not be confused with normal grief and adjustment after traumatic events.

Spiritual abuse is a very real threat to not only your life here which is enough for anyone to contend with, but with spiritual abuse one has very great fears for the next life.

Notes

1. *Diagnostic and Statistical Manual of Mental Disorders*

CHAPTER TWENTY ONE

In my suffering I penned this poem.

The Black Tear

The Black Tear fell and rolled away to another place of sorrow
To another weeping valley where there is no tomorrow
As it gathered with the others, clear ones that fell in times past
A vast ocean of pain and grief, tangible evidence of brief relief
No solution no diminution.

Marcia Van Outen 2006

Helpful website

Recovery from Mormonism
www.exmormon.org

A site for those who are questioning their faith in the Mormon Church
and for those who need support as they transition their lives to a normal
life. Not affiliated with any religion. Does not advocate any religion

Some sample letters

"Utah has the highest rate of Depression in the United States.
Psychiatrists point to several factors that could contribute to Utah's high
levels of depression: limited mental health resources, restricted access to
treatment as a result of cost, poor quality of resources and a varied list
of other factors, including an under funded educational system and a
culture deeply rooted in the Mormon faith.

Interesting! From the time I moved from LA to Orem, Utah my emotional condition went downhill. I had no help, no companies my hubby worked for offered insurance, so I was on my own to pay for massive psychiatrist bills. I was thoroughly depressed the entire 6 years I lived there. I noticed depression in other women, too, though everyone tried to put on their show. I was Visiting Teacher for the bishop's wife... she was crying many of the times I went to see her. Now I'm out of Utah, thankfully, and out of the cult. Not on meds, not depressed...

I just cringe at these stories where Utah LDS are trying to pin the depression, suicide and antidepressant use rate on anything and everything other than Mormonism. Utah has twice the national average of anti-depressant use and Utah is 70% Mormon. DO THE MATH!"

****

"When I was married, Mormon, and living in Utah I'd been on Prozac, Paxil, Effexor and I can't even remember what else. I was all smiles on the outside, held Church jobs that took a lot of time, made my children's' clothes and dressed them alike, always picture perfect. I canned, decorated cakes, did 100% Visiting Teaching, made cute little things for my Relief Society sisters, cross-stitched beautiful pics for my home, blah, blah, blah. I wanted to DIE! I didn't want to take my own life, but I prayed for the Lord to take me. But still... smile, smile, smile!"

"Haven't been on meds since leaving the Church 7 years ago. Did things that improved my career and found wonderful, fun, intelligent friends, I'm not only happIER than I've ever been in my life, but maybe truly happy and fulfilled for the first time ever. Being in total control of my life and not worrying about God and Satan trying to micromanage my life, lifts 90% of any depressive thoughts right out of me.
Sorry, but my very-unprofessional opinion, based on real life experience, is that there is ONLY one reason for the high depression, suicide and anti-depressant use in Utah... L-D-S-Inc."

****

The state of Utah, which is predominately Mormon, has a higher than the national average of...teenage suicide.

The state of Utah, which is predominately Mormon, has a higher than the national average of wife-beating.

Attorney Fighting against the Latter Day Saints for Enabling Child Sexual Abuse

The Latter Day Saints

The Latter Day Saints have a unique culture that provides a haven for sexual abusers. Of course, child sexual abuse is not meant to be part of the culture -- but the Latter Day Saints leadership enables child sexual abusers to continue destroying people's lives long after they become aware of the crimes. Because the Latter Day Saints leaders do not bring known abusers to justice, and even cover up the abusers' crimes, they are guilty of supporting this behavior and making it possible for more children to be victimized.

In his practice representing victims of child sexual abuse, attorney Timothy D. Kosnoff has launched many lawsuits against the LDS Church Corporation on behalf of people who were sexually abused as children. Attorney Kosnoff has learned exactly how child sexual abuse has become rampant among the Latter Day Saints, and he is committed both to stopping individual abusers and to fighting the Latter Day Saints church's enabling the abusers.

A Culture that Enables Child Sexual Abuse

When either children or adults abused as children come forth to complain about a sexual predator, they come forth to the adult men of the Latter Day Saints congregation. The Latter Day Saints are an insular religious community: its bishops and stake presidents insist on handling all such allegations internally and strongly discourage any intervention by outside authorities. Church leaders too often cover up or turn a blind eye to evidence of child sexual abuse and attempt to deal with paedophilia exclusively as a matter of sin and not as a crime and a grave threat to children and families. LDS Church General Authorities in Utah have known of the wide-spread nature of this problem but continue to deny it and refuse to implement meaningful reforms that can better protect LDS children.

Anyone raised in the Church of Jesus Christ of Latter Day Saints is taught great reverence for the power and authority of the priesthood. Too often, protecting the power and image of the male leaders who possess the priesthood is the driving rationalization for covering up their crimes against children.

Dealing with Abuse "In-House" Does Not Work

Unfortunately, these church leaders treat child sexual abuse as a mere sin, not a crime, and do nothing to prevent the abusers from continuing their crimes. Many people who are abused within the Church know that nothing will be done if they report abuse, and they suffer in silence instead.

Quite simply, this method of handling child sexual abuse allegations is criminal. There are mandatory standards for child abuse reporting that leaders of the LDS church habitually violate. LDS Church officials and its lawyers typically attempt to evade responsibility by hiding behind the "free exercise of religion" clause of the Constitution, statute of limitations technicalities and clergy-penitent privilege statutes -- and while they protect themselves, the paedophiles in the Church are free to continue their horrific abuses.

One Lawyer Fighting against Latter Day Saints Sexual Abuse
Attorney Kosnoff was involved in a recent case against the Church of Latter Day Saints in which one individual was paid $3 million to settle out of court. The pattern of abuse supported by the Church was outrageous -- the abuser had victimized people in 7 states over 18 years, and after each incident, he was simply moved to a different ward. No organization, and especially not a church, should knowingly allow such a thing to happen.

Used with the kind permission of Timothy D. Kosnoff. Attorney

Thomas Murphy Anthropologist said:

"With the Book of Mormon we don't have a single, not one source from Ancient America outside of the Book of Mormon validating a single place, a single person, a single event in both the Book of Mormon. We don't have any of that so the problems that DNA poses for the Book of Mormon in a sense exemplify the difficulties that we already have in archaeology. There's never been any evidence that would show us that there was an Israelite migration to the New World, none in genetics or for that matter in any other source Historical, Archaeological, or Linguistic. We are in a dilemma now. The genetic evidence shows clearly that the Native American Indians are not Hebrew, they are not Israelites. Not only do the ancestors of Native Americans not come from Israel, but we know where in fact they came from and that's from the Northern part of East Asia"

Conclusion

Randall Shortridge Ph.D.

"If this was taken into a court of law, it would be an open and shut case and that's because the DNA fingerprinting evidence is unquestionable. The American Indians came from Asia"
There was **no angel Moroni,** there was **no First Vision,** there were **no plates,** there were **no people from Israel** on the American Continent whatsoever. Jesus did not appear to the Book of Mormon people because **they did not exist.** There was no emigration of a group of Jews to the New World.
(Emphasis added)

New Testament

21. Neither shall they say, Lo here! Or Lo there! For, behold, the kingdom of God is within you.

Luke chapter 17 verse 21

Letter from the author

Leaving the Mormon Church doesn't mean that everything goes back to the way it was before joining it. Some people were born and raised in that faith and know nothing else. A great many years will have been spent in the confines of the church. Years that could have been spent in growing, changing and learning in the real world. Doctrines and teachings that were ingrained will take some time to dissipate, if ever. A whole world view is changed. Self-identity has to be re-examined and this can be difficult and frightening, even more so for those who were raised in that faith for they know nothing else. Ex-members then have to find what it is that they believe in when Mormon teachings are found to be false. They will experience a great sense of loss for the time, energy and money given to the church. The Mormon Church takes a great deal of time and money, time that could have been given to their loved and friends. They will also carry the pain of how their being a member affected their loved ones, if their loved ones were not members of the church. And what about life after death? We thought we had all the answers! And what are we now? Christians, Catholics, Protestants, Methodist, Atheists, or whatever we were before the Mormons came.

I feel very fortunate that I found out the truth and I still (I hope) have some time left to live in the real world and, more importantly to be here and now, not always looking to the Second Coming when everything will be put right. I try to live in the present, take one day at a time and try to be a good person. That's all I can do. I penned my findings and experiences to hopefully help others who are on the same journey. May you find great strength and courage for the remainder of it.

Live in the present, using the past, to build your future

Marcia Van Outen

Lyrics from the song "Good News" from the album " Dream Harder" by the Waterboys.

I'm preparing for birth
I'm not the only one

I'm a part of the earth
I'm a drop of the sun

I'm in step with the stars
I'm in league with the land

I'm a functioning part
of the Master's plan !

New Testament

And ye shall know the truth, and the truth shall make you free

John 8 verse 32

The End

BIBLIOGRAPHY

The Book of Mormon

Milton V. Backman, Jr., and Ronald K. Esplin, *History of the Church, Encyclopaedia of Mormonism*

Bennett, John Cook *A HISTORY OF THE SAINTS OR AN EXPOSE OF JOE SMITH AND MORMONISM.*

Baskin, R.N. Remininicenes of Early Utah, 1914

Boston Recorder Published by Nathaniel Willis April 8, 1839

Young, Brigham *Journal of Discourses*

Booth, Ezra *Letters For the Ohio Star, Nelson, Portage County, 1831*

Boston Recorder Published by Nathaniel Willis April 19, 1839

Baskin, R.N. *Reminiscences of Early Utah, 1914*

Daily Bulletin Vol lX No 1273 Honolulu March 11, 1886

The Deseret News

Creigh, Alfred *History of Washington Pa.* (Harrisburg B.Singerly, Pub, 1870, 71)

Codman, John. "*Mormonism*" *The International Review* Xl: 3 (NYC: A.S. Brarnes &Co, Sept. 1881)

Clark, D.D. Rev. John A. *GLEANINGS BY WAY*

The Doctrine and Covenants

Deming, Arthur B. *NAKED TRUTHS ABOUT MORMONISM*

Deming, Arthur B. *Naked Truths About Mormonism* ll December 1988 No 1 (Berkeley, California: A.B. Deming Society)

Daily Press Vol. 11. No 40 Honolulu, Thursday, April 15, 1886

Daily Missouri Republican Vol LXXVll May 29, 1885

Diagnostic and Statistical Manual of Mental Disorders

Evangelical Magazine and Gospel Advocate, April 9,1831

Frazer's Magazine, February, 1873

Ford, *Thomas* Gov. History of Illinois. *(Chicago: S.C. Griggs & Co.* 1854

Nelson Winch Green, Mormonism its rise, progress, and present condition... 1858, 1870 ed.

The Holy Bible King James Version

Hayden, Amos S. *History of the Disciples* (Cincinnati: Chase & Hall, 1875)

Hale, Isaac affidavit of published in the Susquehanna Register, May 1, 1834

Howe E.D. *Mormonism Unvailed* [Sic]

History of Illinois

Hickman,William *(Danite) Brigham Young's Destroying Angel,* 1964

Harris, William *Mormonism Portrayed* (Warsaw: Sharp & Gamble, 1841)

History of the Church, vol.2

Jonas, Larry S. *Mormon Claims Examined*

Journal of Discourses, vol. 6

Johnson, Benjamin F. *Autobiography (1818-1846) My Life's Review*

Johnson, Benjamin F. 1903, Letter as printed in the Testimony of Joseph Smith's Best Friend

Kinney, Bruce D. D. *MORMONISM The Islam of America*

The Lion of the Lord New York, 1969

Lee, John D. Confessions of. 1880

Livesey, Richard 1838. *An exposure of Mormonism, being a statement of facts relating to the self-styled "Latter Day Saints," And the Origin of the Book of Mormon.*

Millennial Star, vol. 28

The Manuscript Story.

The Manuscript Found Published by the Reorganised church of Jesus Christ of Latter Day Saints

Mace, Wandle *Journal of Wandle Mace*

Mormon Portraits 1886

McConkie, Bruce R. *Mormon Doctrine 1958*

Mc Conkie, Bruce R. Mormon Doctrine (1979 printing of 1966 edition)

Nauvoo: Kingdom On The Mississippi

The New York Spectator, September 23, 1843

Patterson, Robert Jr. *Who Wrote The Book of Mormon?* (Philadelphia: L. H. Everts & Co., 1882)

Patterson, Robert Jr. *Who Wrote The Book of Mormon?*

REPRINTED FROM THE ILLUSTRATED HISTORY OF WASHINGTON COUNTY

Pratt, Orson .*Apostle The Seer.*

Pratt, Orson, Orson Pratt's Works, *Divine Authenticity of the Book of Mormon, Liverpool 1851*

Purple, William D. *Joseph Smith, The Originator of Mormonism*

Quest for Empire

Quincy, Josiah, *Figures of the Past From the Leaves of Old Journals*, 3rded (Boston, 1883)

Revelation received West of Jackson County, Missouri, July 1831

Race Problems- As they affect the Church, speech delivered at Brigham Young University, August, 1954

Stricker, Marion *LIFE AFTER MORMONISM and THE DOUBLE-BIND.*

Sunderland, La Roy, Mormonism Exposed 1842

Shook, Charles A. *The True Origin of Book of Mormon* (Cincinnati: Standard Pub. Co., 1914)
(Rebecca Johnston Eichbaum Statement of September 18, 1879)

Smith, William, Temple Lot Case p.98

Smith, Joseph Jr., *History of the Church*, v. 2&5

Smith, Joseph. *The Man And The Seer*

Smith, Joseph, *Seeker After Truth*, Salt Lake City, 1951

Smith, Joseph Fielding. Jnr.*Doctrines of Salvation*, 1954

Smith, Lucy, *Biographical Sketches*

The Salt Lake Daily Tribune Vol. XXXIIII. Salt Lake City, Utah, Sunday, April 15, 1888. No. 155.

The Saints' Herald, May 19, 1888

Tanner, Jerald & Sandra., *The Changing World of Mormonism*

Tanner, Jerald & Sandra. *Mormonism—Shadow or Reality?*

Tiffany's monthly, published by Joel Tiffany 1859

Von Wymetal, Wilhelm Ritter (under the pen-name of "W. Wyl") (1838-1896)
Mormon Portraits 1 Joseph Smith (SLC: Tribune Printing & Pub., 1886)

Whitmer, David. *An Address to All Believers in Christ, Richmond, Missouri 1887*

Walters, Wesley P, Affidavit. Oct. 28, 1971

The Way to Perfection, Salt Lake City, 1935

The Young Woman's Journal, 1892

Zion's Harbinger and Baneemy's Organ, St. Louis, 1853

ACKNOWLEDGEMENTS

Love and hugs to my children, for help with the editing process and the constructive criticism. To my brother and to my good friends for their support, they know who they are! Many thanks to my good doctor. To Author house Publishing and a special thank you to Scott, his patience knows no bounds!

Thanks to those who have shared their knowledge and wisdom and made a difference for good.

Marion Stricker *Author*
Sandra Tanner *Author*
Thomas Murphy *Anthropologist*
Randall Shortridge *Molecular Biologist*
Dr. David Glenn Smith *Molecular Anthropologist*
Dr. Stephen L. Whittington *Bioarcheologist*
Simon Southerton *Molecular Biologist*
Dr. John Mc Laughlin *Linguistic*
Dale Broadhurst
Richard Packham
Contributors to www.exmormon.org.
Sony Music Publishing
Timothy D. Kosnoff *Attorney at Law*

To all those who put pen/quill to paper long ago and kept the records.

To God, I still have my faith!

And finally to the most important man in my universe, my husband, who with his own quiet faith kept us all together. Words cannot express.

Helpful websites
www.exmormon.org
www.ultm.org

"Truth Will Out"

The truth will become known eventually. **The Merchant of Venice, 1596: Shakespeare**

Lightning Source UK Ltd.
Milton Keynes UK
UKOW030607161112

202255UK00002B/4/P